MARLBOROUGH
HIS LIFE AND TIMES

VOLUME IV
1704–1705

BY WINSTON S. CHURCHILL

MARLBOROUGH

HIS LIFE AND TIMES

By

THE RIGHT HONOURABLE

WINSTON S. CHURCHILL, C.H. M.P.

VOLUME IV

1704–1705

NEW YORK

CHARLES SCRIBNER'S SONS

MCMXXXV

CONTENTS

VOLUME IV

ILLUSTRATIONS

VOLUME IV

PLATES

FACSIMILES OF LETTERS

MAPS AND PLANS

MARLBOROUGH

ILLUSTRATIONS

ABBREVIATIONS

B.M. = British Museum Library.
H.M.C. = *Report of the Royal Historical Manuscripts Commission.*
S.P. = State Papers at the Public Record Office, London.

For further details as to footnote references see the Bibliography (pp. 257–261, Vol. IV).

In quoting from old documents and letters the original text has been preserved wherever it is significant. Letters of Marlborough and Sarah which enter directly into the narrative have been modernized in spelling, grammar, and punctuation so far as is convenient to the reader. But the archaic style and setting has been preserved, and occasionally words are left in characteristic spelling.

Documents never before made public are distinguished by an asterisk (*). In the case of unpublished letters to and from Marlborough preserved in the Blenheim collection no further reference is given.

All italics are the Author's, unless the contrary is stated.

In the diagrams, except where otherwise stated, fortresses held by the allies are shown as black stars and those occupied by the French as white stars.

METHOD OF DATING

Until 1752 dates in England and on the Continent differed owing to our delay in adopting the Reformed Calendar of Gregory XIII. The dates which prevailed in England were known as Old Style, those abroad as New Style. In the seventeenth century the difference was ten days, in the eighteenth century eleven days. For example, January 1, 1601 (O.S.), was January 11, 1601 (N.S.), and January 1, 1701 (O.S.), was January 12, 1701 (N.S.).

The method used has been to give all dates of events that occurred in England in the Old Style, and of events that occurred abroad in New Style. Letters and papers are dated in the New Style unless they were actually written in England. In sea battles and a few other convenient cases the dates are given in both styles.

It was also customary at this time—at any rate, in English official documents—to date the year as beginning on Lady Day, March 25. What we should call January 1, 1700, was then called January 1, 1699, and so on for all days up to March 25, when 1700 began. This has been a fertile source of confusion. In this book all dates between January 1 and March 25 have been made to conform to the modern practice.

MARLBOROUGH
HIS LIFE AND TIMES

VOLUME IV

CHAPTER I

THE STORM OF THE SCHELLENBERG

1704, JULY 2

THE junction of the two armies was effected on the 22nd at Launsheim, and their full concentration was complete by the end of June. It was the largest and strongest force of cavalry and infantry yet massed in Europe in all these wars. After providing the army for the Rhine the line of battle was formed of 177 squadrons and 76 battalions. Its weakness was in artillery. Marlborough had only been able to bring field-pieces with him in his six weeks of marching, and the Imperialists were woefully deficient even in the lighter guns. Together they could muster but forty-eight cannon. However, three-quarters belonged to the English Artillery, which, under Colonel Blood, was of exceptional quality and mobility. Siege train as yet there was none, and only twenty-four pontoons were available for throwing bridges.

Ever darker became the suspicions which Marlborough and Wratislaw entertained against the Margrave. General Goor, who was at this time entirely in Marlborough's confidence and who acted in many ways as his staff officer, a second Cadogan, inflamed these suspicions with all the knowledge he had gathered about the Margrave from the year he had served under him. Everything that the Margrave suggested, whether on military manœuvres or in the negotiations which he still continued with the Elector, was scrutinized and discussed between these three. It had been agreed to march to Giengen on the 25th and court a battle. This would bring the hostile armies face to face. But at midnight on the 24th the Margrave sent Baron Forster to Marlborough asking him whether he would not make the 25th a day of rest, for he, the Margrave, had a plan for forcing the Elector to fight at a disadvantage. Marlborough assented to the day of rest, and the army did not march. In the morning Wratislaw was

charged by the Margrave to explain his scheme to Marlborough. "When I proposed these details to my lord . . ."
reported the envoy, "he was quite amazed by them and said
to me, 'Is this really the best plan the Margrave has been
able to think of to make the Elector fight?'"[1] He proceeded to riddle it with criticism. The Margrave himself
evidently had no confidence in his proposal, for when he
came to Marlborough's headquarters in the afternoon he did
not advance it. On the contrary, he spoke only of his wish
to separate the armies and proceed himself to the Upper Iller.
Marlborough replied that it would not be safe to divide the
armies till the Danish cavalry had arrived, which could scarcely
be before July 5 or 6. Accordingly it was once more decided
to march upon Giengen and the enemy. Wratislaw says:

> The same evening Marlborough asked that General Goor
> whom he [the Margrave] had put under arrest a year before,
> should be brought to him, and this was at once done. This Goor
> revealed to us that the Lieutenant-General had first protested to
> him profusely that he wished to maintain his friendship with
> Marlborough, but after this had attempted to prevent the march
> to Giengen.[1]

The suggestion was evidently present to both Marlborough
and Wratislaw that the Margrave had wished by losing a day
to make sure that the Elector got safely within his lines of
Lauingen. This view was strengthened when the march began
on the early morning of the 26th, and it was seen that the
Elector was already retiring in haste, but in time.

No sooner on the 26th had the Elector made good his
retreat to his line and the allied army encamped than the
Margrave sent the Comte de Frise to Marlborough with a
new project. The army should be divided; Marlborough,
with 40 battalions and 65 squadrons, would watch the
Elector in his entrenchments, while the Margrave, marching
down the Danube, would force a passage near Neuburg.
By this arrangement the army would be divided into two
halves, and Marlborough would give up 9 battalions and
20 squadrons of the troops in Anglo-Dutch pay to his

1 Wratislaw to the Emperor, Giengen, June 29; *Feldzüge,* vi, 830.

colleague. This did not commend itself to him. He replied that to separate now, when within a few days he was to receive the Danish, and the Margrave the Swabian, reinforcements, "would be indefensible should the slightest misfortune arise out of it."

The Captain-General had, in fact, other cares and other designs. Although in superior strength to the enemy, he sat with only passes through the mountainous, unfertile

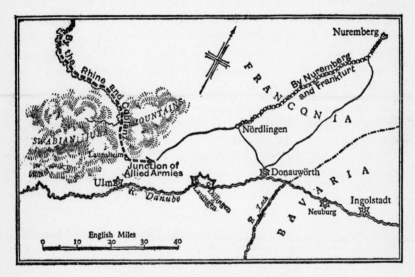

THE NEW COMMUNICATIONS

country behind him. But the long, delicate flank march was now over, and he was independent of the middle Rhine, with its many points of weakness. To subsist and be secure he must at once move east and pick up his new line of communications with Franconia. All this had been duly prepared. Under cover of the Margrave's army at Ulm he had been for some weeks past forming large magazines and hospitals at Nördlingen, whence his line of supply stretched back to Nuremberg and its fertile regions. His financial base at Frankfort was already linked up with the new area, and his agents and contractors were actively purchasing supplies and hiring transport throughout the whole valley of the Pegnitz. It was necessary to draw the allied army from the broken, barren foothills of the Swabian Jura and place it at the head of these far safer communications. It was, moreover, urgent to force the Danube and seize a fortified bridgehead upon it. There was only one place which suited both these requirements. Curiously enough, Villars, as history has revealed, had given a prescient warning to the Elector in the previous year: "Fortify your towns, and above all the Schellenberg, that fort above Donauwörth, the importance of which the great Gustavus taught us." [1] The warning had passed unheeded, and now it was upon this same fort that Marlborough's eye had for some time been fixed. On June 8, the day before he had met Eugene and four days before Prince Louis had arrived, he had written to Godolphin, "I shall in two days after the junction [of Marlborough's and the Margrave's armies] march directly to Donauwörth. If I can take that place, I shall there settle a magazine for the army."

The capture of Donauwörth would give crossings for both the Danube and the Lech and direct entry into Bavaria. Its fortified possession would enable Marlborough to bestride the Danube and manœuvre on either bank as events might require. From Donauwörth his new line of communications, and if necessary of retreat, would run back naturally into Franconia almost at right angles to his front.[2]

1 L. P. Anquetil, *Vie du Maréchal Duc de Villars* (1784), i, 289.
2 An army thus placed is able to withdraw directly upon its communications, finding depots and meeting reinforcements and food convoys at every stage (A).

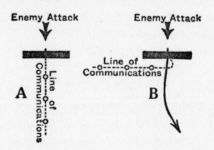

An army whose communications are in prolongation of its front is said to be 'formed to a flank.' This is a dangerous and unsound strategic position. If driven back only a few miles this army is cut from its supplies and base, and in the greatest danger of entire destruction (B).

The Duke was therefore only awaiting the arrival of his infantry to do what he had for some time intended. He now replied to the Comte de Frise that "he would ask the Margrave to make him a present of Donauwörth, and until this had been done not to think of a separation or of any other design." He added that "he must confess to the Margrave that his troops had this failing, that they could not remain in the field without bread. It was therefore necessary to capture some place where magazines could be formed." The discussion was continued on the 27th. The Margrave remarked that he had information that the enemy intended to fortify the position on the heights of Donauwörth, and to this end had already collected a great many peasants from the district. Now Donauwörth had assuredly been mentioned in the conference of the three generals at Gross Heppach, and it seemed odd to both Marlborough and Wratislaw that the Elector should have gained such timely intelligence. He replied sternly that the Schellenberg must be stormed even if it cost ten or twelve thousand men. Here was a clash of wills.

There was therefore not only the sharpest difference of opinion between the two commanders, but Marlborough and Wratislaw had the deepest misgivings about the Margrave's good faith. "I am doing all that is humanly possible," wrote Wratislaw,

to quench this fire, and I am certain that Marlborough will never break out publicly against the Margrave, but will, on the contrary, caress him on every possible occasion. It is not however altogether possible to calm his suspicions, because I am myself beginning to have doubts as to the Lieutenant-General's conduct, for it is certain that without me the artillery from Philippsburg and the Rhine would not be on its way, *and what could we do with great armies if we had not artillery with which to make a hole through the wall?* Marlborough said to me that in a few days it would be possible to come to a definite conclusion on the conduct of the Margrave, and if his conduct is not correct, two alternatives are open: either to arrest him or to send him to the Rhine at your Imperial Majesty's express command and to bring the Prince of Savoy here. The first is safer, but not perhaps quite fair; for we have nothing positive to bring forward against the Margrave, and never shall have, because he is too clever and wily to allow himself to be caught in the act.

He then proposed to the Emperor to strip the Margrave of his two most trusted officers, Baron Forster and the Comte de Frise. The one was to be sent to Vienna and kept there, *"once you have got him,"* during the whole campaign. The other was to be sent to the Rhine. He concluded this remarkable dispatch with the following words:

> It is unnecessary to impress upon your Imperial Majesty the secrecy of this letter; for you will yourself recognize . . . if the slightest thing leaked out, a faithful servant would probably lose his life—or at least my person would be exposed to the implacable revenge of the Margrave. . . . My fidelity compels me to say to your Imperial Majesty that at the moment the stake at issue is not the Spanish monarchy, but the very preservation of your Imperial Majesty's sacred person and your whole Imperial house.[1]

Nothing could show more vividly than these words the grim and even terrible relations which festered in the allied headquarters.

Amid these various tensions Marlborough remained serene, calm, patient, efficient, and good-humoured as ever. His repose and conviction were imperturbable. His letters to Sarah show his care of his troops, his poise, and his resolve.

June 25

> As I was never more sensible of heat in my life than I was a fortnight ago, we have now the other extremity of cold; for as I am writing I am forced to have fire in the stove in my chamber. But the poor men, that have not such conveniences, I am afraid will suffer from these continual rains. As they do us hurt here, they do good to prince Eugene on the Rhine, so that we must take the bad with the good.[2]

And:

GIENGEN
June 29

> Since my last, I have had the happiness of receiving yours of the 30th of the last month, and the 1st and 2nd of this. It is not

1 Giengen, June 29, 1704; *Feldzüge*, vi, 832 *et seq.*   2 Coxe, i, 346.

only by yours, but by others that I find that there are several people, who would be glad of my not having success in this undertaking. I am very confident, without flattering myself, that it is the only thing that was capable of saving us from ruin, so that whatever the success may be, I shall have the inward satisfaction to know that I have done all that was in my power, and that none can be angry with me for the undertaking, but such as wish ill to their country and their religion, and with such I am not desirous of their friendship.

The English foot and cannon joined me two days ago, but I do not expect the Danish horse till six or seven days hence, till which time, we shall not be able to act against the Elector of Bavaria, as I could wish. You will easily believe that I act with all my heart and soul, since good success will in all likelihood give me the happiness of ending my days with you. The Queen's allowing you to say something from her is very obliging. I shall endeavour to deserve it; for I serve her with all my heart, and I am very confident she will always have the prayers and good wishes of this country.

He adds, with that peculiar power of being interested in all sorts of things great and small at the same time which was a characteristic both of Frederick the Great and Napoleon:

You have forgot to order Hodges to send me a draught of a stable, as I directed him, for the lodge; for it ought not to be made use of till the year after it is built; and as I see you set your heart on that place, I should be glad all conveniences were about it.[1]

Meanwhile the allied army waited at Giengen, opposite the entrenched camp and at an equal distance from Ulm and Donauwörth. Thus the enemy was still left in doubt where they meant to strike. After the argument of the 27th the Margrave resisted no further, and resigned himself to an attack on Donauwörth with united forces. Marlborough waited at Giengen till Churchill came in with all his infantry and cannon, and had a good day's rest. On June 30 the whole army was moved eastward downstream, parallel to the Danube, to Balmershofen, within four miles of the Lauingen-

1 Coxe, i, 347.

Dillingen lines. The march was resumed the next morning, Marlborough taking sixty squadrons as flank guard. Though the cavalry rode as close as possible to the enemy's works, the defenders lay low, and not a shot was fired. The allies camped near Amerdingen, fifteen miles from Donauwörth. Marlborough sent out a reconnaissance of four hundred horse with officers of high rank to view the Schellenberg and learn what was happening there. With this went the quartermasters of the army with orders to choose a camp behind the

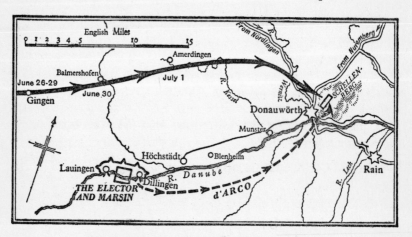

THE ADVANCE TO THE SCHELLENBERG

Wernitz stream about four miles from Donauwörth, and also to report on the roads, bridges, and tracks. The officers reported strong enemy camps on the Schellenberg, and that the troops were working hard on their entrenchments. During the afternoon various peasants and deserters came to Marlborough's tent and were carefully examined.

The Elector had neglected the advice which Villars had given him, and it was not until the third week in June that he began any work upon the defences of the Schellenberg. The lines of defence to be constructed were more than two miles in extent, and it seems that the engineers began upon the extreme right flank by the Danube, which was then entirely open, and worked their way round towards the Old Fort and the fortress, finishing as they went and leaving this sector till the last. The Elector had felt bound to delay the reinforcement of the garrison of Donauwörth until he could learn clearly the intention of his more numerous opponents. But as soon as he saw the continuous procession of the allied army across his front during the 30th he sent Comte d'Arco with fourteen thousand men to defend Donauwörth and complete the fortification of the Schellenberg. He had no reason to suppose that Donauwörth could be attacked before the morning of the 3rd. His enemies had still two fifteen-mile marches to make, and even their advance guard could hardly reach their objective before the evening of the 2nd. They would certainly not attack so late in the day and with wearied troops, and by the 3rd d'Arco should be strongly entrenched. In spite of having delayed so long to fortify the Schellenberg, the Elector had good reason to hope for success.

It has been erroneously supposed that Marlborough and the Margrave agreed to command the whole army on alternate days, whereas in fact, as we have explained, the alternation only affected the ceremonial and the watchword. Even about this there is a serious conflict of evidence upon the initial date. Wratislaw in his dispatch of June 23 says, "On the 22nd one troop found themselves actually entered into the Lieutenant-General's camp. . . . On that day, as the first of concentration, the Margrave issued the watchword." We have seen again how at midnight on the 24th the Margrave sent to ask Marlborough whether he would not make the 25th a day of rest, the inference being that the 25th was Marlborough's day. If this was true the odd-numbered days fell to Marlborough and the even to the Margrave. Thus the Margrave commanded on July 2 at the battle of the Schellenberg. The English authorities, on the other hand, are unanimous that the battle was fought on Marlborough's day. Dr Hare, whose account was "perused by Marlborough" shortly after the action, says distinctly, "It being His Grace's turn to command the next day, he resolved to attack." [1] General Kane and Captain Parker confirm him. The conflict of

1 *Dispatches,* i, 332.

testimony is direct. The evidence of events favours the view that July 2 was the Margrave's day, and that he issued the parola immediately after midnight on the 1st.

The point, however, is not one of substance. There is no foundation for all the well-known arguments that Marlborough felt bound to attack on the 2nd as he could not trust the Margrave to attack on the morrow. This consideration did not influence the operations. Whatever the sequence, there is no doubt that Marlborough's will prevailed continuously throughout these days, and that, while taking pains to carry his co-general with him, he acted during them and afterwards reported upon the battle as if he were the sole Commander-in-Chief. It was, of course, inherent in their co-operation that the two commanders should seem to act together as one, and that no divergence or contradiction in policy should be apparent to the troops.

During the afternoon Marlborough issued orders which could only portend action the next day. One hundred and thirty men were to be drawn from every battalion of his own army to form a special force nearly six thousand strong of what would now be called 'storm troops.' Such a selection could not be made hurriedly, and must have been carried out in daylight before the troops lay down to sleep. Six o'clock was, in fact, the latest moment for such orders, as well as for many of the other necessary preparations. When darkness fell and while all this was going on, Marlborough visited the Margrave. There is no record of the details of their interview, but it is certain that he procured the agreement of his colleague, for we know that at 10 P.M. an officer was sent to Nördlingen with a letter from the Margrave to the local authorities to collect surgeons and prepare for the reception of a large number of wounded. Moreover, three battalions of Imperial Grenadiers were added by the Margrave to Marlborough's 'storm troops,' evidently to make it plain that the two commanders were united. The special force of infantry with 35 squadrons and strong parties of pioneers for road- and bridge-making were ordered to march at 3 A.M. under Marlborough's personal command. A forlorn hope of eighty volunteers led by Lord Mordaunt, Peterborough's son (one of the suitors of Lady Mary, and the 'Raskell' of her father's letter), was formed to head the assault. The rest of the army was to follow with the Margrave at daylight.

Every one learned from these orders the desperate character of the operation and the unusual measures which were to be adopted. It seemed to many a plan of hardihood. The army was still fifteen miles from Donauwörth. They had to cross the Wernitz stream in their march and deploy for battle at the end of it. They could not hope to come to grips before about six o'clock in the evening, and there would only be two hours' daylight left. There is no doubt that nearly all the generals on both sides, friend and foe, thought it inadmissible for the allies to fight a battle before the 3rd. But by the 3rd d'Arco would be well entrenched and the Elector would be moving to his aid. Victory was more than doubtful on the 3rd; failure was certain on the 4th, or later. Nothing could avail unless the battle were set forward a day. Marlborough saw that exceptional risk must be run if the campaign was not to miscarry. A supreme effort must be demanded of the troops; a bloody price must be paid by them; and their commander must stake his reputation upon the outcome. To the questionings which arose he replied, "Either the enemy will escape or will have time to finish their works. In the latter case the delay of every single hour will cause the loss of a thousand men." There was little sleep that night in the allied camp. The thrill of excitement and the stir of preparation ruled the few remaining hours. A stern effort was required of the English and Dutch, who had travelled a long way to make it and upon whom the brunt was evidently to fall. The hour was come, and they were ready.

Early on the morning of July 2 Marshal d'Arco, with Count Maffei and other general officers, was a-horse upon the Schellenberg watching the working parties of troops and labourers entrenching the hill. Though nothing like a mountain, it is a fine, high, "bell-shaped" [1] hill, giving a

1 Hare's Journal.

splendid view of all the country to the west and south. Beneath lay the town of Donauwörth, in those days a place of some note, surrounded by its zigzag ramparts with their stone-backed parapets and long, smooth grass slopes. Donauwörth was a fortress of the second order, not, indeed, up-to-date—for the war-like arts were progressing—but complete in all the regular layers of defence. On the left, then, of Marshal d'Arco, and five hundred feet below him, lay this star-shaped Donauwörth, bristling with roofs and spires, traversed by the silver ribbon of the Danube, across which the all-important bridge lay like a buckle. On his right, reaching almost to the summit of the hill, lay a dense wood. Nowadays a wood like this would not afford the slightest protection to a flank. In fact, the riflemen and machine-gunners of an attack would regard it as the best means of approach. But in 1704 it was an impenetrable obstacle. Individuals could push their way through, but at the worst could only fire a shot or two before they would be killed with bayonet or sword. It was true that beyond the wood, farther to the right, there was more than a mile of open ground stretching down to the river. But in this space the lines had been completed and could be occupied easily while the enemy were making the necessary détour. Therefore Marshal d'Arco was at this moment concerned with the thousand-yards stretch between the low fortress and the high wood.

The old fort of Gustavus divided this space again into two. The cannon of Donauwörth gave considerable protection to the ground in closest range. There only remained from three to four hundred yards between the Donauwörth cannonballs and the obstacle of the wood. Here, then, was the place to fortify and where to mass the troops and field artillery (sixteen guns). It was on this space that all d'Arco's men were digging and binding together the long faggots called fascines which held up their breastworks. How many men d'Arco had is much disputed. Some say thirty-two thousand, some seven. Marlborough's estimate after the battle gives him fourteen thousand men, including 5 good French regiments and 16 battalions of the cream of the Bavarian infantry, besides 9 to 15 squadrons: evidently a very tough proposition.

About eight o'clock in the morning enemy horsemen, many in red coats, began to appear at the edge of the woods and scrub, five or six miles away on d'Arco's left front to the north-west. They were probably the advanced cavalry of the great army marching against him, or perhaps they were only another reconnaissance. As the hours passed more and more horsemen made their appearance, trickling out of the woods, and forming into squadrons upon the heaths and meadows. Then the perspective glasses disclosed rivulets of infantry flowing down the hillsides. So it was the army, as expected, that was coming. But about ten o'clock a very familiar sign became apparent. The allied quartermasters were marking out a camp. They could be seen four miles away beyond the Wernitz stream setting up all the flags upon which the tent lines of the various regiments would presently be pitched. This confirmed d'Arco and his staff in their most reasonable expectation that the enemy after a full march would sleep behind the Wernitz, and deliver their attack the next day. Dig then, like moles, and make this narrow strip between the gunfire of the fortress and the tangles of the wood impregnable! Having reached these well-grounded, serious, but not unsatisfactory conclusions, Marshal d'Arco and his principal officers rode down about noon into the town of Donauwörth for their midday meal. To-morrow fateful battle; to-day dig, and meanwhile dine. However, between two and three o'clock reports arrived that the enemy had not stopped at the marked-out camp. They had thrown several bridges and plankways across the Wernitz, and were moving steadily across these and the old stone bridge into the cup-like space beneath the Schellenberg. It was surely too late to make so grave an attack before sundown; but anyhow one must ride out and see. The horses were brought, and the Command clattered up the hill to their toiling troops. The scene was now much changed. The whole of the opposite slopes descending to

27

the foot of the Schellenberg were crowded with brightly clothed regiments and brigades, horse, foot, and guns all moving forward as fast as they could and with an air of resolute aggression. Large numbers were already across the Wernitz, and long columns were streaking towards that very space between the wood and the fortress cannon which Marshal d'Arco and his assistants admitted was the most likely point of assault.

There are few surer tests of the virtue of a military movement than the impression it produces upon the best mind in the other army. D'Arco did not say to himself, "They are foolish to attack so late—what could be better for us?" On the contrary, he showed a marked uneasiness; and this exposure arose from the fact that he was a better soldier than actor. Indeed, his plight was most disagreeable. He had a strong position and excellent troops, but his defences were not finished, and now in an hour or two fifty or sixty thousand men under famous generals were going to fall upon him, apparently without regard to the fatigue of their march or the price they would have to pay. The question had been whether they would pay the price. If they thought it worth while to do so, he would almost certainly be destroyed. If he and his fourteen thousand men were blotted out before dark, the Franco-Bavarian army would be hopelessly inferior to the invaders. The gateway into Bavaria would be open, and the vengeance of the allies would fall upon his country. It was noticed that, while other Bavarians mocked at the imprudence of the allies' proceedings, their ablest soldier was plunged in the deepest depression. His distress was not due to any want of courage. He was in fact weighing the unpleasant question whether he should, while time remained, retreat, preserve his corps, leave the fortress to its fate, and in a few days lay Bavaria open to the invader. He could not bring himself to this, though on general grounds there was much to be said for it. His force, probably too weak to withstand the masses which were advancing upon it, was nevertheless large enough to be a fearful loss to the Elector's army.

Meanwhile, time and space were playing their appointed

parts. The fringe of Bavarian outposts and covering troops came hurrying back before the advancing tide. They set light before retiring to the village of Berg and other hamlets and dwellings spread in a half-circle beneath the Schellenberg. The smoke drifted across the landscape, and as it died down at five o'clock a battery of ten guns opened fire from below Berg upon the deadly passage near the wood. All work had been abandoned for an hour past, and the defenders had drawn themselves up in battle order behind their unfinished breastworks. The heavy blue and scarlet columns hugging the wood and just out of range of the fortress were already massed in a dip in the ground—easily recognizable to-day— only two hundred and fifty yards away. The tips of all their standards could be seen, suggesting the number of battalions crammed together in this small space. Behind them, sub-tending both the fortress and the intervening ground, were certainly more than forty thousand men moving forward, line behind line in battle array. They were willing to pay the price for what they meant to have. Well, let them pay it.

According to the Imperial report of the action:

At the request of the Duke of Marlborough, the Imperial Lieutenant-General continued his march on the morning of the 2nd, but since the march was very long and the army being obliged to change formation frequently found it extremely arduous, camp was not pitched till four o'clock in the after-noon . . . an hour's march from Donauwörth, where it was found that the previous information was correct—namely, that the enemy with a part of his army had finished great and advan-tageous entrenchments on the Schellenberg above Donauwörth and had in fact encamped part of his troops within them, and had made the rest of his encampment alongside the river across the Danube.[1]

Marlborough had come on the scene about nine o'clock, and directed the advance of the army. He reserved the old bridge which still stood across the Wernitz for the march of the storm troops. He had three pontoon bridges thrown for the main army. He sent the bulk of the cavalry into the

1 Imperial Official Report; *Feldzüge,* vi, 835.

thickets to cut fascines with which the infantry could fill any
ditch that the enemy might have had time to dig in front
of the breastworks. The storm troops, delayed by the soft,
miry track, did not cross the river till noon. He then rode
out with the Margrave and the generals concerned in the
attack, and, as was his custom, personally reconnoitred the
whole of the enemy's position. Their escort having driven
in the enemy's outposts, they were able to examine the whole
front minutely. So close did "the high generality" [1] press
that the fortress guns and even the field batteries opened
a lively cannonade upon them which was continued during
the whole of their inspection. The Duke had hoped that he
could pass some at least of his troops through the dense wood,
and thus extend his attack beyond it. But what he saw of the
wood at close quarters convinced him that this was not
practicable. The fortress cannon-balls bounding along among
the staff showed how narrow was the space upon which the
first and main assault must be delivered. He also saw how
densely the enemy were gathered upon this threatened point.

It was nearly four when the generals joined their troops
and the enemy's guns became silent. The main body of the
army was now about to pass the bridges, and the storm troops
were approaching the foot of the Schellenberg. The formidable aspect of the position had become only the more apparent
at close quarters, but when Marlborough looked across the
Danube beyond Donauwörth he could see the considerable
camp marked out for the enemy's reinforcements. The tents
of the cavalry were already pitched on either flank, and between them a broad space was reserved for infantry who
would certainly arrive during the night. To-day the price
would be heavy. To-morrow the Schellenberg might be un-
purchasable. This was the opinion which General Goor, who
was to lead the first and main assault, most vigorously
expressed. There are no signs that Marlborough had any
second thoughts, for the advance and deployment of the army
continued at the utmost speed; but if any spur had been
needed a travel-stained officer who had arrived from the

---

[1] Imperial Official Report; *ibid.*

Rhine front in the morning would have supplied it. This was Baron Moltenburg, Prince Eugene's Adjutant-General, who brought the news that Villeroy and Tallard "were marched to Strasburg, having promised a great reinforcement to the Elector by way of the Black Forest." Thus the final decision was agreed to by all.

> . . . And notwithstanding that the infantry was very tired from the long march, that the enemy's entrenchment was found perfected and that the evening was beginning to fall, the Duke of Marlborough proposed and the Imperial Lieutenant-General agreed . . . that the advantageous enemy entrenchment should be attacked that evening with the utmost vigour. . . .[1]

In this action Marlborough used the same method which he afterwards, with modifications, pursued at Blenheim and at Ramillies. He thrust a mass of English infantry, conspicuous by their scarlet coats, soon to be dreaded for their prowess, upon what the enemy felt was the key of their position; and he pressed these attacks with a disregard of human life unusual in these prolonged and stately wars. By this means he attracted disproportionate forces of the enemy to the threatened point, and strove with might and main to crash through them. Success here meant victory. If he did not succeed, the dislocation of the enemy's forces produced by this ferocious effort gave him the battle elsewhere upon the denuded portions of their front. Surplus troops from his feints could in every action carry his ultimate attack. This simple, ruthless theme, applied with the highest technical skill, and with cool judgment in the measuring and timing of events, exactly harmonizes with Napoleon's processes, and may well have suggested some of them. It comprised an aggressive dominant of the first order, followed by an opportunist change or a further unfolding, when the enemy's reaction was pronounced. His feints were often realities from which he would above all things have been glad to profit, but which, though failing of success, fatally deranged the enemy's battle, and enabled him to make a second or a further move, foreseen in all its values from the beginning, to which there could be

1 Imperial Official Report; *ibid.*

no effective resistance. A hideous violence directed upon a deadly spot, even if frustrated, prepared a victory elsewhere. By five o'clock the striking-force was already close to the wood half-way up the Schellenberg. To their right upon all the approaches the lines of battle were formed, and extending

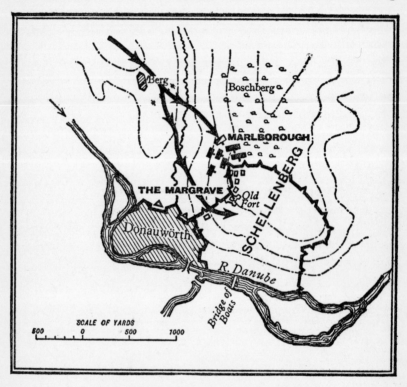

THE STORM OF THE SCHELLENBERG

as the main army came up. The cavalry delivered a short fascine to every officer and soldier in the assaulting infantry. Leaving the Margrave to direct the advance of the army, Marlborough rode to the storming column, the infantry of which was now deployed about three hundred yards broad, in the dip a furlong from the hostile breastworks. Behind the six thousand picked men in three dense lines he had brought eight battalions in support and eight more echeloned right-handed in reserve. These large bodies were sustained

32

by 35 squadrons, including all the English cavalry, formed close behind and somewhat farther to the right of the storm troops. The Margrave's army was now also partly formed, and growing every minute as the marching columns deployed. At about a quarter-past six the drums beat, and Lieutenant-General Goor, who commanded the assault, preceded by Mordaunt and the forlorn hope, led the English infantry up the hill. The battery which d'Arco had posted in the angle formed by the wood and the works fired with deadly effect, while the fortress cannon galled the other flank. The leading troops of the 1st Guards; Ingoldsby's, now the Royal Welch Fusiliers; two battalions of Orkney's, now the Royal Scots; and Meredith's, now the 1st Hampshires, fell by scores; but the whole array rolled forward at a slow step, the soldiers with shouldered arms and clasping their fascines with their left hands.

When half the distance was covered the Bavarian guns fired case instead of ball [1] and tore long lanes through the ranks, while at the same time the breastworks began to blaze with musketry. At the first volley General Goor fell dead. Undaunted, all the English now raised cheers, heard everywhere above the firing, and shouts of "God save the Queen!" as they broke into the charge. But an unlucky accident cost them dear. A deep, unexpected gully, dry though made by water, ran across the enemy's front about fifty yards from the breastworks. Mistaking this for the actual ditch, the troops cast their fascines into it, and thus the survivors of the first line reached the breastworks without the means of crossing them. The rest of the assault coming steadily on behind them, the whole force was brought to a standstill in the unfinished ditch while the exultant Bavarians fired into them from the parapet. A protracted struggle followed. By all reports nothing like the fury of the musketry-fire had ever been heard before. "Incredible" is the word which occurs in various foreign accounts. And all at a few yards' distance into solid masses! At length the assault slackened. Men

---

[1] Parcels of bullets instead of a single cannon-ball.

33

began to double to the rear, the Bavarians leaped out in counter-attack, and a panic began. But the 1st Guards, who had now lost half their men and nearly all their principal officers, turned, faced the foe, and drove the Bavarians back to their trenches.

We must now introduce a new character to our readers. M. de la Colonie, whose *Memoirs of an Old Campaigner* afford by far the most modern and vivid picture of these wars from the enemy's side, commanded the battalion of French Grenadiers whom Marshal d'Arco had personally posted behind the breastworks at the point where the wood came to an end on the summit of the hill. The colonel did not like the situation any more than did his chief. But as a brave veteran soldier he made the best of it. His rôle was to make quite certain the enemy did not come through the wood or on the far side of it, and, once assured in this respect, to meet the main attack wherever it might fall. For this purpose his grenadiers had to be drawn up in strict parade on ground so high that the breastworks gave them no protection from the artillery. At the first discharge of Colonel Blood's batteries he was himself splashed in the blood and brains of a company commander, who with twelve grenadiers was destroyed by a single cannon-ball. He records the accuracy of the fire, and states that he lost five officers and eighty men out of perhaps six hundred before a musket-shot was fired on either side.

La Colonie's regiment soon moved to a portion of the breastworks. He says:

> The enemy broke into the charge, and rushed at full speed, shouting at the top of their voices, to throw themselves into our entrenchments.
>
> The rapidity of their movements, together with their loud yells, were truly alarming, and as soon as I heard them I ordered our drums to beat the 'charge' so as to drown them with their noise, lest they should have a bad effect upon our people. By this means I animated my grenadiers, and prevented them hearing the shouts of the enemy, which before now have produced a heedless panic.

34

The English infantry led this attack with the greatest intrepidity, right up to our parapet, but there they were opposed with a courage at least equal to their own. Rage, fury, and desperation were manifested by both sides, with the more obstinacy as the assailants and assailed were perhaps the bravest soldiers in the world. The little parapet which separated the two forces became the scene of the bloodiest struggle that could be conceived. Thirteen hundred grenadiers . . . bore the brunt of the enemy's attack at the forefront of the Bavarian infantry.

. . . During this first attack, which lasted a good hour or more [actually less than half an hour], we were all fighting hand to hand, hurling them back as they clutched at the parapet; men were slaying or tearing at the muzzles of guns and the bayonets which pierced their entrails; crushing under their feet their own wounded comrades, and even gouging out their opponents' eyes with their nails, when the grip was so close that neither could make use of their weapons. I verily believe that it would have been quite impossible to find a more terrible representation of hell itself than was shown in the savagery of both sides on this occasion.

At last the enemy, after losing more than eight thousand men [*sic*] in this first onslaught, were obliged to relax their hold, and they fell back for shelter to the dip of the slope, where we could not harm them. A sudden calm now reigned amongst us, our people were recovering their breath, and seemed more determined even than they were before the conflict. The ground around our parapet was covered with dead and dying, in heaps almost as high as our fascines; but our whole attention was fixed on the enemy and his movements. We noticed that the tops of his standards still showed at about the same place as that from which they had made their charge in the first instance, leaving little doubt but that they were re-forming before returning to the assault.[1]

It is probable that more than three thousand of the assailants had fallen in this first attack, and lay in a space perhaps three to four hundred yards square. Marlborough immediately ordered a second attempt. And now the generals, brigadiers, and colonels dismounted from their horses, and, with

---

[1] *Memoirs of an Old Campaigner,* p. 185.

the remnants of Mordaunt's forlorn hope, formed a glorious front line. At the head marched Lieutenant-General Count Styrum, soon mortally wounded; but this renewed effort, though nearly as bloody, was repulsed more easily than the first. Most of the generals and colonels were soon shot down, and the wave recoiled a second time from the terrible defences. But General Lumley brought his squadrons up in close order within musket-shot, thus heartening the infantry and preventing all retreat.

Wratislaw, watch in hand, was spectator from the opposite slope behind Berg. According to his timing, the Margrave's attack began only a quarter of an hour after Marlborough's; Hare's account says half an hour. The discrepancy is no doubt explained by the fact that the storm troops had been massed in the dip hard by the enemy's trenches, whereas the main army deployed nearly a thousand yards farther from them. But at about seven o'clock the Margrave, advancing valiantly at the head of his troops, was already in close action. The Duke in the dip, unmoved by the bloody disaster around him, sent an officer with a platoon of infantry to test the defences farther to the right of those he had attacked. They were found to be almost empty, the bulk of the defenders having been drawn into the struggle by the wood. Marl-borough therefore directed the eight battalions of his reserve to attack in the new direction more to the right, in conjunction with the Margrave's general advance. At the same time he called upon his shattered battalions for a new attack over the same deadly ground. Most of the high officers were now killed or wounded, but at about a quarter-past seven a new onset was organized and began to move forward, though less confidently than its precursors. So obstinate was the temper at this point that Lumley ordered Lord John Hay's regiment of dragoons, now deathless as the Scots Greys, to dismount and attack with the infantry.

The defenders still resisted with the utmost constancy. But at last Fortune, who had remained insensible to sacrifice, began to declare herself on the side of numbers. Marshal d'Arco had told the governor of Donauwörth to spread two French

TAPESTRY OF THE SCHELLENBERG
By permission of the Duke of Marlborough.
Photograph by permission of the Victoria and Albert Museum

battalions along the covered way, and had assigned to two Bavarian units the task of guarding the curtain of entrenchments which joined the fortress to the scene of the struggle. But the governor had withdrawn all his troops within the ramparts, and the others were too few to defend their front against the forces now coming into action. The Margrave's horse was shot under him, and he himself was wounded; but the enemy's fire, whether from the trenches or the fortress, could not cope with the crowds of troops which now pressed upon them. The ditches were filled with fascines, and about the same time as Marlborough on the left was organizing his third attack large bodies of German infantry pierced the centre of the entrenchments with little loss. D'Arco was on the spot. The intruders were charged by his cavalry, but they were already too many to be driven out. The cavalry charge failed, and the Imperialist infantry, pouring through the gap and spreading to the right and left, advanced upon the flank of those who had so bravely and successfully defended the summit of the hill. The Imperial official report states:

> It is impossible to describe the vigour with which the left wing attacked and what a ceaseless fire it had to sustain. On the right wing the fire was by no means so heavy. Indeed, the Imperial troops reached the trenches without firing a shot, threw in the fascines (the English as well as the Imperial cavalry supporting them in the changed line), and after prolonged hand to hand fighting forced their way right into the entrenchments where they were able to maintain themselves in good order. After some twenty minutes more firing they repulsed the enemy reserves, and then came to the help of the left wing, the cavalry attacking the enemy in the rear. This provided the left wing with openings, so that they succeeded in breaking into the entrenchments in all directions. . . .
>
> The continual volleys of the musketeers lasted without a break for a complete hour and twenty minutes, and all experienced officers of both wings acknowledge that they never saw such a heavy or continuous fire, such a hearty attack and vigorous defence, from which it will be readily understood that the losses on both sides must have been great.[1]

1 *Feldzüge*, vi, 837.

What followed is best told by La Colonie.

> Never was joy greater than our own at the very moment when we were in the greatest danger.
>
> We pictured to ourselves all the advantages produced by our successful resistance, and the glory of the action itself, perhaps the most memorable in the history of the world; . . . our ten battalions . . . having sustained, unbroken, two determined assaults of a formidable army. . . . About 7.30 . . . I noticed all at once an extraordinary movement on the part of our infantry, who were rising up and ceasing fire withal. I glanced around on all sides to see what had caused this behaviour, and then became aware of several lines of infantry in greyish-white uniforms on our left flank. From lack of movement on their part, their dress and bearing, I verily believed that reinforcements had arrived for us, and anybody else would have believed the same. No information whatever had reached us of the enemy's success, or even that such a thing was the least likely, so in the error I laboured under I shouted to my men that they were Frenchmen and friends. . . .
>
> Having, however, made a closer inspection, I discovered bunches of straw and leaves attached to their standards, badges the enemy are in the custom of wearing on the occasion of battle, and at that very moment was struck by a ball in the right lower jaw, which wounded and stupefied me to such an extent that I thought it was smashed.[1]

This was the moment when Marlborough's final attack began to struggle forward across the shambles. All resistance now became impossible. The ten battalions, exhausted by their ordeal, and finding their left flank turned and their retreat menaced by overwhelming numbers of fresh troops, retreated a few hundred yards in order, and then broke and ran as hard as they could down through the cornfields towards the river and a pontoon bridge across it. But this had already been broken asunder by the flight of the wagon-train, and the Margrave's forces separated all these men from Donauwörth. Marlborough, entering the captured position with the leading squadrons, had his dazed infantry stopped and re-formed while he launched all the 35 squadrons of

---

[1] *Memoirs of an Old Campaigner*, p. 191.

English and Prussian cavalry, including the Greys (now remounted), after the fugitives. The pursuit was merciless. The troopers, infuriated by the slaughter of their foot, gave no quarter. "Kill, kill and destroy!"[1] was the word. So they rode them down and killed them all, or chased them into the Danube.

La Colonie, weakened by his wound, hampered by his "richly embroidered uniform" and long, very tight boots, ran for his life. The wife of a Bavarian soldier, also a fugitive, helped him to pull off these impediments. He lay exhausted in the standing corn till a group of horsemen approached, when he plunged into the river. They fired at him from the bank, but the swift current bore him out of their reach, and after a desperate swim he scrambled to shore on the opposite bank, and was succoured by a friendly sergeant. It was the merest chance we did not lose his memoirs.

The battle was over and the allies had won. When the Margrave came riding up to the bloodstained summit he called out to Marlborough, "I am delighted that your proposal has proved such a success." The Duke replied, "I am thankful that you have supported me so well with your troops, and relieved the pressure on me."[2] Of Count d'Arco's fourteen thousand men scarcely five thousand rejoined the Elector's army. The capture of the Schellenberg involved the surrender of Donauwörth, which could not be held for many days against the fire of batteries planted on the hill. The governor did not await this trial. During the night of the 3rd he quitted the fortress in such haste that he failed either to burn the town or effectively destroy the bridge as ordered. The allies now had their bridgehead on the Danube, and valuable stores found in Donauwörth formed the nucleus of the magazines Marlborough had planned to establish there. The prize had been gained, but the cost of nearly six thousand casualties, fifteen hundred killed outright, was shocking in an age when soldiers were hard to find, and human life narrowly valued. The resources of Nördlingen were overwhelmed by the wounded. All who could walk or

[1] Rutland Papers, *H.M.C.*, ii, 181. [2] Imperial Official Report, *Feldzüge*, vi, 837.

crawl were dispersed in the surrounding villages with only the most primitive arrangements. Marlborough's correspondence of the 3rd and 4th is full of directions for their care.

The English were the hardest hit. Out of four thousand in action fifteen hundred were killed or wounded. Many weary, faithful feet that had trudged from the Thames to the Danube here came to rest. The proportion of loss among the senior officers was beyond compare. Six lieutenant-generals were killed and five wounded, together with four major-generals and twenty-eight brigadiers, colonels, and lieutenant-colonels. The gazettes and news-letters of Europe were adorned with the names of those notables, including princes and commanders long celebrated in the wars.

There is a pathos in Addison's tribute to his countrymen:

> How many generous Britons meet their doom,
> New to the field, and heroes in the bloom!
> Th' illustrious youths, that left their native shore
> To march where Britons never marched before,
> (O fatal love of fame! O glorious heat,
> Only destructive to the brave and great!)
> After such toils o'ercome, such dangers past,
> Stretched on Bavarian ramparts breathe their last.[1]

Various reflections may be made upon this action. That it was vital to the army and the campaign to secure this bridge-head on the Danube is obvious. But Marlborough admitted in a letter to Overkirk that the prize *a coûté un peu cher*. It is arguable, though by no means provable, that if he had waited till the 3rd and brought the whole army into play on both sides of the wood, the enemy even though reinforced could not have held so extended a line, and possibly life might have been spared. But the fear of the reinforcements was decisive upon him.

England, though startled by the casualties, was proud of the victory and thrilled by the prowess of her troops. But it was soon easy to put another complexion on the event, and the Tories were not alone when they asked, "What was the sense of capturing a hill in the heart of Germany at such heavy loss? Were there not many such hills?" And if it

[1] *The Campaign.*

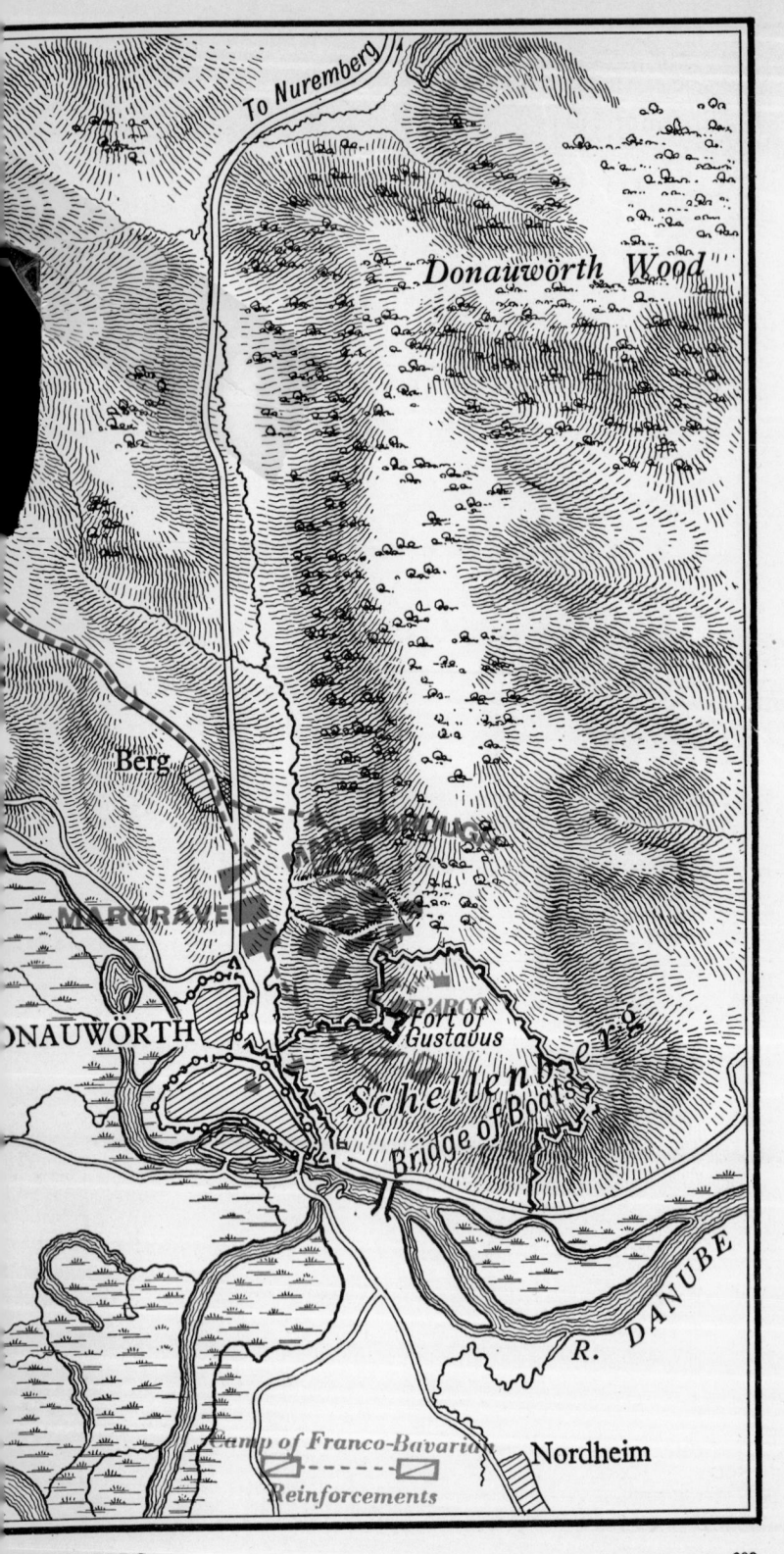

To Nuremberg

Donauwörth Wood

Berg

Schellenberg

Fort of
Gustavus

ONAUWÖRTH

Bridge of Boats

R. DANUBE

Camp of Franco-Bavarian
Reinforcements

Nordheim

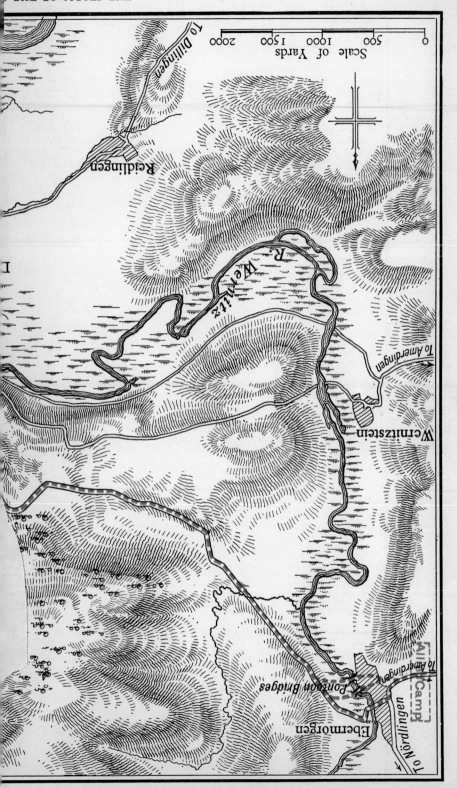

To Dillingen

Reidlingen

Scale of Yards

0   500   1000   1500   2000

R. Wernitz

To Amerdingen

Wernitzstein

To Amerdingen

Allied Camp

Pontoon Bridges

Ebermorgen

To Nördlingen

cost six thousand men to rout eight thousand Bavarians (for
so they put it) how many would be wanted to dispose of the
armies of the Elector and Marsin, reinforced by those of
Villeroy and Tallard? Moreover, it was said both at The
Hague and in London that the victory belonged to the
Margrave. Marlborough had plunged on obstinately into the
strongest part of the enemy's line and squandered life to no
purpose, while the Margrave, experienced soldier, had pounced
upon the gap in the defences, and saved his impetuous colleague from utter defeat.

The Court of Hanover, whose troops had suffered more
than a thousand casualties, took a similar view. The Electress
Sophia in a letter to Leibnitz wrote:

> The Elector is saddened at the loss of so many brave subjects
> in consequences of *the mistakes made by the great general Marl-
> borough*. He says that the Margrave of Baden did very much bet-
> ter, and that without him there would have been complete failure,
> as on the other wing proper measures had not been taken.[1]

The Dutch, who the year before had endeavoured to
placate Marlborough by the medal "Victorious without
slaughter," were now out of humour with him, and,
resentful of his distant operations, struck a medal for the
Schellenberg, on the face of which they displayed "a busto
of Prince Louis" with the inscription, "The enemy defeated
and put to flight and their camp plundered at Schellenberg
near Donauwörth 1704." This, as will be seen, did less than
justice to their Captain-General, and inadequately compre-
hended the strategic setting in which their own fortunes
were involved.

1 Leibnitz, *Werke* (1873), ix, 91.

CHAPTER II

THE DEVASTATION OF BAVARIA

1704, JULY

FAME and fortune, which had hitherto journeyed with Marlborough, halted on the frontiers of Bavaria and awaited his return. The month which followed the battle of the Schellenberg is gloomy for his record. It would seem that his vision and calculation had carried him no farther than this. He had foreseen with uncanny accuracy all the milestones of his long march and the reactions upon friend and foe which would be imposed as each one was passed. He had marked Donauwörth as the gateway by which he would enter the promised land. He was there. The European situation, military and political, was for the moment transformed. But what was he to do next? He had always made it plain that he meant to compel the Elector to return to his allegiance under threat of destroying his country. Accordingly when, on the 8th, the allied army crossed the Lech, they began to burn and lay waste all within their reach. In vain did the despairing inhabitants offer the largest sums of money they could scrape together to placate the wrath of the invaders. Marlborough could have enriched himself vastly by such a process. The precedent of Cohorn in the Pays de Waes only a year before was but too well known to him. He does not seem to have thought of it. His military needs conquered both his avarice and his humanity. He replied—"nobly," says Lediard—"The forces of the Queen of England were not come into Bavaria to get money, but to bring their prince to reason." Thus the army advanced to Aicha, which they reached on the 22nd, spreading terror on all sides and leaving a blackened trail behind them.

The Elector had not awaited the forcing of the rivers. To tarry was to be cut off. As soon as the news of the Schellenberg reached him he evacuated his entrenched camp beyond the Danube and retreated to Augsburg. He fortified himself in a strong position partly protected by the Lech and under the cannon of the fortress. Here he hoped to maintain himself until a new French army came to his aid. He had in fact no other military choice. However, his retreat had carried him forty miles farther from his hoped-for succours, and his weakness prevented him from protecting the country. Simultaneously he gave up Neuburg and withdrew its garrison to Ingolstadt, the sole fortress remaining in his hands on the long course of the Danube from Ulm to Passau.

Marlborough to Godolphin

[DONAUWÖRTH]
July 4, 1704

* I sent an express yesterday to acquaint Her Majesty with the success we had on the second. The garrison of this place, observing that we used our utmost diligence to make a bridge over the Danube, set fire to their magazines and with the last of their troops burnt the bridge, which was not in our powers to hinder; but we came so quick into the town that there is but little of it burnt, so that we are now taking what care we can for the forming a magazine, and we hope to get our bridges finished, so that we may pass the Danube to-morrow, upon which we no ways doubt that the Elector will be obliged to cover his army with the River Lech, which will oblige him to eat his own country, and I think make it almost impossible for the troops to join him which are promised him by Mons. de Villeroy. If he will ever treat, it must be now; for if we get a passage over the Lech before he gets more troops his country is ruined; and you may assure Her Majesty that I shall not be amused by any treaty, but pursue the advantage we now have over him.

P. Louis has desired me to make his compliments to Her Majesty and I believe he will very soon give himself the honour of writing. He does assure me that *he will act in everything as I shall think it best for the common cause*; and we are agreed that whatever colours, cannon, or other ammunition are taken one-half shall be for Her Majesty and the other for the Emperor. The value of this will not be great, but for after-time it will remain for the honour of Her Majesty in their history. As I have no Deputies of the States in this army, I am forced to give money for all the extraordinaries, so that you will easily believe that the ten thousand pounds which I made serve in Flanders will fall very short here; for there the Dutch paid all the carts and horses that were furnished by the country, and all the pay that is given to the soldiers when they work, all which I am now forced to do, as far as concerns the 86 squadrons and 44 battalions which is the number of troops I command. Those which compose the right wing commanded by Prince Louis are only 24 battalions and 85 squadrons by which you may see the certain ruin they must have had if the troops I command had not been here. Having been a-horseback ever since daylight I must defer answering your last two letters till the next opportunity.

John to Sarah

DONAUWÖRTH
July 4

I writ to my dearest soul yesterday, giving her an account of God's having blessed us with a victory the day before, the effect of which has been that we are now masters of this town, which will be of great advantage to us; since it will oblige the Elector to retire into his own country, and give us the opportunity of posting ourselves between him and the French troops he expects. We should not have taken this place in ten days, if the garrison had not been frightened by the action they saw two days ago; for the Bavarians were under the shot [*i.e.,* the protection] of their cannon, when we forced them.

I am in great hopes we shall succeed, which will be for the eternal honour of Her Majesty; for not only the country, but the generals and soldiers all own their being saved, to her generous proceedings; as in truth it is very plain, that if Her Majesty's troops had not been here, the Elector of Bavaria had been now in Vienna.

Since this action I have hardly had time to sleep, for Lieutenant-General Goor helped me in a great many things, which I am now forced to do myself, till I can find some other officer I can rely on for it.[1]

Marlborough to Godolphin

July 6

We are now taking care for a passage over this river of Lech, and then we shall be in the heart of the Elector's country. If he will ever make propositions it must be then. The Marshals de

---

[1] Coxe, i, 366.

Villeroy and Tallard are separated. The latter is to join the elector of Bavaria, and the Duke de Villeroy is to act on the Rhine. Prince Eugene will be obliged to divide his army; so that he may observe each of their motions. *As for his person, it will be with that army that is to observe M. Tallard.* . . .

By all the intelligence we have, our last action has very much disheartened the enemy, so that if we can get over the river to engage them, I no ways doubt but God will bless us with the victory. Our greatest difficulty is that of making our bread follow us; for the troops that I have the honour to command cannot subsist without it, and the Germans that are used to starve cannot advance without us. The duke of Wirtemberg has sent orders to his country for two hundred wagons, to help bring on our stores, and I have promised to pay them for a month, which time I hope will finish our business in this country.[1]

John to Sarah

July 9

The garrison which we have at Neuberg will give us the advantage of having bread for the army out of Franconia. I should not trouble you with this, but that I am extremely pleased to know, that I have it now in my power that the poor soldiers shall not want bread. I know that I make my court to my dear life, when I assure her that I take all the pains I am capable of to serve the public, and that I have great reason to hope that everything will go on well; for I have the pleasure to find all the officers willing to obey, without knowing any other reason than that it is my desire, which is very different from what it was in Flanders, where I was obliged to have the consent of a council of war for everything I undertook.[2]

The small fortified town of Rain, on the Lech, resisted for seven days. La Colonie and the remains of his Grenadiers had rallied there, after escaping from the battlefield, and, strengthened by several hundreds of local troops, their stubbornness required siege operations. Now was the need for the Imperial siege train which Marlborough had been promised would be ready. It was late, weak, and ill-equipped. The artillery which the Empire was to provide from Mainz and Philippsburg had not arrived. Not till the 14th did the

---

1 Coxe, i, 367.   2 *Ibid.*, 370.

first "great guns" from Nuremberg make their appearance. Trenches had been opened meanwhile, and the bombardment begun. Ammunition was scanty, and the gunners unskilful. It was thought prudent to induce the garrison to capitulate by the offer of easy terms, and on the 16th they marched out with the honours of war, and were allowed to rejoin their army at Augsburg. La Colonie plumes himself, not without reason, on this result.

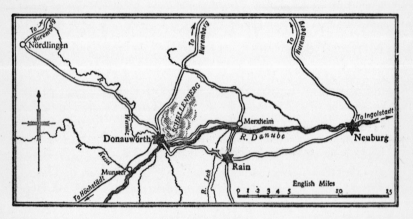

THE TRIANGLE

Marlborough, who had promptly occupied Neuburg, had now a satisfactory technical position, at the head of his communications with Nuremberg, astride of the Danube and the Lech, and with enough fortified bridges to enable him to manœuvre with ease on either side of both these rivers. The defended triangle Donauwörth—Rain—Neuburg was the central structure upon which all his movements depended. He could hold out his right hand for a junction with Eugene, and with his left he dominated Bavaria. He could concentrate for battle on either side of the Danube. It is important here to notice also that as soon as the Elector had quitted the Lauingen-Dillingen lines Marlborough had them levelled by local labour, and placed small garrisons in the towers of Dillingen and Höchstädt. This foresight was later rewarded.

Until Tallard joined the Elector the numbers of the allies

were sufficient to pin the Elector in Augsburg, and also undertake an important siege. Of course, Munich was the prize, and lack of heavy artillery and siege stores was decisive against this. Twelve twenty-four pounders were all that could be gathered.

Wratislaw wrote:

> Marlborough's consternation at it is indescribable; for if we had not had the present successes, the whole campaign might have had to be ended fruitlessly owing to his departure; but now one will try to make the best of it.[1]

Marlborough wrote to Godolphin at the end of the month:

> For want of cannon and the King of France doing all he can to succour the Elector, we shall be obliged to take measures such as our wants will permit us; but you may be assured that if they give us any opportunity, we shall be glad to come to a battle; for that would decide the whole; because our troops are very good. But our misfortune is that we want everything for attacking towns, otherwise this would have been dated from Munich.[2]

And again to Sarah:

> The army I am joined with has neither cannon nor money, which are two very necessary things for success, but I am very far from complaining, knowing very well that they are as desirous of having it as I am. . . .[3]

The threads of negotiation with the Elector had not been severed. Marlborough earnestly desired a settlement. The transfer of Bavaria from the party of the Two Crowns to the Grand Alliance was the hinge on which the whole war seemed at this time to turn. For the reasons which have been explained he did not trust the Margrave as an intermediary, and still less would he trust Frederick I. Heinsius had long opened to him, and had recently warned him of, the Prussian designs. But a direct negotiation in the field with the faithful, accomplished Wratislaw as the agent at once of the

---

1 To the Emperor, Ebermergen, July 4, 1704; *Feldzüge*, vi, 841.
2 July 31, 1704; Coxe, i, 373.   3 *Ibid.*

Empire and the Maritime Powers, even if it led to nothing, must certainly be tested to the end.

Wratislaw set the matter before the Emperor in a pithy dispatch, which shows incidentally his feelings towards the Margrave.

> As to disgusting the King of Prussia, there is nothing in it, for this King has himself written to Marlborough that he, Marlborough, must now conclude the treaty *in loco*. As far as the Margrave is concerned there is even less difficulty. He has often said it was his business to conduct the militaria but not the negotia; besides he can be handled with the greatest ease, since *there can be no hesitation in trusting him with what will have to be communicated to the Elector himself in a few hours*.
>
> *The Margrave is lying in bed with his wound, or I should say contusion of the toe,* and we were with him yesterday. . . .[1]

It was Max Emmanuel's interest to bargain with the allies for peace, and with France for help. No appeal to France could be so potent as the open threat to change sides. There was besides the hope of gaining time from the enemy. The plight to which his ambitions had led him was unenviable. Huddled round Augsburg with no news of succour, he was condemned to watch the torment of his country. The confederate generals had, as we have seen, agreed from the outset that while they treated with him seriously for a separate peace they would not relax or alter the course of their military operations. They proceeded to ravage Bavaria before its ruler's eyes. From many points on the horizon rose pillars of smoke. By every pathway open his terrified subjects implored from their prince either protection or peace. At the same time Wratislaw, sceptical but persuasive, offered grand bribes. If Max Emmanuel would return to the loyalties from which he had been seduced by the lure of the Imperial Crown there should be full forgiveness. He might resume his place among the Germanic princes of the Empire. His dominions should be restored to him. Nay, they should even be increased. Pfalz-Neuburg and Burgau would be added to his hereditary lands upon the guarantee

1 Wratislaw to the Emperor, Ebermergen, July 4; *Feldzüge,* vi, 841.

MAX EMMANUEL, ELECTOR OF BAVARIA
From a print in the British Museum

of the Queen of England, the Emperor undertaking to compensate the lawful owners. Two hundred thousand crowns would be paid to repair the damage—which was, however, increasing daily. Marlborough, now duly empowered from London, added the promise to hire twelve thousand Bavarian troops for service in Italy at the current rates of pay. On two points only was the Emperor insistent. "You must and shall at all times reject the claim to the title of King, and also refuse the French troops permission to depart freely."[1]

On the other hand stood Marshal Marsin and the French army. Under the duress of rapine the Elector had dispersed his own troops throughout his territory to guard towns and properties, especially his own. In Augsburg the French were far the stronger. The Great King had sent them there at his request. If he made his peace with the Emperor what would Marlborough do with them? He asked through his secretary, Reichard, who had been in touch with the allied headquarters since June 6, that they should be granted safe-conduct home. The most that Marlborough would allow was that he should not be compelled himself to fight against them. Nevertheless, the negotiations went forward, and by July 12 what was virtually a draft agreement had been framed. The Elector had even fixed the Monastery of Fürstenfeld as the place, and the 14th as the date, when he would himself personally meet Wratislaw to sign the bond.

But now Marsin in dire straits used his power. He suggested to Max Emmanuel that the allies might well seize his person and make him a prisoner of State. Further he declared that if he went to the rendezvous, the French troops would burn their baggage, march at once towards the Rhine, and shake the dust of Bavaria off their feet. It is possible even that these threats did not stop there. Certainly the feelings of the French officers can be understood. Under their weight the Elector yielded. He would not go himself. But in the absence of any further help from France he insisted that the parleys should be kept alive. Marsin and his generals held a council of war at which the Elector was present. Each

1 The Emperor to Wratislaw, July 23, 1704; *Feldzüge*, vi, 845.

gave his opinion. Here it appeared that the main anxiety of the French was to get out of the country safely. One of the generals, Blainville, whom we shall presently see for the last time on the field of Blenheim, voiced a latent opinion that the best that could now be hoped for by Louis XIV was the neutrality of the Elector and the escape of the French army. Max Emmanuel seized upon this as ground for continuing to treat, though not in person. He had meanwhile been confronted with the menace that Marlborough would systematically burn and destroy the whole of Bavaria, which lay open to his cavalry, unless he came to terms.

On the 13th the Electress, daughter of the hero King of Poland, John Sobieski, came to Augsburg. She cared little for the French and much for Bavaria. She implored her husband to make peace. Marsin spent the day in fierce anxiety. But on the morning of the 14th, when Wratislaw was already waiting at the Monastery of Fürstenfeld, came the longed-for letter from Tallard. Written on the 8th, it announced that Tallard and his whole army of 40 battalions and 60 squadrons were marching through the Black Forest upon Villingen. This was decisive. The Elector, unstable, unprincipled, but torn by strains which few could bear, saw once again his dream of empire revive. He decided that Bavaria must burn. He sent Reichard to the monastery to explain to Wratislaw that Marshal Tallard was coming to his aid with thirty-five thousand men, and that therefore his 'honour'—this had not arisen before—precluded him from entertaining the proposals, which were otherwise satisfactory.

Marlborough had not counted much upon the negotiations. He had known for some time that Tallard was on the march. He had wondered when the news would reach the Elector. Still, the refusal, and even more the reason for it, were grave for him. The arrival of Tallard would end his stay in Bavaria. The failure of the Empire to provide an adequate siege train as promised made any first-class siege most uncertain. He had not been able to agree upon a satisfactory plan of action with the Margrave. That General talked of Ingolstadt. But this was a strong fortress. The means for taking it were probably lacking, and its investment spelt retreat from Bavaria. Finally, the Margrave had protested against the policy of devastation. From about the 12th it had been stopped. Marlborough's apologists have presented us with abundant proof that he loathed the whole process. He would not allow, we are told, the British troops, or at least the British cavalry, to take part in it. It is pretended that the Margrave as the Imperial General would naturally have the chief say in a work of this kind upon the soil of the Empire. The responsibility, we are assured, was only indirectly Marlborough's. But this is the reverse of the truth. Not only the Margrave, but the Emperor, objected strongly to what they considered the brutalities of a foreign gang, on whom however they depended for salvation.

Wratislaw took Marlborough's view. The friction between the two headquarters was aggravated by a difference upon a hateful issue. The burnings were for the time being suspended. But no other plan was put forward. It is possible the confederates might have taken Munich at certain moments in the campaign, not by a siege, but by something like a raid. But the Margrave was averse from running risks, and Marlborough in unwonted perplexity declared that it was for the commander who knew the country to propose the plan. Thus nothing was done. A large brewery was organized at Aicha for the English troops, and the army marched on the 22nd to Friedberg to confront the Elector and Marsin four miles away in their strong position around Augsburg. There seemed to be no possibility of bringing them to battle. Meanwhile the negotiations, in a broken-backed condition, still lingered on. The threat of burning all Bavaria still hung over the Elector, and Tallard, though nothing further had been heard of him by either side, was presumably approaching. His arrival would bring about a crisis. Tallard had only to move along the north bank of the Danube against Marlborough's communications alike with Eugene and with his Nuremberg supplies to bring about a battle somewhere between Ulm and Donauwörth. If the Elector joined himself to Tallard Marlborough must recross the Danube with an army strong enough to fight them both. In either case the reign of the allies in Bavaria was limited. What could be done must be done quickly.

John to Sarah

July 13

Since my last I have had the happiness of yours of the 13th and 16th of last month, and am very sorry to see that you have had a return of the illness that I saw you have once at St Albans. I conjure you not to neglect taking advice and doing what may be proper for preventing it in future; for if you will make me happy now, you must live long, and not have melancholy thoughts of what is passed; for I do assure you I place all my hopes in ending my days quietly with you, and to be contented with the children that it has pleased God to continue to us.

My blood is so heated that I have had for the last three days a violent head-ache; but, not having stirred out of my chamber this day, I find myself much easier, so that I hope to-morrow morning to be very well. Lord Treasurer will let you know all the news that I have writ to Mr Secretary Harley. Pray tell my dear children that I hope in ten days time to have so much leisure as to write to them. I hope in God my next will tell you I am quite well.[1]

Marlborough to Godolphin

CAMP AT BURCKHEIM
July 16, 1704

* I had the favour of yours of the 20th of the last month yesterday, by which I find our business in Portugal goes very ill. I think you have taken the only way that is capable of setting it right. You will have seen by my two last letters to Mr Secretary that we were in treaty with the Elector, who was to have signed on the 14th, but instead of meeting the Comte de Wratislaw, he sent his secretary to let him know that he had received assurances that the Maréchal de Tallard would join him with 35,000 men by the 22nd, so that it was not for his honour, nor in his power to quit the French. But, as we have heard nothing from Prince Eugene, we are very confident that Tallard is not

1 Coxe, i, 371.

advanced as the Elector thinks. We being in the Elector's country puts it out of our power of hindering this junction: *but I depend very much on the vigilance of P. Eugene.* We have sent him 4000 horse as he desired with assurances of more troops if he thinks they can come in time: for should Tallard join the Elector, it would draw this business to a greater length than is for the good of the Common Cause. For if we could be so happy as to finish suddenly by a treaty; we should not fail of sending troops to the Duke of Savoy; but it must be Mr Hill's business to see that they are employed as you seem to desire in yours of the 20th of the last month. . . . We are doing all the mischief we can to this country, in order to make the Elector think of saving what we cannot yet reach; for as we advance we burn and destroy; but if this should not make him come to a treaty, I am afraid it may at last do ourselves hurt for want of what we destroy. The town of Rain has this day capitulated, so that we march to-morrow, and I am so tired that I have not strength to say more than that I am ever yours. . . .

John to Sarah

FRIEDBERG
July 23, 1704

* I have none of yours to answer, and, having been on horseback most part of this day, I shall not be able to write much to you. We are now in the finest camp I ever saw, and out of my own window I can see both armies. The Elector expects M. de Tallard should join him in four or five days. When he does I do not think he will venture to quit the strong camp he now is in. If he does not his whole country is in our power; for we have it behind us, and he may be sure, if he does not make peace, we will destroy it before we leave it. You will I hope believe that my nature suffers when I see so many fine places burnt, and that must be burnt if the Elector will not hinder it.

I shall never be easy and happy till I am quietly with you, my dearest soul, whom I love above my own life.

Marlborough to Godolphin

FRIEDBERG
July 27, 1704

* Yours of the 27th and 30th of the last month I have received, by which I find Ld Galway is to be gone in two days. I no ways doubt but this change will have a good effect in Portugal; but would it not have been as well for the Service, if it had been done

53

with less harshness to the Duke of Schomberg; *for it is impossible to give a more mortal stroke to a General than to recall him in the middle of a campaign.*

I am glad that Donauwörth has been worth something to you, which may enable you to bear the loss of any other wagers that you may have made; for all the great boastings the French made of what they would do on the Rhine are vanished and they are now changing the scene. Monsr de Tallard after having attacked Villingen five days without success raised the siege, and was to be at Dutlingen [?] the 24th, so that he may be the 1st or 2nd of the next month with the Elector. We are also assured that Monsr de Villeroy has orders to march with those under his command into the country of Würtemberg, that there will be no men left in Alsace, but such as refused to pass the Rhine. *These resolutions of the French have hindered the Elector from making his peace, and have brought the seat of War into this Country,* so that we must now take our measures for the finishing this campaign on this side, which I still hope with the blessing of God will end for our advantage.

You will know by the letters from Vienna the orders that are given for the reinforcing the Emperor's army in Italy which takes away some troops that were ordered to reinforce us here. However, I can't but be pleased that they are sent to that country; for if we should miscarry here, it will not be so much for the want of men, as for that of Cannon.[1]

Thus the month in Bavaria passed. These precious days gained by toil and daring slipped swiftly by. Tallard was drawing near, and, more dominating than Tallard, winter was but three months away. Parliament must meet in November. London and The Hague would inquire why their troops were so far afield; what authority had there been for this excursion; and what had their Captain-General to show for it all. The shock of the Schellenberg had passed. The helplessness of the Empire to provide the promised siege train had robbed that victory of its natural fruits. Neither Munich nor Ulm could be taken. The Elector had been neither crushed nor gained. We see Marlborough for a while in the flicker of that baleful sunlight which was to

1 Extract.

54

play at Moscow upon Napoleon, who also sought a treaty or a battle at the end of a long march far from home.

We left Eugene at the end of June at Rastatt with his army hastily jumbled together guarding the Lines of Stollhofen and watching Villeroy and Tallard beyond the Rhine. Although now the commander of an army in the field, subordinate in rank to the Margrave, Eugene was president of the Emperor's war council, and day by day from his headquarters he supervised the theatres of war in Hungary, on Lake Garda, and in Piedmont. He gave advice and he gave decisions upon the whole war policy of the Empire, and above all he preserved his strategic relation to Marlborough in Bavaria, upon which everything hung. At this moment we can perceive and admire the comprehensive and flexible quality of Eugene: commander of an all-important local operation, the defender of the lines; a pledged essential unit in Marlborough's combination to the eastward; and the supreme director of the military efforts of a vast, disintegrating Empire. He discharged all these variously graded functions with perfect harmony. Like Marlborough, he could conduct a local action and ride in person with the charge without losing in the slightest degree his general sense of values. Like him, he could mix, sword in hand, in a mêlée and, if not injured, emerge with judgment undistorted.

Eugene soon became conscious of the lack of results in Bavaria. He imparted his misgivings to the Duke of Savoy in an illuminating letter. After explaining that it was his task, and likewise that of Wratislaw, "to contribute to a good understanding" between the Margrave and Marlborough, he wrote, "Up to now everything has gone well enough between them; but I fear greatly that this will not last. And to tell the truth since the Donauwörth action I cannot admire their performances."

Of Marlborough we have his impressions from their long talks at Gross Heppach.

To draw a true picture of Marlborough: here is a man of high quality, courageous, extremely well-disposed, and with a keen

desire to achieve something, all the more as he would be ruined
in England should he return empty-handed. With all these qualities he understands thoroughly that one cannot become a general
in a day, and he is diffident about himself. General Goor, who
was killed in the Donauwörth affair, was the kind of man on
whom he leaned, and he is a grave loss at this juncture, being a
man of courage and capacity, who by all accounts brought about
the attack that evening, sure that to wait for the next morning, as most of them wanted, would have been to waste half the
infantry without succeeding. I have been made conscious of the
death of this man by seeing the Duke, according to the news,
more than a little hesitating in his decisions.

They have been counting upon the Elector coming to terms.
They claim of course that no time has been lost over that; nevertheless since the action nothing has been done, although the
enemy so far has let them have all the time they wanted. They
have amused themselves with the siege of Rain and burning a
few villages instead of, according to my ideas, which I have put
before them plainly enough, marching straight upon the enemy.
If unable to attack him; take up a position, encamp half an hour
away from him, and by their being so superior in cavalry in an
open country, cut his communications with Augsburg and Bavaria
and stop him from foraging; it being certain that he has no
supplies in Augsburg and would have been obliged to quit that
post. Then would be the time to exploit the retreat and pursue
the enemy so closely that he would not have been able to avoid
a battle. It was even in their power to prevent his junction with
Tallard, who is already near Villingen and has delayed there
longer than I can explain. . . . But to put things plainly, your
Royal Highness, I don't like this slowness on our side, the enemy
will have time to form magazines of food and forage, and all
our operations will become the harder.[1]

This does less than justice to Marlborough's difficulties, the
lack of artillery and supplies and the unavoidable delay in
taking Rain. It underrates the considerable magazines at
Augsburg, which were certainly sufficient to maintain the
Elector's army till long after the date when Tallard could join
him. But most of all it ignores the perpetual annoyance of a
joint command. Even with the utmost goodwill on both

1 Undated; *Feldzüge,* vi, Supp., 131.

sides, even with the understanding that the general direction of the campaign lay with Marlborough, the process was fatal to sustained vigorous action. But there was no longer good-will between the commanders, nor even a pretence of it between their circles. The story of the Schellenberg became an irritant, and the officers and troops of the two allies asserted the claims of their respective chiefs to the honours of victory. The attitude of the English was judged by the Imperialists to be patronizing. The Margrave's men complained of their saying "that they had come to Bavaria to put spirit into the Imperialists and spurs into the French." We know enough of Marlborough to be sure that he was not the author of such a phrase. He never boasted, he never joked; he rarely coined a phrase, and never uttered a taunt. No such assurances can be made about our countrymen.

On the other hand, Marlborough's correspondence shows a real dislike of the Margrave and a repulsion from his military outlook. It was increasingly difficult to come to any agreement with him. Prince Louis now made objections to all Marlborough's proposals. He longed to divide the armies and escape from this tutelage and interference. When it was seen that there was no use in remaining any longer at Friedberg, Marlborough and the Margrave at last agreed that the siege of Ingolstadt was the best measure still open. This had been Prince Louis's wish ever since the capture of Rain on the 16th. The siege train, such as it was, was assembling at Neuburg. To Harley and other correspondents Marlborough wrote on July 31:

> We are endeavouring to get together thirty pieces of cannon at Neuburg for the siege of Ingolstadt, which, when we have taken it, will make us masters of the Danube from Ulm to Passau and by that means we shall always have a free passage into Bavaria.[1]

As a preliminary to the siege it was decided to move the army back to Schrobenhausen, two marches to the eastward.

Before making what was obviously a retrograde movement from Friedberg Marlborough demanded a renewed and far

[1] *Dispatches*, i, 381.

more extensive devastation of Bavaria. The Margrave again objected. He would not make war "like a hussar," but only "like an experienced general." He did not on this date, July 28, know that the Emperor had expressed the strongest abhorrence of the policy. Marlborough was insistent. Wratislaw, who agreed with Marlborough, challenged the Margrave fiercely. Hard words passed between them. Was this another instance of his pro-Bavarian sympathies? Under this pressure the Margrave gave way. More than this: Marlborough required that the Imperial cavalry should do the work. The Margrave again submitted. Later he wrote to the Emperor:

> As the result of the ravaging, the fires, and the forced contributions, in a short time there may be little of Bavaria left. I hope that I have taken the right course for Your Majesty's service in accepting other people's opinion.[1]

Sixty squadrons were now sent forth upon this lamentable duty. Not only on either side of the great Munich road, but as far as they could reach in the countryside, all villages and townships were destroyed. All grain which could not be collected was burned. By an ingenious refinement the personal properties of the Elector, which were numerous, were scrupulously spared, in order no doubt to prejudice him with his subjects.

The object of the first burnings had been to torment the Elector into compliance. Though there had been much smoke, no great harm had been done. Anger at the Elector's proved bad faith in the negotiations, disappointment and anxiety at their having come to nothing, had no doubt caused exasperation at Marlborough's headquarters. But these were not the motives for his action. Now that he was being forced to leave Bavaria, the military need of denying the whole region and its supplies to the enemy is plain. But there was another reason not noted by English writers which seems far more important. The proposed ravaging of the country, and the threat to destroy it entirely wherever a cavalry

1 Röder, ii, 65.

brigade could ride, had already induced the Elector to disperse a large part of his army in protecting valuable places, and among these particularly his own estates and salt-mines. Out of 35 battalions and 60 squadrons at his disposal he had at the end of the first week in August only 5 battalions and 20 squadrons to combine with the French in Augsburg. We shall see presently what Tallard, when he arrived, thought of this squandering of vital forces at the climax of the campaign. The fact in itself affords a military explanation of Marlborough's action. It was not senseless spite or brutality, but a war measure deemed vital to success and even safety. But to the wretched sufferers it made no difference what the motive was.

Marlborough's letter to Sarah show his disquiet.

July 30

The succours which the Elector expects on Sunday have given him so much resolution that he has no thoughts of peace. However, we are in his country, and he will find it difficult to persuade us to quit. We sent this morning 3000 horse to his chief city of Munich, with orders to burn and destroy all the country about it. This is so contrary to my nature that nothing but absolute necessity could have obliged me to consent to it, for these poor people suffer for their master's ambition. There having been no war in this country for above sixty years, these towns and villages are so clean that you would be pleased with them.[1]

But there is not much in all this. Men in power must be judged not by what they feel, but by what they do. To lament miseries which the will has caused is a cheap salve to a wounded conscience.

Although perhaps four hundred villages were burned, the devastation of Bavaria was neither so sure nor so widespread as that which France had inflicted upon the Palatinate a quarter of a century before. It was, of course, incomparably less efficient than the destruction wrought by the Germans in their withdrawals from France and Belgium in our own times. But we must make allowances.

1 Coxe, i, 375.

Explosives were then in their infancy, and fire often leaves cottage walls standing. Moreover, Marlborough would not allow the beautiful trees to be cut down, as was systematically done in the orchards of Northern France in 1917. Thus the policy was not applied with the thoroughness which our broader civilization has achieved. Still, in those days when the civil population was as far as possible kept out of the war, when the habitations and property of mankind were on so humble a scale, when often a house was a welcome sight, when a mill or granary betokened riches, when a spread of cultivated fields was a cheerful relief to the landscape, the measure meted to Bavaria seemed most grievous. The French, forgetting the Palatinate, of course proclaimed that this barbarism was worthy only of the Turks. Its military usefulness cannot be disputed.

CHAPTER III

MARSHAL TALLARD

1704, JULY

AT the moment of his setting out upon his fatal expedition Tallard was one of the most distinguished figures in the circle of Louis XIV. Not only was he reputed an excellent soldier with recent exploits to his credit, but his diplomatic qualities and experience had raised him to the highest Ambassadorial posts. He combined a knowledge of war with a wide outlook upon European politics. He might have been a Foreign Minister of France if he had not been needed as a Marshal. He was a great gentleman, of polish, taste, and learning, who wielded the pen, though at too great length, as readily as the sword. It was with deep misgivings, which have already been described, that he obeyed the commands of the King to proceed to the rescue of Bavaria. He had protested that neither the policy nor the force supplied him was suited to the occasion. He was reluctant and perplexed as he entered his coach, and with his son at his side journeyed towards his ruin.

On June 28 Tallard's army had begun to move towards the Strasburg bridges. On July 1 it crossed the Rhine, and, turning away from the lines, wended southward up its valley with obvious intention of marching towards the Danube. This confirmed the news which Eugene had sent by the responsible officer who had reached Marlborough when he was about to storm the Schellenberg. Even more remarkable was Marlborough's own Intelligence, for on July 3 he already knew almost exactly the number of battalions and squadrons which the King had so secretly assigned to Tallard only ten days before at Versailles.[1] A messenger could hardly have covered the distance quicker. The Marshal, his army crawling on its belly, being fed with great difficulty

_____
[1] *Dispatches*, i, 331; Pelet, iv, 496.

along the broken tracks which threaded the Black Forest, arrived on July 16 before the town of Villingen. This was a properly garrisoned second-class fortress of the Holy Roman Empire, made to block the only serviceable road. Tallard's supply problem had not been solved even up to this point. He required another week to bring his army through the barren country and to carry forward his food. He wished to take Villingen and afterwards Rothweil, and open a regular line of communications from the Rhine valley to the Danube plain. He had written to the King a month before that Villingen "by itself could not last two days." [1] He had brought some siege cannon ahead with him, and he planned to reduce Villingen with his vanguard while the rest of his troops and their supply-trains trickled forward through the gorges and caught him up. When the French cannon opened fire upon the fortress on the 16th the Marshal was in a more sanguine mood. A report had reached him during his march of a battle on the Danube on July 2 in which the allies had lost fourteen thousand men: "the Prince of Baden having been wounded and all his Generals killed or wounded." Not only did Tallard believe this tale, but, since it came from enemy sources, he thought it was probably understated.

No one can comprehend the movements leading up to the battle of Blenheim unless he realizes that Eugene and Marlborough were working like two lobes of the same brain. They were in constant touch with one another. Not only were messengers sent with dispatches, but trusted, proved, high-class officers, who saw through the eyes of the commanders, rode to and fro upon the three-days journey. Sometimes there was a gap of three or four days, but we may assume that the mutual understanding was very complete between Marlborough, holding on to his Danube triangle, and Eugene at Rastatt, behind the Stollhofen lines. Now, on July 18, when Tallard is cannonading Villingen, Eugene with eighteen thousand men has slipped away from the Lines of Stollhofen and presents himself at Rothweil, whence he

1 Tallard to the King, Lauterburg, June 16, 1704; Pelet, iv, 481.

glares at Tallard. If Tallard is to join the Elector, Eugene will keep pace with him and join Marlborough in good time. But what will happen if in his absence Villeroy storms the Lines of Stollhofen? Everything must be done by Eugene to prevent this; but if it happens, the misfortune must be

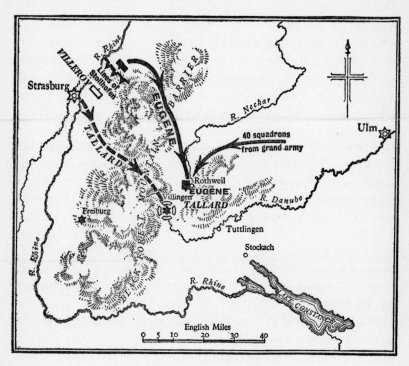

TALLARD ATTACKS VILLINGEN

endured for the sake of the greater climax maturing on the Danube. Thus we see that one facet of the art of war is the disregarding of secondary forfeits, however painful or disastrous in themselves.

Late on July 16 Tallard first learned the truth about the Schellenberg. Earlier messages from Marsin had miscarried; but now he knew that the allies, whatever their losses at the Donauwörth bridgehead, were ravaging Bavaria, while the Elector and Marsin were penned around Augsburg. Marsin's letters left him in no doubt that Bavaria would

63

desert to the allies unless effective help came at once. He was now committed to the siege of Villingen. The garrison proved stubborn. They resisted with spirit. The French batteries were awkwardly placed, and suffered severely from the fortress fire. Red-hot shot set light to the town; but the German inhabitants extinguished the flames. Meanwhile Eugene in considerable force had appeared at Rothweil and threatened to intervene. For Tallard to pursue the siege to its conclusion was probably to be involved in a festering local crisis; and meanwhile no aid to the hard-pressed and faltering Elector. Tallard decided, no doubt rightly, to abandon the particular for the general situation. Marsin assured him that he could keep him fed upon the forward march. He therefore on the 22nd, after four days' bombardment, raised the siege of Villingen, put his army on short commons, and made for the Upper Danube at Tuttlingen, whence he reached Ulm, hungry, tired, but essentially intact, on July 29. He was disturbed to find in that fortress only six thousand sacks of flour.

Eugene's movements after Tallard skirted round Villingen and took his plunge are easy to understand, now that we know the whole story. From Rothweil, where he was joined by 40 squadrons sent from Marlborough's army, he could come to Donauwörth and link up with the Marlborough triangle at least four days before Tallard could reach Ulm, and a week before he could join the Elector at Augsburg. But Eugene had to think constantly of Villeroy and the Lines of Stollhofen, now only thinly held by the corps of the Prince of Anhalt. He wished therefore to give the impression to the enemy by spies and deserters, who were numerous, that he was moving back to his old position. Accordingly, after repairing Villingen he marched with ostentation twenty miles northward to Tübingen, which he reached on the 27th of July. At that point he vanished from the French view among the desolate hills of Swabia.

Frequent instructions reached Villeroy from the King, who at Versailles received news from all quarters. Louis XIV was too far from Strasburg to control the swiftly changing

MARSHAL TALLARD
By permission of David Minlore, Esq.

scene. At first, impressed by Eugene's strength upon the Rhine, he had ordered his Marshal to concern himself with holding the enemy upon his front and defending Alsace. But when he heard that Eugene was on the march apparently towards the Danube he sent orders in the opposite sense. Villeroy, since Alsace seemed no longer threatened, was to follow Tallard towards Bavaria, secure his communications, and be ready to act if necessary upon the Danube plain. These were good orders; but by the time they reached Villeroy the Marshal thought them out of date. He was convinced that Eugene was still close to the Lines and showed no sign of moving to Bavaria. He had also been directed to send a reinforcement of five thousand men to Bedmar, in Flanders, and felt himself considerably weakened thereby. He therefore remained near Strasburg; and the King, lulled by his assurances, approved.

What greater tribute can be paid to the masterly manœuvres of Eugene? He had fulfilled both his objects. He had deceived Villeroy: he was about to join Marlborough. The King, at the moment when he had the right idea, was persuaded to abandon it; and Villeroy, gaping at the half-vacant Lines of Stollhofen, need no longer be considered as a factor in the fateful decisions impending upon the Danube.

Much foolishness has been written of the sudden surprising arrival of Eugene to the rescue of Marlborough, and how he appeared in the nick of time where he was most needed. But that all these operations were most closely concerted between the two commanders is evident, not only from the common sense of the matter, but from Marlborough's official correspondence. On July 27 he wrote through Cardonnel a series of letters in which the same information was imparted in different degrees to various high personages with whom he had to keep in touch. The accuracy of his information about the enemy, and also the speed with which it reached him, is remarkable. He knew on the 27th exactly what had happened at Villingen, and where Tallard was baking his bread and would march. He had heard of the King's orders to Villeroy almost as soon as that Marshal.

He had known for some time about the Swiss having refused to cross the Rhine; and also about the detachment Villeroy had sent to Bedmar. He derived all this from his own secret service, and confirmed it where necessary from Eugene's field reports. He credited Tallard with three days' more expedition than he actually made. But this was an error on the side of prudence. To Harley he said:

> . . . I am of your opinion, that he [the Elector] will not be brought to terms till the last extremity, and that we could not [ought not to] buy him at too dear a rate; he relies entirely on his succours, which are advancing from the Rhine. . . . M. Tallard after lying six days before Villingen, with four twenty-four-pounders and eight sixteen-pounders, had been obliged that day, upon the approach of Prince Eugene, to retire; . . . and was to march the same day [the 22nd] to Tuttlingen on the Danube, where he had sent before to bake bread for his troops, resolving to march with all expedition to join the Elector. If this news be true, of which we are hourly expecting the confirmation, the junction [of Tallard and the Elector] may be made about the 2nd of the next month. We are told that the Maréchal de Villeroy has orders to fall with the troops under his command into the country of Würtemberg, so that the enemy's vast designs on the Rhine are vanished, and the whole war like to be brought on this side. They will have in Alsace only the Swiss that refused to pass, and a few battalions more under the command of M. Coigny. . . . Since the closing my letter we have one from Prince Eugene which confirms the news relating to M. de Tallard.[1]

And to M. Schmettau:

> . . . You will have heard that this general has had a check at Villingen. He has since advanced with all diligence and, as we calculate, will join the Elector about the 2nd of next month. *Prince Eugene keeps by his side and will be within reach of us about the same time,* so that the war will drag on at the expense of Bavaria which is likely to be for the most part ruined.[2]

[1] Friedberg, July 27; *Dispatches,* i, 373.
[2] "M. le Prince Eugene le cotoye, et sera a portée de nous environ le meme temps de sorte que la guerre va trainer encore aux depens de la Baviere, qui en apparence sera pour la plupart ruinée." (*Ibid.*)

And to Secretary Hedges:

> . . . M. Tallard . . . now is marching this way with all the expedition possible, so that he may probably join the Elector about the 2nd of next month. *Prince Eugene is likewise advancing this way, and I hope will be within reach of us about the same time.*[1]

And the bulletin of Marlborough's army, on the 27th:

> As soon as the French retired from Villingen, Prince Eugene went thither and returned the same evening to Rothweil, *from whence he will march on the other side the Danube as the French advance on this.*[2]

Here we see how all was foreseen, prescribed, and combined between the two Generals. Eugene knew that, whatever might miscarry behind him on the Rhine, or in Würtemberg, he must arrive on the Danube somewhere between Ulm and Donauwörth at the same time that Tallard joined the Elector. Marlborough in all his conduct counted upon him to do this, and his own arrangements made the junction sure and certain.

We are commonly assured that Marlborough and Eugene planned together to send the Margrave out of the way to besiege Ingolstadt while they themselves sought battle upon the Danube. One must beware of trying to find a pattern everywhere among the facts of history. It is only sometimes that design is truly present, and even then there are often many events happening unexpectedly or disjointedly from day to day which are inconsistent with it. It is therefore necessary to set out the facts exactly.

Upon the agreement to besiege Ingolstadt the Margrave wrote to Prince Eugene. He submitted his letter to Marlborough before sending it, and Marlborough wrote his own comments upon it to Prince Eugene without showing them to the Margrave.

Marlborough to Eugene

FRIEDBERG
July 31

> Your Highness will see by the Prince of Baden's letter what he feels about the siege of Ingolstadt, and that he is bent upon

[1] Friedberg, July 27; *Dispatches*, i, 373.　　[2] *Ibid.*

67

making it with the troops we have here without any reinforcements from your side. I have pointed out to him that there is no military reason for keeping so many troops in the Lines [of Stollhofen] or in Würtemberg, because Tallard is here, and Villeroy, having sent off a detachment towards the Low Countries, cannot have a corps of more than twenty thousand men to oppose us from the Rhine [*de ce côté-là*]. On the other hand, when Tallard has joined the Elector and Marsin, they will have at least an army of more than forty thousand men; and when we shall be occupied with the siege they, being between us and their garrisons, will be able to draw [from them] to the very last man, and raise themselves to fifty thousand; whereas, when we have furnished the troops for the siege—which the Prince of Baden believes he can conduct with twenty-three battalions and thirty squadrons, which in my opinion is too little—the enemy will nevertheless have a considerable superiority over our army of observation; and we shall run the risk not only of a setback, but of losing the whole fruit of the campaign. Instead of which if we pushed this siege with vigour, we might still find ourselves able to besiege Ulm. With this object (without however broaching a word to anyone) I have written to Mainz to get ready the twenty pieces of cannon belonging to the States-General which could come in time for that. . . .[1]

Besides this letter Marlborough enclosed a formal memorandum called a *projet* under three heads. The first declared that the Palatine troops were sufficient to defend the lines against Villeroy. The second showed in detail down even to individual battalions how *un petit corps* could be scraped together from various quarters as a reserve to cover Würtemberg. The third paragraph must be stated in full:

> For the siege of Ingolstadt there can march the Prussian corps, the Danes, and the rest of the cavalry now with the army of Prince Eugene, which troops will be reinforced for the siege so that *the grand army will always be in a position to make head against the Elector joined by Tallard.*[2]

Nothing can exceed the precision with which this plan is stated. The bulk of Eugene's troops are to go to the siege of Ingolstadt, strengthened by enough troops from the

[1] *Dispatches,* i, 379.   [2] *Ibid.,* 380.

Marlborough-Margrave army to push the siege with vigour, *provided always that the covering army or "grand army," as Marlborough called it, shall be capable of fighting a battle with the whole combined forces of Marsin, the Elector, and Tallard.*

Marlborough concluded his letter to Eugene with a sentence which shows the contrast between his relations with Eugene and with the Margrave.

I request Your Highness to look closely into this [*examiner de près*], and if you find yourself in agreement, as I have to be very careful how I handle the Prince of Baden [*comme il est nécessaire que je garde des mesures avec M. le Prince de Bade*], I would beg you to settle it thus, and put it up to him as if it were your own idea [*de prendre le tout sur soi comme ses propres pensées*].

Eugene replied to the Margrave on August 2 from Heidenheim. It is instructive to see how he and Marlborough already worked together. He adopted Marlborough's view in its entirety, and after a lengthy survey of the situation presented it to the Margrave as his own. He declared that the whole of the forces with him could be spared from the Rhine for the rest of the campaign, and he offered to undertake the siege of Ingolstadt himself with them. Hitherto the personal question of command had not been discussed. Prince Louis keenly desired it for himself. He had always favoured the operation. He now felt bound to offer Marlborough the choice whether to conduct the siege or cover it. Marlborough did not immediately announce his decision. For some days the question rested in suspense. Meanwhile Eugene's letter arrived.

The fact that Eugene was himself willing to take the siege was not calculated to lessen the Margrave's desire. With Eugene before Ingolstadt, the Margrave saw himself tied up with Marlborough in the covering army. The joint command had led to unceasing friction and a widening breach. All the time Marlborough, with Wratislaw in his pocket, had dominated or overridden him on every occasion. All he had been able to do was to resist and make trouble, and he must by now have felt that whatever he proposed was treated as suspect, because of his alleged Bavarian sympathies. And here was this prize, the capture of Ingolstadt, the virgin fortress, his own original plan, to which the others had at length come round—was it to be taken from him? But Marlborough had not yet given an answer to his only too courteous offer. There is no doubt that on the night of August 3 the Margrave of Baden desired above all things to conduct the siege of Ingolstadt himself.

Marlborough to Godolphin

FRIEDBERG
August 3rd, 1704

* I find by yours of the 7th [18th N.S.] of the last month you were impatient to know what further steps we had made. If we had had cannon we should have been a week ago at Munich; for the consternation was so great that we might have done everything if we had wherewithal to act. P. Lewis thinks that he shall have it in his power to have Cannon on the Danube sufficient for the attacking of Ingolstadt. It is the strongest place in this country, which makes me very much apprehend the success; for I am very sure that one-half of what will be promised will not be performed. Complaints can do no good, so that I beg you will let nobody know it, but such as will say nothing of it; for we must do the best we can. If we succeed in this undertaking and can possess ourselves of Ratisbon [Regensburg], the next thing we shall think of is if possible to attack Ulm; in order to which you will see by the copy of my letter to P. Eugene that I have sent for 20 pieces of Cannon which belong to the Dutch. If I should let them know it here, they would be so negligent that they would neglect the getting their own. P. Louis makes me the compliment of my choosing either to make the siege or cover it. I have not yet taken my resolution; but in the next camp I must, for there the troops for the attack must be named. As yet Monsr de Tallard has not joined the Elector and we begin to be afraid that his design is to pass [re-pass] the Danube at Ulm, by which he would give us a great deal more trouble than if he joined the Elector. . . .

Meanwhile, as can now be seen, there was no doubt about what Marlborough's choice would be. Although he kept up appearances even with Godolphin, Wratislaw on August 3 reported to the Emperor, "Marlborough is

70

willing to satisfy the Margrave and let him take command
of the siege for fear lest the Margrave should leave him
short of the needed supplies." We cannot therefore doubt
that when the time comes the Margrave will succeed in gaining his heart's desire, nor that Marlborough will make the
sacrifice, when the time comes, out of respect to the first
general of the Empire.

Marshal Tallard reached Augsburg on the 5th, and the
next day the full concentration of the Franco-Bavarian
army was effected at Biberbach. Marlborough moved to
Schrobenhausen on the 6th and to Sandizell on the 8th,
the bulk of the Margrave's forces lying close by, but
rather nearer to Neuburg. The two hostile armies lay
about twenty miles apart. Simultaneously the army of
Prince Eugene had appeared on the Danube at Höchstädt,
in the tower of which, it will be remembered, Marlborough
had a post. The confederate position was at this moment
thoroughly sound. The enemy could not advance towards
Donauwörth or Rain, where all the crossings were fortified
against them. Unless they wished to force a battle at a
disadvantage, their only offensive movement was against
Eugene beyond the river. By this also they would assail
Marlborough's communications through Nördlingen with
Nuremberg. There could be little doubt they would take
this course. Marlborough and the Margrave could join
Eugene in front of Donauwörth in time to meet such a
menace with their three armies united. But they would
only just have time; for the distance they would have to
march, from Sandizell to Donauwörth, was twenty-two miles,
while that from Biberbach by the bridge of Lauingen to
Donauwörth was thirty-three miles. There was only one day's
march in favour of the allies. Marlborough—for he was in
fact the directing authority—had superior forces, interior
lines with well-prepared roads and fortified bridges within
them, and satisfactory communications with his advanced base,
Nördlingen, and even better *via* Neuburg with his ultimate base, Nuremberg. The enemy would have to march
round and see what part of this closely wrought structure

71

they would attack; and all the while they would be courting a battle with perhaps sixty thousand men against more than seventy. So far prudence and advantage rested with the allies.

On the afternoon of the 6th Eugene had arrived at Schrobenhausen. Sergeant Millner saw him as he rode through the camp of the Royal Irish, "attended by only one servant." He was welcomed by Marlborough alone.

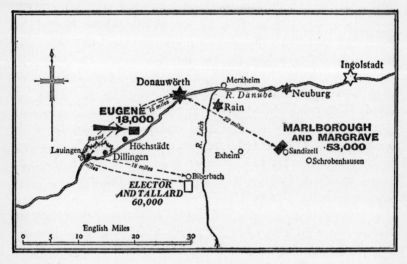

AUGUST 8

The Margrave had already started from Neuburg to inspect the siege train and make arrangements for the siege. That night he wrote to Marlborough that he had found everything ready, and had therefore given orders to invest and isolate Ingolstadt by a cavalry brigade. Marlborough and Eugene had twenty-four hours together, with Wratislaw at hand. The Margrave returned on the evening of the 7th, and the three commanders discussed the situation. They decided that the arrival of Tallard should not deter them from the siege of Ingolstadt. Marlborough then stated he would prefer to serve with the covering army. Before Eugene could speak the Margrave declared that he was ready to conduct the siege, and pointed out that his troops were

72

nearer to the fortress than those of Prince Eugene. The latter therefore remained silent, and the Margrave had his wish. After the battle Prince Louis viewed the story in a different light; but he had surely no ground for complaint. His was the decision, and that it was agreeable to the two superior minds with whom he was working is not a fact for which they can be reproached.

Early on the 7th Marlborough and Eugene with a large escort rode forth to examine for themselves all the country between them and the enemy. A battle might be fought here, and they must know the ground thoroughly. They did not return till nightfall. On the 8th they moved to Sandizell. On the 9th Prince Louis's besieging force of 20 battalions and 15 squadrons, or fifteen thousand men, most of whom were camped along the Neuburg road, marched across the river towards Ingolstadt. Eugene returned to his command at Höchstädt, and Marlborough set the main force on a short march to Exheim, five miles nearer to Donauwörth and his military triangle. He had not gone far when news arrived that the whole Franco-Bavarian army was in motion towards the Danube at Lauingen. A similar report met Eugene just as he had got through Donauwörth. He immediately turned his horse and rode back to Marlborough at Exheim.

Now comes the surprising event. Marlborough, with Eugene's agreement, allowed the Margrave to continue his march to besiege Ingolstadt twenty miles in the rear. He thus discarded his numerical superiority. He left himself with only thirty-eight thousand men (who could, indeed, join or be joined by the eighteen thousand under Prince Eugene on either side of the Danube before a battle) but opposite to more than sixty thousand Franco-Bavarians. The chronicles of disaster no doubt afford innumerable precedents, but we know of no similar defiance of the sound principle of gathering all forces together for a battle by any of the successful captains of history. We have therefore a new situation deliberately created by Marlborough and Eugene in which the odds in numbers were turned against

73

themselves. They could certainly unite, but when united they would have to fight with about five men to six and barely half as many guns. Judging in the after-light, we may admire the confidence of these masters of war in themselves and in their soldiers.

That they had by now—and probably at this moment—resolved to attack the enemy and fight a battle on which the whole result of the war would be staked is suggested by a curious incident. The Emperor Leopold had been from the beginning of the month grievously depressed. Suddenly on the night of the 12th, which was the earliest a swift courier from Exheim could have reached him, he sent for the Bishop of Vienna, and directed him the next morning to begin a solemn Triduum, or three days' invocation of divine protection for the armies of the Holy Roman Empire. Such ceremonies were not unusual in these troublous times, but the court and the capital were puzzled because no special object was assigned for their prayers. During the 13th, 14th, and 15th of August there were intercessions of a general character. The Emperor was several times heard to say, "In these three days the fate of the House of Austria will be decided." No one knew what he meant until nearly a week later. Then his words were on every lip, and many avowed he had received a divine premonition. The English Ambassador was sceptical. In his dispatch of August 20 he wrote, "I am not so superstitious as to believe that the pious emperor possesses the gift of divination, and yet I do recall it as remarkable that August 13, the day of the victory, was also the first day of the Triduum." [1] He evidently suspected—and we may share his view—that the two generals had sent word through Wratislaw that they meant to put everything to the test, and had even specified the 13th, 14th, and 15th as the days within which they would make their attack upon the enemy.

Yet even now they did not attempt to recall the Margrave. It would still have been possible for his troops to have marched back from Neuburg to join them between Donau-

1 Stepney's dispatch, August 20; Klopp, xi, 184.

wörth and Höchstädt on the afternoon of the 12th; and his cavalry could have arrived there that morning. On the contrary, we find Marlborough sending him ten more squadrons, or fifteen hundred horse, to put him at his ease. He and Eugene must have felt very sure of their own skill and comradeship and of the quality of their troops. Their decision was scarcely complimentary to the Margrave. His military epitaph for all time must be that the two greatest captains of the age, pre-eminent and renowned in all the annals of war, rated, by actions more expressive than words, his absence from a decisive battlefield well worth fifteen thousand men. And this before a Europe whose military society, evolved by twenty years of war, measured all the facts and values with professional eye. No wonder Prince Louis never forgave them!

Once the Margrave had departed, Marlborough's problem became intricate, and as critical as an actual battle. He now had two vital objects to safeguard: he must be able to cover the Margrave and the siege of Ingolstadt, and to pass the Danube and join Eugene in time. Which of these tasks would predominate depended upon the movements of the enemy. Even now the situation was not clear. Marlborough could not move with his whole force to join Eugene's army until he was sure Tallard and the Elector had definitely committed themselves to passing the river. Their march might be a feint, and meanwhile he must preserve the power to cover the Margrave. We have his letter from Exheim on August 9 to the Margrave, which lucidly explains the position.

> I have received sure news to-day upon the march which the whole enemy army made this morning towards Lauingen. Prince Eugene, who had left me, came back this afternoon to confirm this, and has since left to rejoin his command. On this news we have ordered twenty-seven Imperial squadrons to march to-morrow before daybreak [*de grand matin*] to join him, as I shall do at the same time with the whole army to put my right on our bridges over the Danube and to pass this river if the enemies pass it with all their army.[1]

1 *Dispatches*, i, 387.

His concern is to reassure the Margrave that he will not be exposed.

> In this case Prince Eugene will send forthwith a reinforcement to Your Highness of ten Imperial squadrons. I will take care moreover to stand myself always between the enemy and the siege of Ingolstadt and to detach troops [for your protection] in the same proportion that they can.
>
> We have also information that the whole garrison of Munich or the bulk of it marched last Friday from the direction of Augsburg. I will not fail to let Your Highness know all I can learn.[1]

In the midst of this tense crisis, which he was measuring and controlling from hour to hour, we find Marlborough with time to write one of his periodical series of letters to his Cabinet colleagues and to the States-General, dealing on this occasion mainly with the financial contribution which the Dutch should make to the cost of the expedition to Portugal and with the command in that country. All this, apart from his orders to the troops, was written while the uncertainties and crisis of the 10th were at their height, and may be read at length in Murray's *Letters and Dispatches*. Thus we see him measuring accurately and functioning with cool routine, while resolved upon moving towards an event which, if it miscarried, would be fatal not only to himself and his army, but to the whole cause of the allies, for the sake of which the risks were run. But thereafter Cardonnel's office shut down. When it reopened four days later the destiny of Europe and its leading nations had been settled for nearly a hundred years.

The sun was setting on Marlborough's camp at Rain when an officer galloped in with a decisive letter from Prince Eugene.

> CAMP OF MUNSTER, *two hours from Donauwörth*
> *August 10, 1704*
>
> * MONSIEUR,
> The enemy have marched. It is almost certain that the whole army is passing the Danube at Lauingen. They have pushed a Lieutenant-Colonel whom I sent to reconnoitre back to Höchstädt. The plain of Dillingen is crowded with troops. I have

1 *Dispatches*, i, 387.

held on all day here; but with eighteen battalions I dare not risk staying the night. I quit however with much regret, [the position] being good and if he [the enemy] takes it, it will cost us much to get it back.

I am therefore marching the infantry and part of the cavalry this night to a camp I have had marked out before Donauwörth. I shall stay here as long as I can with the cavalry which arrived to-day from Your Excellency's camp and my own dragoons. As soon as the head of your infantry comes up, I will advance again with mine, if the enemies have not occupied the position.

Everything, milord, consists in speed [*diligence*] and that you put yourself forthwith in movement to join me to-morrow, without which I fear it will be too late. In short, all the army is there. They have left at least twelve battalions at Augsburg under Caraman. . . .

While I was writing sure news has reached me that the whole army has crossed. Thus there is not a moment to lose and I think you might risk making the march by the Lech and the Danube. That will shorten it a good deal, and the road is better. I await your answer, milord, to make my dispositions. It is above all important not to be shut in [? cramped] between these mountains and the Danube.[1]

This vibrant letter, hitherto unknown, and especially its last sentence, are revealing. After the open plains of Höchstädt and Blenheim are passed the hills draw in towards the river, and there is no battle-ground suitable for a main trial of

---

*[1] "Monsieur. Les ennemis ont marché. Il ny at presque pas a douter que toute l'armée ne passe le Danube a Laüingen. Ils ont poussé un lieutenant collonel que j'avois envoyé pour reconnoistre, jusqua Höchstetten. La plaine de Tillingen est remplie de monde. J'ay tenu tout le jour ici, mais avec 18 bataillons je n'oserois hazarder de rester cette nuit ici. Je quite cependant avec beaucoup de regret, estant bon et s'il le prenne nous aurons beaucoup de peine a le reprendre. Je fais donc marcher cette nuite l'infanterie a un camp que jay fais marquer aupres Donavert et une partie de la cavallerie. Je resteré ici aussi longtemp que je pourré avec la cavallerie qui est arrivée aujourdhui du camp de V.E. et les dragons que j'ay avec moy. Dabord que la teste de Vostre infanterie arriverat je feré ravancer la mienne si les ennemis nont pas occupé le poste. Le tout milord consiste en la diligence et que vous vous mettiez dabord en mouvement pour me joindre demain, sans cela je crains qu'il sera trop tard. Du reste toute l'armée y est. Les ennemis ont laissé aumoins 12 bataillons a Ausbourg avec Chamarante lieutenant. Pendant que j'ecris jay nouvelle sure que toute l'armée est passée. Ainsi il ny at pas un moment de temp a perdre, et je crois quon pourroit hazarder de faire la marche en passant le Lek et le Danube cela la raccourcit beaucoup et le chemin est meilleur. J'attens une reponse milord pour me regler, il depend du tout de ne se pas laisser enfermer entre ces montagnes et le Danube.

strength until after Donauwörth and even Neuburg have been passed. Hence the desire of Eugene not to retreat beyond the Münster position, and that the concentration point of the army should be as far up-stream as possible. This shows that the decision to fight a battle had already been taken by the two commanders, and that this was recognized between them as their main purpose.

Much praise has been bestowed upon the smoothness and celerity of the concentration which followed. But the dia-

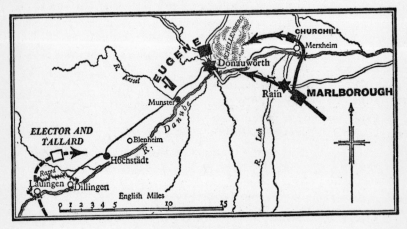

AUGUST 10

gram shows how conveniently the divisions of Marlborough's army lay at the moment when the sudden but expected call came, and how short were the distances. Part of his cavalry had already joined Eugene. His brother Churchill, who had crossed the pontoon bridge at Merxheim in the morning, was seven miles from Donauwörth, where Eugene's infantry had spent the night. Marlborough himself, taking the short cut across the Lech to Donauwörth, as Prince Eugene recommended, was equally close. Starting at midnight on the 10th, they could both be at Donauwörth during the next morning by marches of only seven miles. A further four miles would bring the combined army into the line behind the Kessel stream. Knowing that Churchill and Marlborough were on the march and close at hand, Eugene at daybreak on the 11th

78

arrivée aujourd'huy du camp de X. et les dragons que jay avec moy dabord que la teste de notre infanterie arr je feré radancer la mienne si les ennemis nont pas occupé le poste le tout milord consiste en la diligence et que vous mettiez dabord en mouvement

Camp or Munster
Th 16 Aug. 1704
from the Prince of Savoye

EUGENE TO MARLBOROUGH, AUGUST 10
Blenheim MSS.

du camp de munster
a deux heures de donner
ce 10 aoust 1704

Monsieur

les ennemis ont marché
il ont et presque pas-
a blouster que toute
l'armée ne passe le danube
a lauïngen, ils ont poussé
un lieutenant collonel
que jauvois envoyé pour
reconnoistre, visque

pour me ioindre demain
sans cela je crains qu'il
seroit trop tard, elle reste
toute l'armée y est, les-
ennemis ont laussé au moins
12 bataillons a auβbourg
avec chamarante lieuten...
pendant que iecris...
jay nouvelle seure-
que toute l'armée est
passée, ainsi il ny at...

höchste
billing...
monde,
jour il
bataille
hazar...
nuit icy
avec be...
estant
nous a

temp a
quoi p...
de fair...
paββa...
danube
beaucoup
est the...
seront
regler,
faut

... la plaine de— coup de peine a
... est remplie de reprendre, je fais ...
... jay tenu tout le marcher cette ...
... mais avec 18 l'infanterie a un ...
... je noserois— que jay fais mar ...
... de rester cette cuisses donnaient, ...
... quite cependant une partie de
... coup de regret cavallerie, je ne ...
... il sen ... icy aussi longtem ...
... rons beau— je pourrai avec ...
cavallerie et qui ...

... montagnes et le ...
... et je crois personne n'est ...
... hazardé avec plus de ...
... la marche en deff.
... le ... et le—
... la raccourcit
... et le chemin
... jattends une
... pour me
... dépend du—
... ce pas laisser

très h...
et très ...
jenni...

led his infantry back to join his cavalry, who were watching the enemy. He thus laid strong hands upon the position and freed the roads for the movement of Churchill's twenty battalions, followed by Marlborough and the main body. Of course, when so large a force is marching by a single road, as after Donauwörth, the rear must be a day behind the van. But the last of the cavalry and infantry were closed up and came into line by 10 P.M., after a total march of only eleven miles. The enemy by a fifteen-mile march from their bridge-heads might have drawn up before the allies' position at the same time, but not sooner, and neither army would have had their artillery ready for a battle till the next day.

We must now take advantage of our passports to the opposite camp. When Marshal Tallard had reached Augsburg on the 4th, one of his first complaints to the Elector was that he had dispersed the Bavarian force. He recurred to this in bitter words in his letter to Chamillart a month later.

> In addition, there was the total ignorance of the enemy's strength, and M. de Bavière having all his troops, except five battalions and about twenty-three squadrons, spread about the country to cover his salt-works, a gentleman's private estate in fact, instead of what they should have guarded—his frontiers.[1]

Marsin supported Tallard.

> This reinforcement [Eugene's army] makes it necessary for M. Tallard to press to the utmost his Electoral Highness to recall some of his troops who are in Bavaria to make this army equal in number to the enemy, and even if possible stronger, so that we can go where we like. The Elector has 35 good battalions and 43 squadrons of good troops, of which since the entry of the enemy into Bavaria he has had 23 squadrons and 5 battalions with the army, the rest being spread about in his properties in small bodies, which produced no effective result, and which would be much more useful for the service of the King and of the Elector in reinforcing the army. Love for his country has induced him to take this course, though he has done his country no good thereby.[2]

---

[1] Tallard to Chamillart, September 4, 1704; Pelet, iv, 565.
[2] Marsin to Chamillart, August 8; Pelet, iv, 550.

The ravaging of Bavaria had plainly produced important military results.

The Elector was conscious of these reproaches. He promised to recall his troops as soon as the enemy evacuated the country. He ordered forthwith four battalions and four squadrons to join him from Munich. Apart from this the three enemy chiefs were satisfied that they had the whip-hand of the confederates. They took it for granted that Marlborough's retreat from Friedberg was the first stage in a general withdrawal from Bavaria. At no time, till they had ceased to count at all, did they contemplate even an allied siege of Ingolstadt or know about it. The conviction that once Tallard had arrived the allies would retire upon their communications by Nördlingen towards Nuremberg obsessed their minds. The only question was how best they could inflict punishment upon them. Thus Tallard to the King on August 5:

> From the heights of Biberbach we shall see what the enemy will do and regulate our own movements accordingly until the thirteen battalions and sixteen squadrons with which the Elector has undertaken to strengthen his army have enabled us to grip the enemy tighter, and then we shall not let him get off cheaply [*et ne les point marchander*].[1]

They agreed to march on the 9th to Lauingen, cross the Danube there, and await in a strong camp the arrival of the Bavarian reinforcements. Meanwhile they would threaten Marlborough's communications at Nördlingen and oblige him to quit Bavaria.

On the night of the 9th they slept at Lauingen by the banks of the river. On the 10th they crossed to the northern bank. It would have suited their plan to rest in the Elector's old entrenched camp of Lauingen-Dillingen. But they found all the fortifications levelled. Feeling themselves decidedly the stronger, they were in no mood to begin digging them up again. They therefore moved forward to Höchstädt on the 11th. During this day they learned that Marlborough

---

1 Pelet, iv, 548.

was joining Eugene. They did not know whether the Margrave was with them both or not. The initiative, they conceived, rested with themselves. The allies would naturally retreat upon Nördlingen and along their communications. The only question open was whether they could not maul Eugene's rearguard as he and Marlborough withdrew into the hills. Upon this there was considerable debate. The Elector, nominally the commander of the army in which he had hardly any troops of his own, was all for the offensive. He called for an immediate advance along the river towards Donauwörth. Tallard resisted. He judged rightly that time was upon their side. The Bavarian reinforcements would come in. Soon Marlborough would have to go home. The King's interests would best be served by their entrenching themselves where they were. If only the lines of Lauingen-Dillingen had not been destroyed, this is probably what they would have done. Feeling ran high at headquarters. Tallard even said to the Elector who mocked at his caution, "If I were not so convinced of Your Highness's integrity, I should imagine that you wished to gamble with the King's forces *without having any of your own*, to see at no risk what would happen." [1] On this unkind presentation of the facts the Elector subsided. The French officers around Marsin who agreed with him muttered, however, that if the allied armies occupied Höchstädt without a battle *"in a week there would be fifty letters written to Versailles."*

It was decided as a compromise to move three miles farther forward to the open ground in front of Höchstädt. On the 11th and the next morning they captured the small posts of eighty and a hundred men respectively which the allies held in the towers of Dillingen and Höchstädt. They marched into their new camp on the morning of the 12th. It never entered into their minds that they might be attacked themselves. In this warfare of marches and counter-marches battles were so rare that if reasonable precautions were taken, and the military movements were

1 Tallard to Chamillart, September 4; Pelet, iv, 564.

correct, they might almost be ruled out. They had been so long accustomed to the war of manœuvre and of engagements with limited risks that the idea of a ferocious death-grapple, where the destruction of the whole of one side or the other was at stake, did not present itself. For three years a world war had raged without any decisive battle having been fought. That the armies before which they were grimacing in the orthodox fashion would suddenly fall upon them and try to kill them all or perish in the attempt, seemed as unlikely as that a chess-player should knock over the board and seize his opponent by the throat. These experienced generals in no way contemplated such violent behaviour. They therefore passed the 12th in great composure. They lay behind a marshy stream. Their front was covered by a line of loop-holed and defended villages. Their right lay upon the Danube; their left upon the wooded mountains. They felt safe and comfortable, and when Tallard proposed to build a few redoubts, the Elector begged him not to break the soil.

On the morning of the 12th, as they were moving into their laid-out camp behind the Nebel stream, they could plainly see the enemy six miles away in considerable numbers at the mouth of the gorge between the hills and the river. And they were struck by the fact that, instead of a retirement while time remained, a broad expanse of tents began to spring up at the beginning of the plain. Evidently the allies were not in a hurry. What did this mean? Was it not a fine opportunity to fall with their whole army upon a portion of the other? Opinions were again divided, but prudence pre-vailed. Before attacking they must know whether the Mar-grave was with Eugene and Marlborough or not. So a reconnaissance of forty squadrons under the Marquis de Silly went forward to probe the enemy and take some prisoners. The reconnaissance soon found itself opposed by equally large numbers of the enemy's cavalry, and at one point not far from the river they came upon a number of pioneers apparently engaged in making approaches across a swampy water-course. This odd fact did not disturb their preconceived opinions.

But they caught four prisoners or deserters, who were subjected separately to sharp examination. Each of these men told the same tale. They one and all declared that the Margrave and his troops had arrived. And secondly that the whole allied army was going to move off towards Nördlingen the next morning. This intelligence seemed to be confirmed in the first part by the reports of the French cavalry scouts who had watched the dust clouds above Marlborough's baggage column marching the day before from Rain to Donauwörth, and in the second part by the rumours which came in from the countryside. Thus the two Marshals and the Elector were all in the end agreed, first that they should not attack so strong an army, and secondly that it was naturally responding as might be expected to the strategic compulsion of their move. Of course these prisoners or deserters had been 'planted' upon them in order to deter them from making any attack on the 12th, which would have deranged the deployment of the allied offensive on the 13th.

During this day Marlborough and Eugene from the church tower of Tapfheim had gazed long and intently at the French camp, and both had ridden out with their cavalry to drive back the French reconnaissance. With pride and pleasure they rejoiced in each other's companionship and in their conviction that the whole war must be put to the test at dawn. But in the French and Bavarian camp no one expected anything of importance to occur on the morrow, and generals and soldiers went untroubled to their rest.

The Count of Mérode Westerloo, a Flemish officer of distinction who commanded a Belgian contingent in the service of Spain forming part of Marshal Tallard's army, has left us sprightly memoirs of this and other campaigns. He dined that night in Blenheim village with the generals and colonels of his division. Never was he in better spirits than when, having eaten and drunk excellently, he returned to his quarters. These were in a grange which overlooked the Nebel. His retinue had carpeted the floor and set up his bed. "Never I believe have I slept a sleep more sound and tranquil than this night."[1] He was still sleeping profoundly at six o'clock in the morning when his trusty valet, all out of breath, entered the barn. "Milord, the enemy are there!" "Where," said the count, mocking him; "there?" "Yes, there, there," reiterated the servant, and, throwing open the door of the barn and the curtains of his master's bed, he revealed a brilliant and astounding spectacle. The wide plain, bathed in the morning sunlight, was covered with hostile squadrons and battalions, already close at hand and steadily marching on. But behind this magnificent array, if the count could have discerned them, were the shapes of great causes and the destinies of many powerful nations. Europe protested against the military domination of a single Power. The Holy Roman Empire pleaded for another century of life. The ancient rights of the Papacy against Gallicanism and the ascendancy of a Universal over a National church— despite the mistaken partisanship of the reigning Pope—were, in fact, fatefully at stake. The Dutch Republic sought to preserve its independence, and Prussia its kingdom rank. And from across the seas in England the Protestant succession, Parliamentary government, and the future of the British Empire advanced with confident tread. All these had brought their cases before the dread tribunal now set up in this Danube plain.

1 Mérode Westerloo, *Mémoires,* p. 298.

CHAPTER IV

THE BATTLE OF BLENHEIM

1704, AUGUST 13

MARLBOROUGH had spent some of the night in prayer. He received the sacrament from Dr Hare. "The religion he had learned as a boy" fortified his resolution and sealed his calm. While the advance guards were moving into the night he visited Prince Eugene, whom he found writing letters. They mounted their horses. It is said by several authorities that on being in the saddle he declared, "This day I conquer or die." Nothing was more unlike him. Months before in England he had used such words to Wratislaw, and assuredly they did not go beyond the truth. But, arrived at the point of action, it is more probable that he made some considerate inquiry about his horse's forage or his man's rations.

The army filed off at three o'clock in eight columns, preceded by 40 squadrons, along tracks which had been carefully marked and prepared, through darkness intensified by the gathering mists of dawn. As day broke they crossed the watercourse by Tapfheim, and here the advance guards were merged in their respective columns. Here also a ninth column was formed close to the river. It comprised all the troops of the outpost line, and included the two English brigades of Rowe and Ferguson, in all 20 battalions and 15 squadrons. Of this powerful body Lord Cuts took command. The artillery and the pontoons marched by the main road with the Duke's six-horse coach at their tail. The whole force numbered 66 battalions, 160 squadrons, and 66 guns, or about fifty-six thousand men. Daylight came, but at first the sun only drew more vapours from the marshes and shrouded densely the crawling masses. Thus the heads of the columns arrived in line with Schwenningen village, scarcely two miles from the enemy's camp, about six.

Here Marlborough and Eugene remained together for

85

some time in company with the Prussian Major-General Natzmer, who had fought at Höchstädt in the previous year. The plan of the two commanders was that Eugene should attack and hold the enemy's left wing while Marlborough overwhelmed his right. If Marlborough succeeded he carried forward Eugene's battle with him. The more decisively

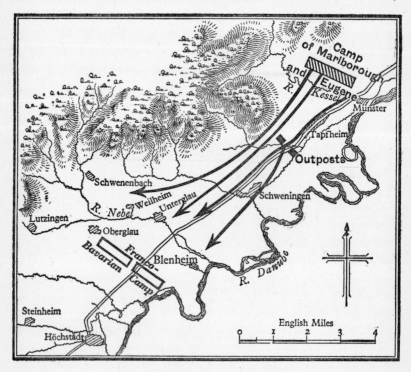

THE ADVANCE TO BLENHEIM

Eugene could attack, the greater the chances of Marlborough's success. If both allied wings were defeated, retreat would be difficult, especially for Eugene, most of whose troops could only have fallen back into trackless wooded heights. On the other hand, the advance of Marlborough along the Danube and towards Höchstädt would not only conquer the enemy in his own front, but would threaten the retreat of the whole of the French opposite Eugene.

The mists began to thin as the sun rose higher, and the

enemy outposts became aware of large numbers of men gathering along their front. They sent back speedy warnings, and at the same time the mists dispersing revealed from the French camp large forces covering the whole space from the Danube to the hills. Even now the Marshals and the Elector held to their prepossession that the confederate army was retiring under a bold display through the shallow valley which led back to Nördlingen. Tallard had finished a letter to the King, but before dispatching it he added the following postscript:

> This morning before daybreak the enemy beat the *général* at 2 o'clock and at three the *assemblée*. They are now drawn up at the head of their camp, and it looks as if they will march this day. Rumour in the countryside expects them at Nördlingen. If that be true, they will leave us between the Danube and themselves and in consequence they will have difficulty in sustaining the posts and depots which they have taken in Bavaria.[1]

Incredible as it may seem, the Marshal penned these words about seven o'clock or even a few minutes afterwards, *and sent off the messenger*. We see that the possibility of the allies forcing a battle did not even enter his mind. This also gives us the measure of the audacity of Marlborough and Eugene in relation to the military conventions of the period as understood by the French High Command.

However, the columns still moved forward, and when, shortly after seven, they began to deploy into a long wall of blue, red, and buff, gleaming with steel, the truth broke suddenly upon the French and Bavarians. They were about to be attacked! There was no time to retire, even if they wished to do so, without abandoning their camp and baggage. They must now prepare to fight for life and honour. This sudden revolution of ideas had an effect not only upon the commanders, but upon their troops. It was a moral surprise.

---

1 "Ce 13, au point du jour les ennemis ont battu la générale à 2 heures, à 3 l'assemblée. On les voit en bataille à la tête de leur camp, et suivant les apparences ils marcheront aujourd'hui. Le bruit du pays est qu'ils vont à Nordlingen. Si cela est, ils nous laisseront entre le Danube et eux, et par conséquent ils auront de la peine à soutenir les établissements qu'ils ont pris en Bavière." (Marshal Tallard to the King, dated Leitzeim, August 12, 1704; *Campagne de monsieur le maréchal de Tallard en Allemagne 1704* (Amsterdam, 1763), ii, 140.)

Count Westerloo, who had mustered and mounted his own squadrons upon his first sight of the enemy, had been perturbed at the unbroken silence of the French headquarters. But now Tallard came hurrying along, thanked him for his promptitude, and ordered him to tell the artillery to fire the signal guns to recall the foragers, and meanwhile to sound the alarm incessantly.[1] The camps sprang into activity. Aides and messengers galloped to and fro, the soldiers hustled out of their tents, formed in their companies, battalions, and brigades, and moved forward to their appointed places in the order of battle.

This had, of course, subject to the final dispositions of the commanders, already been prescribed. The allied army, whose formation developed and broadened continually, was soon within cannon-shot, and at half-past eight the powerful French artillery which covered their front opened fire upon them. The English field batteries began to reply as they came into range, and the cannonade became general. Its thunders rolled down the Danube Valley. The Margrave, forty miles away in his camp before Ingolstadt, was writing to the Emperor. His officers drew his attention to the distant thudding which loaded the air, and he inserted in his letter the words, "The Prince and the Duke are engaged to-day to the westward. Heaven bless them."

The French position had been selected for its military advantages. Its flanks rested securely on the Danube and the wooded hills. Its four-mile front was shielded by the rivulets of the Nebel. In those days, when populations were small and only the best soil cultivated, drainage was rare; and a strip of soft or marshy ground, in places a treacherous quag, profuse in rushes and marigolds, laced by streamlets from four to twelve feet broad, carried the springs and rainfall from a wide bay of hills to the river. A spell of dry weather had reduced this obstacle, still however serious to the soldiers of 1704. Along it were three considerable villages. On the French right, a furlong of water-meadows from the Danube, stood Blenheim (locally Blindheim), about three

---

1 Mérode Westerloo, p. 300.

hundred houses, many of stone, with the usual South German gardens and enclosures, clustered round a solid church and stone-walled graveyard. Two miles or more away in the centre rose the roofs and church-tower of Oberglau, and a mile and a half beyond, nestling under the hills, the spire of Lutzingen. Here were three strong points on which to

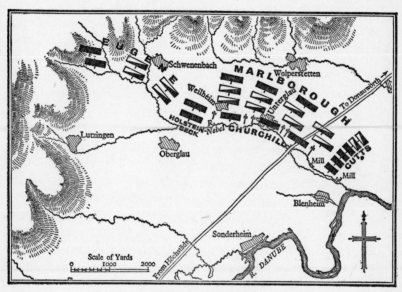

ALLIED DISPOSITIONS

hang the front. From the marshes of the Nebel the ground rose almost imperceptibly but steadily in about a mile to a grassy upland, upon which the four or five thousand French and Bavarian tents were spread in well-drawn rows. On the allies' side the slopes were slightly more pronounced; and here the villages of Weilheim and Unterglau with several smaller hamlets had served as the French outpost line. These had already been set on fire by the retiring pickets and were burning briskly.

Tallard, Marsin, and the Elector met in Blenheim at about nine o'clock to concert their plans of defence. They were somewhat staggered by the stern aggression of which they saw themselves the objects. They assumed that the Margrave

89

had joined the allied army, and that they were to be assaulted by superior forces. But they were not ill-content with their position, and they had time to occupy it advisedly. Tallard's army had been kept distinct from the rest on account of his independent command, and also because glanders or some other disease was rife among his horses. The generals climbed up the church-tower, whence the whole scene was revealed. From this modest height it appeared as a large, flat plain, framed by the mountains and the river. The cannon were firing busily on both sides, and between the bulges of dense white smoke which sprang into being and drifted towards them, and the dark clouds which arose from the conflagrations, long columns of the enemy were seen slowly making their way through the scrub of the foothills towards the head of the valley opposite Lutzingen. Not far away, before Blenheim, four heavy lines of infantry, among which the English redcoats predominated, and two of cavalry were deployed. In the centre, opposite the long, too long, space between Blenheim and Oberglau, the main force of the allies was drawn up in four dense lines. Their arrangement was unusual—indeed, entirely novel. The first line was of foot, the next two lines of horse three or four deep, and in the rear another line of foot. The experience of many years of warfare questioned such dispositions.

It was settled that the Elector and Marsin should hold the front from the hills to Oberglau, and that Tallard, strengthened by thirty squadrons of Marsin's cavalry, should defend the ground between Oberglau and Blenheim, and above all should guard the right flank at Blenheim, including the short gap between Blenheim and the Danube. In fact the stations of the troops and the camps from which they had been mustered broadly conformed to these dispositions. But a difference is said to have arisen upon the method of meeting the impending attack across the Nebel. Marsin and the Elector were for holding the firm ground close to their edge of the marsh, so as to destroy the enemy before they could form in ranks after wading or filing across. Tallard was more ambitious. On his front he would allow at least a considerable part of

90

them to cross. Within well-judged limits the more that crossed the fewer would escape; for then the masses which he would place in Blenheim and the strong force in Oberglau would sally out upon their flanks and rear, while he charged upon them down the smooth glacis between these invincible pillars. If Marlborough persisted in so hazardous an attack

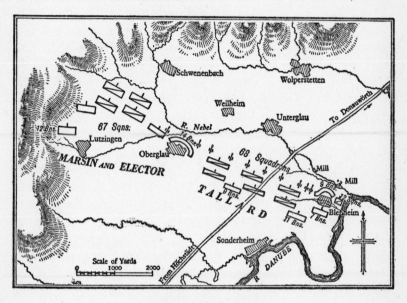

FRENCH DISPOSITIONS

it would be no mere drawn battle. He would take him in a trap. The Elector, on whom all he had heard about the Schellenberg had made a deep impression, uttered a warning. "Beware of these troops. They are very dangerous: you cannot afford to concede anything." "Well, then," said Tallard, "I see that to-day the victory will be my own." On this they descended the tower and galloped to their posts.

The distribution of the troops can be seen upon the plan; but, in short, Tallard placed 12 dismounted squadrons of dragoons, whose horses had died of disease, behind a barrier of carts from the Danube to Blenheim. He assigned 9 battalions to the defence of the perimeter of Blenheim, with another 7 immediately behind them and 11 more battalions

91

a few hundred yards back in reserve. He drew up 68 squadrons, supported by 9 battalions of infantry, a thousand yards from the Nebel on the open ground between Blenheim and Oberglau, and he sent his two remaining battalions to join twelve of Marsin's command in Oberglau. Marsin and the Elector arrayed the remainder of the French and all the Bavarian cavalry from Oberglau towards Lutzingen; and massed their infantry on either flank, posting Count d'Arco with 12 Bavarian battalions in front of Lutzingen with their flank resting 'refused' upon the hills. In all they marshalled 84 battalions, 147 squadrons, and 90 cannon, or about sixty thousand fighting men, against the allies' 66 battalions, 160 squadrons, and 66 cannon, or fifty-six thousand men.

Prince Eugene, with the troops he had brought from the Rhine and the cavalry which had joined him three weeks before at Rothweil, was meanwhile toiling through the rough and broken country in front of the Elector and Marsin. His progress was slow, and all the time he was harassed by the enemy's artillery, to which his own cannon, being still on the march, could for some time make no reply. Lord Cutts' column, the ninth, had now deployed by the river against Blenheim. At ten o'clock his leading British brigade,[1] having expelled the enemy from two water-mills upon the Nebel, crossed the marsh and lay within a hundred and fifty yards of the outskirts of the village. Here they endured for the next three hours with fortitude the severe fire of a heavy six-gun battery posted on a small eminence near Blenheim and to their right. The rest of Marlborough's army sat or lay in their ranks on the forward slope, the horse dismounted, and they too endured the cannonade of an artillery nearly twice as strong as their own. Marlborough's pioneers and working-parties, protected by infantry from the first line, repaired a stone bridge across the Nebel, and with the planks of the pontoons and seven hundred fascines

1 Rowe's Brigade:

Howe's	. .	15th Foot: the East Yorkshire Regiment
Ingoldsby's	. .	23rd Foot: the Royal Welch Fusiliers
Marlborough's	. .	24th Foot: the South Wales Borderers
Rowe's	. .	21st Foot: the Royal Scots Fusiliers
North and Grey's	.	10th Foot: the Lincolnshire Regiment

which had been cut by the rear line of cavalry, constructed five additional bridges or causeways across the marsh between Blenheim and Oberglau. The artillery fire caused serious losses in both armies, but by far the heavier to the allies. An officer who accompanied the French artillery commander, M. de Frézelière, upon his rounds wrote, "We were excited by the extraordinary effects produced by our fire, each discharge piercing their battalions, and some slant-ways; and from the very order in which the enemy were posted, every shot told."[1] The cannon-balls struck, bounded, and shore their way through the lines of men and horses on the plain, and caused nearly two thousand casualties before the attack could even be begun. Divine service was held at the head of every regiment, and the prayers and psalms rose to a grim accompaniment of crashes and cries of pain. But no unwounded man stirred from his place. The pioneers were a special target; but the bridges grew steadily.

The services being ended, the waiting soldiers, unsheltered from the fire, ate their midday meal. Marlborough, resplendent in scarlet, wearing his Garter ribbon and riding his white horse, paced slowly in front of his harassed lines. A roundshot, striking at his horse's feet, enveloped him in a cloud of earth, and wrung an anxious gasp from the watching troops he had led so far from home. But he continued his progress uninjured. He had found the time to choose the sites for the field hospitals, such as they were, and had posted every battery himself. He spent the dragging hours in watching their shooting or conversing with the commanding officers. After a while he dismounted and lunched with his attendants, probably on the rising ground behind Unterglau village. In these conditions, where every man's bearing could be so closely scrutinized, he seemed entirely free from care; yet a grave anxiety was growing in his heart. What had happened to Eugene? He should have been in position by eleven. It was now nearly noon. Messengers had gone and returned with vague reports. The columns were struggling on as fast as they could. At length

[1] Baron de Quincy to Chamillart, September 18, 1704; Pelet, iv, 576.

he sent Cadogan to find the Prince, and to see for himself. Cadogan returned shortly after twelve with the news that Eugene was nearly ready. All the bridges were now finished, and so far the enemy opposite Marlborough showed no mind to dispute the passage. But the day was wasting. Each minute now acquired a value. At last an aide-de-camp arrived at a gallop. "His Highness will give the signal for attack at half-past twelve." Marlborough rose, called for his horse, and mounted, saying to the group of officers, "Gentlemen, to your posts." All the troops stood up and dressed their ranks. The infantry fixed their bayonets, and Cutts launched his attack upon Blenheim. At the same time the first line of General Churchill's infantry began slowly to move towards the Nebel.

High and proud was the bearing of these regular soldiers as they strode into battle. "All," says Hare, "advancing cheerfully showed a firm and glad countenance and seeming to be confident to themselves of a victorious day." [1] Among those who now advanced was Captain Blackadder, and as he gazed upon the mass and pomp of the enemy covering the whole plain before him his heart was so filled with a sense of the infinite mercy and power of God that he could not help exclaiming aloud to his company, "How easy it would be for the Lord to slay or take captive all those thousands before nightfall!" whereat his men, seeing their commander thus transported, were mightily heartened. "And moreover," adds the Captain, in proof of the efficacy of faith and prayer, "before night it was even so."

The British brigade of five battalions which had been sheltering as much as possible in the stream-bed from the artillery now rose up and marched upon the palisades and enclosures of Blenheim. Their brigadier, General Rowe, had ordered that there should be no firing till he struck his sword upon the pales. The distance was perhaps a hundred and fifty yards, and almost immediately, owing to the ground, the troops passed out of the fire of the hostile battery. They marched in silence and perfect order to within thirty yards

1 Hare's Journal.

JOHN, LORD CUTTS
William Wissing
National Portrait Gallery

of the defences. Then the French fired a deadly volley, and General Rowe, who was still unscathed, struck the palisade with his sword; whereupon the survivors of the leading companies fired in their turn, and came to grips with the French through the palisades and across the obstacles which they tried by main force to tear to pieces. Their efforts were vain. Although here and there small parties penetrated, the French, who so greatly outnumbered their assailants, repulsed the attack, inflicting a loss of one man in three. Here fell General Rowe mortally wounded, and both his staff officers were killed in trying to carry him away. As the assault recoiled

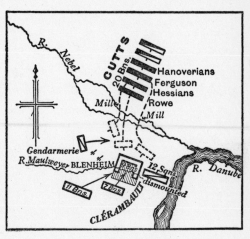

ATTACK ON BLENHEIM VILLAGE

in disorder three squadrons of the celebrated French Gendarmerie, also clothed in red, charged round the outskirts of the village and fell upon their flank. Rowe's own regiment [1] lost its colours. The Gendarmes, pressing on, encountered the Hessian brigade at the edge of the marsh, but these good troops by a well-directed fire routed them in their turn and rescued and restored the colours of the 21st.

Lord Cutts now extended his line to the left with Ferguson's English brigade, and with Rowe's brigade, which had reformed, and the Hessians who still covered the right, delivered a second and even more costly attack. Here the troops broke at various points into the enclosures and pressed the defenders back upon the actual fronts of the houses and the barricades across the streets. More than this they could not win. M. de Clérambault, who commanded all the troops in

1 Now the 21st Foot, the Royal Scots Fusiliers.

95

Blenheim, was so deeply impressed with the weight and fierceness of the attack that he had quite early drawn into the village the seven supporting battalions, and under the pressure of this renewed and more serious onslaught he summoned also the eleven battalions which Tallard had posted as the reserve of his right flank. Thus there were crowded into Blenheim no fewer than twenty-seven battalions, together with the four regiments of horseless dragoons who held the ground between the village and the river. As these excessive reinforcements arrived when the French in the village were already being forced to contract their front line a disastrous congestion resulted. Nearly twelve thousand men were crammed into Blenheim, so closely packed that the bulk could neither move nor use their arms. All the ground before the village was heaped with nearly two thousand dead and wounded, including many hundreds of the British. Lord Cutts had still an intact Hanoverian brigade, and was preparing himself to lead the third attack when, about half-past two, Marlborough, who was watching the struggle at some distance, sent him orders to desist, and to hold the enemy pinned down. Cutts therefore withdrew his infantry just beyond musket-shot, and made his colonels advance their platoons from each company in succession to deliver their fire and retire out of range. Thus the repulse was accepted. At this moment, however, though it was not fully realized, twenty-seven French battalions were occupied by sixteen of the allies. It is probable that **Cutts'** unused Hanoverian brigade, moving to its right, rejoined the main body of Churchill's infantry.

Shortly after midday Marshal Tallard, conceiving that there would be another two hours' delay before the attack, decided to visit the left of the Elector's line to survey the situation there. He had not been with the Elector long when the heavy firing around Blenheim recalled him to his own army. He noticed that Clérambault had drawn the reserve into the village, but he took no steps to alter this decision. As he sat his horse upon the gentle rise on which his cavalry stood his attention was riveted by an episode which made a disconcerting and profound impression upon his mind. Marlborough's first line of infantry was already crossing the Nebel and drawing up in solid bodies on the firm ground. His first line of cavalry were now leading their horses continuously along the causeways. Five English squadrons from Lumley's command who had scrambled across near the burning mills were actually formed in the low ground on the edge of the plain. The eight squadrons of Gendarmerie, some of which had, as we have seen, already been sharply engaged, were ordered by General Zurlauben to charge these intruders. They swept down upon them in an enveloping formation. But the five English

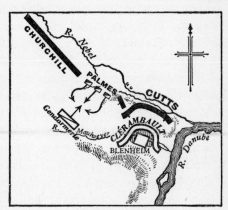

PALMES' CHARGE

squadrons, under Colonel Palmes, charging outward in three directions, broke the wings of the charge, and then, wheeling inward in perfect discipline and horsemanship, fell upon the centre of the Gendarmerie, completely routed them, and pursued them three hundred yards behind the Maulweyer brook, which flows through Blenheim. It was true that these squadrons, carried away by their zeal, came under tremendous fire from the outskirts of the village, and themselves recoiled with many empty saddles to their starting-point. But what Tallard had seen struck a chill into his soul. In the account which he eventually wrote in December of the battle he remarks that, "although there were eight squadrons on our side, the five enemy squadrons sustained their shock and made them recoil." He explains the loss of the battle "first, because the Gendarmerie were not able to break the five English squadrons."[1] Well might Marlborough say, "The troops I carry with me are very good."

1 Pelet, iv, 575.

97

The Elector, who was galloping about in the most dangerous places, and had strayed far from his own troops, now heavily engaged, was also a spectator of this encounter. "What!" he cried to his staff, "there is the Gendarmerie running away! Is it possible? Go, gentlemen, tell them that I am here in person. Rally them and lead them back to the charge." The unfortunate gentleman who endeavoured to obey his behests was severely wounded, taken prisoner by an English officer, to whom he hastily presented his cross of the Order of Würtemberg and a hundred and thirty-seven *louis d'or*, and only escaped as he was being led off because his captor was laid low by the Blenheim musketry.[1]

While these exciting incidents attracted unduly the attention of the hostile High Command, Marlborough's main body was gradually but ceaselessly forming beyond the Nebel. Already the first line of the infantry had advanced far enough to enable the first and a good part of the second line of cavalry to draw up in good order. Tallard now directed a cavalry charge upon the left of this array. Through confusion or neglect only a part of the squadrons he designed to use committed themselves to the charge. Much disorder was caused to the left of the allied line. Four or five English squadrons were rolled up from the flank. It was a dangerous moment, but the fire of the infantry repulsed the horsemen, and General Lumley made good the line by bringing across several fresh Danish and Hanoverian squadrons. Nothing could more plainly illustrate the delicate and hazardous character of the great operation which Marlborough was conducting in his centre, so long as it remained incomplete.

But now around Oberglau a new crisis arose. The Prince of Holstein-Beck, with ten battalions forming the right of General Churchill's infantry, advanced to storm the village. The Prince, with the two leading battalions, had hardly crossed the Nebel when M. de Blainville, who commanded in Oberglau, drew out into the open nine battalions against them. Among these was the Irish Brigade in the French service, known at the wars as the "Wild Geese." At the

---

[1] Pelet, iv, 586.

same time the Prince found himself threatened on his right
by Marsin's cavalry. He sent to ask for aid from Fugger's
brigade of Imperial Cuirassiers, which was covering the left
of Eugene's renewed attack. Fugger replied that he could
not move without Eugene's orders. Blainville's nine battalions now came forward, with the "Wild Geese" yelling
in the van. The two confederate battalions were overwhelmed. Holstein-Beck,
bleeding from mortal
wounds, fell into the
hands of the enemy, and
the other flank, the right
this time, of Marlbor-
ough's ever-growing
formation beyond the
Nebel was laid open to
Marsin's cavalry. Not
only was this danger
grave in itself, but the
French counter-attack

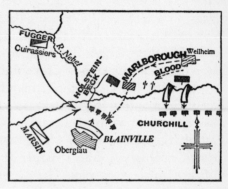

ACTION AROUND OBERGLAU

from Oberglau threatened to break the contact between the
two wings of the allied army.

The whole front from the Danube to the hills was roaring
with fire and conflict. "From one end of the armies to the
other every one was at grips and all fighting at once—a feature
very rare in battles." [1] Marlborough, who had lately been
watching the battle from the rising ground behind Unterglau,
attended by his retinue, now came quickly forward, passed
the burning villages, crossed the Nebel by a causeway, and
took personal control at the danger-point. He led forward
three Hanoverian battalions from Holstein-Beck's reserve.
He made Colonel Blood bring a battery of cannon across
the streamlet. With these he threw the Irish back some
distance towards Oberglau. In this breathing-space the
rest of Holstein-Beck's command began to form a line on
the firm ground. This was the moment for Marsin's
cavalry beyond Oberglau to renew their charges, and

1 Mérode Westerloo, p. 309.

strenuous efforts were made to gather a strong force and set it in motion.

But meanwhile Marlborough had sent a personal message to Prince Eugene asking for the use of Fugger's brigade. Eugene was himself in an intense crisis. His second attack was quavering on the verge of repulse. Marlborough's aide-de-camp found him in the front line. He made his request. Without a moment's hesitation Eugene gave the order. The Imperial Cuirassiers changed front and advanced towards Oberglau. At that moment Marsin's cavalry advanced to the charge. But Fugger's cuirassiers charged at the same time and, striking at a favourable angle and on the bridle hand, threw back Marsin's squadrons in disorder. Marlborough, planting his battery to rake Blainville's line, was now able to move forward again with the three Hanoverian battalions, supported by the growing masses of Holstein-Beck's command. The struggle around Oberglau rose to a climax, both sides being closely engaged and their cannon firing grape and even case. But by three o'clock Blainville's troops were driven in upon the village, and Marlborough, nearly one thousand yards beyond the Nebel, was able to pen them, as Cutts was penning the much larger masses in Blenheim. This was the second crisis in the passage and deployment of Marlborough's centre.

A lull now descended upon the battlefield. The firing had lasted more than six hours and physical contact for nearly two, and everywhere it seemed that the armies reeled. Dr Hare, who followed his chief among the balls, has recorded, "before three I thought we had lost the day." [1] Tallard has declared, "At this moment [the charge upon the left of Marlborough's centre] I saw the hope of victory." These perils had been surmounted. But, indeed, many an experienced officer in Europe, impartially surveying the scene, would have pronounced the allies defeated. They had failed with ghastly slaughter to take Blenheim. Nothing but deadlock existed there. They had equally failed to take Oberglau, and only narrowly escaped a severance of their wings. The

[1] Hare's Journal.

whole of Prince Eugene's attack had come to a standstill. For nearly three-quarters of an hour the two lines of cavalry in this quarter stood facing each other at sixty yards' distance, neither of them able to move forward or strike another blow. In vain did Eugene on one side and the Elector on the other ride along the ranks animating, commanding, entreating,

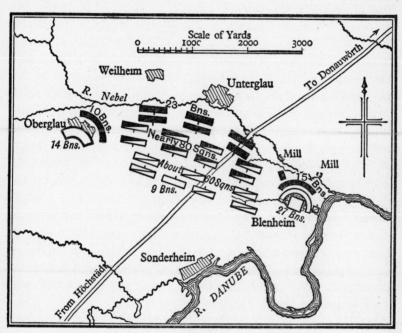

LEFT AND CENTRE AT 4 P.M.

and taunting their exhausted and shaken soldiers to a renewed effort. At no point, it seemed, could the allies move forward. Yet it was certain they could not stay where they were. If they could not advance they must soon retreat. If they retreated they were lost.

Nevertheless at this moment Marlborough was sure of victory. Shortly after three o'clock he sent one of his aides, Lord Tunbridge, to Eugene, announcing that all was well in the centre. From the tumult of battle his design was now emerging. Although his total army had at the beginning been several thousands fewer than the French, and although it had suffered up to this point perhaps double their losses, he was now in a position of overwhelming strength. By four o'clock the whole of the cavalry and the whole of Churchill's infantry were formed in good order on the farther side of the Nebel opposite the French centre. The cavalry now formed the first two lines and the infantry the second pair. The English field batteries were moving forward to join them. Upon the two-mile stretch from Blenheim to Oberglau he had now nearly 80 squadrons, only a few of which had yet charged, against 50 or 60 French, many of whom had been several times engaged. Upon the same front he had 23 battalions against only 9. Leaving the bloody local fight around Oberglau, he now rode to conduct the advance of this formidable array.

The pause in the battle continued for a while. The reason for it is plain. Marlborough wished to concert the attack upon the whole front, and Eugene after his second repulse required time to reorganize. At half-past four, when the Danish infantry had worked their way round the Bavarians on the extreme left of Lutzingen, the battle was renewed at all points. The Prince of Anhalt-Dessau, carrying a regimental colour in his hand, led forward for the third time the redoubtable Prussian Foot. Eugene advanced again at the head of the Imperial cavalry. And now between Blenheim and Oberglau Marlborough's long lines, horse and foot together, were set in motion. The impact of so great a body of troops, comparatively fresh, upon the weakest part of a wasted front everywhere closely engaged, after so many hours, might reasonably be expected to be decisive. It was not in character different from the march of the French centre against the plateau of Pratzen by which Napoleon so suddenly yet so surely gained the battle of Austerlitz. There is a grand simplicity in two or three to one at the decisive point. To procure it—there lies the secret.

Marshal Tallard had still two lines of cavalry with which to fill a threatened front. But he no longer trusted them fully. On the other hand, whether because he was physically short-sighted or because he still counted upon a helpful sortie

TAPESTRY OF THE BATTLE OF BLENHEIM.   *Photograph by permission of the Victoria and Albert Museum*

By permission of the Duke of Marlborough.

by the troops in Blenheim, he does not seem to have at all measured the preponderance of the forces about to fall upon him. "We neglected the great double lines," wrote a French general officer at Tallard's side, "which were forming at the foot of that fatal hill." Still, Tallard had used the interval to interlace his second line of cavalry with the nine battalions which were his last resource in infantry. He does not seem to have attempted to draw any of the surplus troops from Blenheim. He was content to order them to break out and attack the flank of the hostile advance. They had for some time tried to do this; but it was as hard for them to come out of the village as for Lord Cutts to enter it. The English and Hessian brigades which stood around the outskirts could plainly see any gap being opened in the defences for a sortie; and they shot down with a concentrated fire every French party which emerged before it could form a line. In this quarter the tables were entirely turned.

Meanwhile Marlborough's attack was almost abreast of a line drawn from Blenheim to Oberglau, and so far there had been no collision. Tallard, who now saw doom outstaring him, ordered his first line to charge; and they became intermingled with Marlborough's squadrons, who do not seem at this time to have quickened their pace beyond a walk. "All our Brigades," writes the French general already quoted,

> charged briskly, and made all the Squadrons they attacked give way; but these Squadrons *being sustained by several lines of horse and foot*, our men were forced to shrink back, and throw themselves on our second line, which, being at some distance, gave the enemy time to gain ground, which they maintained, *by their numbers, and their slow and close march.*[1]

The French were pressed back; but the allied horse as they advanced now came into the fire of the nine battalions. These young troops, who fought with so much gallantry for France, seconding and sustaining their cavalry, caused a good deal of disorder in Marlborough's first line, and compelled it to halt and then to retire a distance estimated by several observers at about sixty paces. The Marshal called upon his

1 Lediard, i, 429.

cavalry for a further effort. He met with no response. Marlborough now brought forward not only infantry but cannon to rake the devoted French battalions, some of which were formed in square. A battery of nine guns, which was following up the main advance under Colonel Blood's personal direction, fired upon them with grape, while at the same

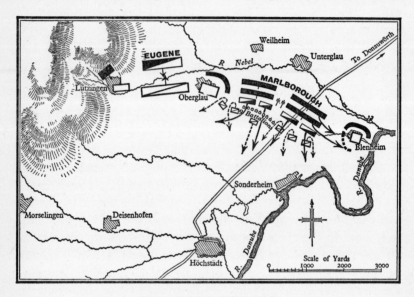

THE BREAK-THROUGH

time the German infantry, coming to the front through the horse, opened a devastating musketry at close quarters. As the French squares would not give way, they had to be very largely destroyed where they stood.

It was probably at this time that an incident occurred which gives us an intimate glimpse of Marlborough in action. One of his general officers was retiring with a force of cavalry in disorder. Marlborough rode up to him and, commanding a halt, remarked with ceremonious sarcasm, "Mr ———, you are under a mistake; the enemy lies that way: you have nothing to do but to face him and the day is your own." [1] Whereupon the general returned with his squadrons to the conflict.[2]

1 *The Lives of the Two Illustrious Generals* (1713), p. 72.
2 *Histoire de Jean Churchill*, ii, 2.

THE BATTLE OF BLENHEIM

We cannot pretend to unravel the details of this uneven struggle, but enough has been said to expose the delusion that the battle of Blenheim was gained by a cavalry charge. It was gained by the onset of a largely superior force of all arms working in close accord with one another at a decisive point. At least an hour elapsed between Marlborough's advance from the foot of the slope, before the moment of the final charge was reached. And by that time the result could hardly be doubtful. At about half-past five Marlborough re-formed both his lines of cavalry in front of the foot. He had time to ride along their ranks, and, being now satisfied that the masses of French infantry and cavalry which still held the field before him were disorganized and could resist no more, he drew his sword and ordered the trumpets to sound the charge. Now for the first time the whole body of the allied cavalry broke into a trot, and sword in hand rode forward upon all who barred their path. The French squadrons did not await the shock. Discharging their pistols and carbines in ragged, ineffectual volleys, they broke and fled, leaving the remnants of the nine battalions to their fate. Of course, when we read of troops being 'cut to pieces' we may be sure that the greater number usually escape somehow. But these poor soldiers of France behaved so bravely that the positions they had held could be plainly seen the next day upon the battlefield by their corpses lying in ranks.

In this part of the field all serious resistance now came to an end. Tallard, who redeemed as a soldier his shortcomings as a general, rallied a body of his cavalry behind the tents of his camp. His one hope and duty was to procure the retreat of the infantry in Blenheim. He sent messages to them to retire, and to Marsin to come to his aid. But all control had passed out of his hands. Marlborough, with Lumley and Hompesch, the Prussian, and over seventy squadrons, was upon them. The French ran in two directions, some towards Marsin's army and the rest towards the Danube. Sending Hompesch to the right with half the cavalry, the Duke with Lumley pursued those who were making for the river. The

105

spectacular tragedy which followed has attracted the attention of many historians.[1] The bank of the Danube near Sonden-heim falls very steeply as much as fifteen or twenty feet. A mob of French horsemen, jammed knee to knee and variously computed at thirty squadrons or two thousand men, were driven headlong over this drop into the marshes and the deep, swift river; of whom the greater part were drowned. Mérode Westerloo, who after much hard fighting was caught in this rout, says that for three hundred paces he was so jammed in the crowd that "his horse never put its feet on the ground," until suddenly he was precipitated "the depth of two pikes" into a marshy meadow and buried beneath several falling cavaliers.[2] Marshall Tallard, trying to make his way into Blenheim, recognized by his Order of the Saint-Esprit, was taken prisoner with several of his staff not far from this point by a Hessian regiment. He was conducted to Marlborough, who with salutes and courtesies placed his coach at his disposal.

This was the moment when John wrote the letter to Sarah. Borrowing a piece of paper, actually a bill of tavern expenses, from an officer, he traced in pencil his well-known message:

August 13, 1704

I have not time to say more but to beg you will give my duty to the Queen, and let her know her army has had a glorious victory. Monsieur Tallard and two other Generals are in my coach and I am following the rest. The bearer, my aide-de-Camp Colonel Parke, will give Her an account of what has passed. I shall do it in a day or two by another more at large.

MARLBOROUGH

The destruction of Tallard's army involved the instant retreat and possible capture of Marsin and the Elector. It was now six o'clock. Eugene's cavalry had failed in their third attack. The Prince, infuriated at a courage not equal to his own, is said to have shot two fugitives with his own hand. Certainly he was himself in the direst peril—his coat

1 Indeed, it is almost the only feature which Klopp has been able to discern in this long and complicated battle.
2 Mérode Westerloo, pp. 310, 311.

account of what
pass'd, I shal give
a day or two by
other more att—
ye
                Marlborough

D R Augst 13 1904

I have not time to
say more, but to beg
You will give my Duty
to the Queen, and let
her know Her Army
has had a Glorious
Victory Mons'r Tallard
and two other Generals
are in my Coach and
I am following the rest.
the bearer my Aidde Camp
Coll Parke will give Her

THE BLENHEIM LETTER
Blenheim MSS.

clutched by the enemy, and his life saved only by the devotion of his troopers. When the collapse of their charge was apparent he left his cavalry with bitter words, saying that he would fight and die with the gallant infantry and not with cowards. Indeed, the Danes and Prussians had made remarkable progress. With only two squadrons of cavalry to aid them, they had driven the enemy's extreme left back more than two miles, scrambling over the spurs and valleys amid the rocks and bushes of the foothills. From these slopes the Prince could see the result of Marlborough's main attack. He saw the whole centre of the enemy break into disorder, and knew that the battle was won.

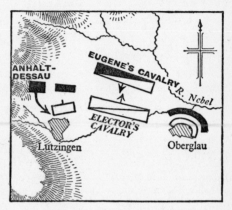

EUGENE'S THIRD ATTACK

Soon the smoke and flames rising from Oberglau and Lutzingen proclaimed the retreat of the army which had so valiantly withstood him. He set to work to organize his troops for pursuit.

When Marshal Marsin saw Tallard's line broken and the wide plain between Oberglau and Blenheim occupied by Marlborough's troops advancing in solid formations, he resolved to retreat. The Elector and the other generals were all in agreement. The disengagement and withdrawal were effected with skill and discipline, and the army of the French left wing marched in the direction of Lauingen in admirable order. This was indeed necessary, for they must expect to have to fight hard to gain the exit between the hills and the marsh of Höchstädt. Marsin's army was by no means exhausted. They had no reason to boast about their battle. With more squadrons, with nearly double the battalions and more than double the cannon of Prince Eugene, they had been hard put to it to defend themselves. They had even ceded important ground to the attack of far less numerous forces. They had fought a self-centred battle, and had been able to give no help to their friends on the right, with whose defeat their own was now involved. These facts attest the glory of Prince Eugene, whose fire and spirit had extorted the wonderful exertions of his troops; who after contending all day against very heavy odds held the initiative and the offensive to the end; and who, moreover, in the midst of local disaster had not hesitated to answer Marlborough's call for the Cuirassier brigade. By seven o'clock the whole of Marsin's army, escorting their prisoners and rescuing on their way two of Tallard's battalions who had already surrendered, were making for the gap above Morselingen, followed by all the troops that Prince Eugene could muster.

General Churchill, with the bulk of his 23 battalions, besides supporting the front, had the duty of protecting both flanks of Marlborough's advance against sorties from Blenheim or a counter-attack from the direction of Oberglau. As soon as Marlborough's cavalry rode on ahead in pursuit of the French his brother wisely turned his main force to the left against Blenheim in order to encircle and capture the mass of French infantry known to be in the village. The process of hemming in Blenheim was thus in full progress. To deter the enemy from breaking out, Churchill at a little after six asked Lord Cutts to make another attack or at least hold the enemy tight. Cutts and his troops responded generously. The remains of Rowe's British brigade headed a new assault, the third, upon the deadly defences. This time they broke in, and fierce hand-to-hand fighting was resumed all along the Nebel side of the village, as well as round the corner between the Nebel and the Maulweyer brook. Marshal Tallard, being conducted down the main road to Marlborough's coach, which we suppose was still some distance behind the Nebel, saw this furious combat flare up on his right hand. He induced one of the officers escorting him to bear a message from him to the Duke offering, if he would "let these poor fellows retire," to prevent all further firing by the French. Marlborough had now joined

Hompesch between Oberglau and Morselingen, and was organizing a cavalry charge upon the flank of Marsin's columns, which could be seen approaching half a mile away. He was surprised at Tallard's presumption. He replied severely, "Inform Monsieur de Tallard that in the position in which he now is, he has no command."

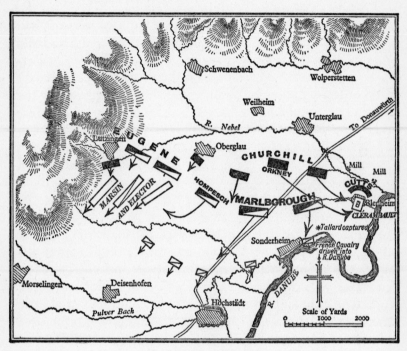

THE PURSUIT

Meanwhile Marsin's army in three columns, the outer ones of cavalry, was drawing near, and Hompesch was about to charge, when another large body of troops in good formation came in sight from behind Oberglau village. These were thought to be Marsin's rearguard. They were so disposed as to take in flank such a charge as Hompesch was about to make. They were in fact the leading brigades of Prince Eugene following the French, and themselves seeking a chance of attack. Marlborough, in no mood to compromise his victory, sent out patrols to make sure of the truth, and meanwhile

109

waited. Eugene in his turn mistook Hompesch for a part of
Tallard's cavalry, and likewise paused to assure himself. By
the time these mistakes were discovered Marsin and the
Elector had made such progress across Marlborough's front
that a new attack meant a new battle. The Duke surveyed
the scene against the setting sun. He observed the firm attitude of the enemy and their superior numbers. He knew that
he had the bulk of Tallard's infantry—how many he could
not tell—behind him in Blenheim, still to be mastered. He
decided to break off the pursuit of Marsin, and in all the
circumstances his judgment should be accepted.

The last scene in the drama of Blenheim lay around the
village which finally gave its name to the battle. The garrison
comprised the best infantry of France and its proudest regiments. They had repulsed every attack with heavy slaughter
and so far with no great loss to themselves. But many had
seen—and it needed no military knowledge to understand—
what had happened on the plain and what its consequences
to them would be. Their army was routed, and they were cut
off. The Marquis de Clérambault, whose nervousness or folly
had crowded Tallard's reserves into the village, saw himself
the cause of the disaster which had befallen the army and
was now to overtake himself and all those for whom he
was responsible. His brain reeled. He sought in flight a
still more fearful safety. Without a word to his subordinates
or giving anyone a chance to assume the command, he rode
to the river, attended only by his groom. The man tried
the passage and escaped: his master followed, "apparently,"
says Saint-Simon cruelly, "intending thereafter to live as a
hermit." But the swirl of the Danube mercifully extinguished
a life for which there was no room on earth. More charitable
tales have been told of his conduct. He had gone to examine
the river-bank—a cannon-ball had startled his horse, and he
had fallen into the river; or again that he sought in its wave
the death he found.

From seven o'clock, when he disappeared, till nearly
eight the twenty-seven battalions in Blenheim had no leader,
and received no orders. Meanwhile they were attacked on

THE FIRST LORD ORKNEY
Sir Godfrey Kneller
By permission of the Duke of Hamilton

every side. Three or four battalions of British infantry under Lord Orkney, with the Greys and the 5th Dragoons and four guns, had cut off all retreat shortly after seven o'clock. Cutts, Churchill, and Orkney assaulted continually. Orkney from the back of the village reached the churchyard, the Buffs in the van, while at the same time every cannon and howitzer

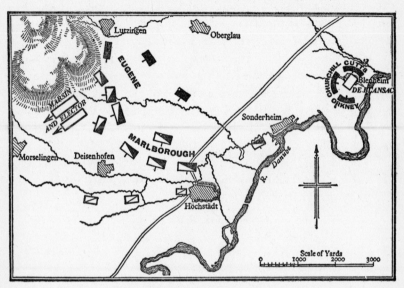

THE END OF THE BATTLE

within reach fired into the crowded streets from the north and the east. All the assailants were driven out. M. de Blansac now assumed command, and strenuous efforts were made to sally forth at several points. The fire of the surrounding troops, which were constantly reinforced, shattered the heads of every formation. The three British Generals, working in spontaneous combination, all realized the tremendous prize they had in their grip. A French brigade which had actually debouched was brought to parley, and its commander allowed himself to be sent in to bring the rest to reason. Agitated argument began about capitulation. Orkney, whose line across the rear of the village was none too strong, used bold language. Resistance was impossible. The Duke, he said, was coming with the whole army. All must surrender

III

at once as prisoners of war. The one concession granted by
Churchill, to whom the issue was referred, was that the officers
should not be searched.

The grief and fury of these unbeaten troops have often
been described. The regiment of Navarre burned its standards, and many officers refused to sign the convention; but
this could hardly avail them much. Before nine o'clock the
surrender was complete. It was not till then that Marlborough's orders arrived. The Duke, concerned at the very
great numbers he now knew to be in the place, would run no
risks. All the troops were to lie on their arms, and by morning he would bring the entire army. But the work had already
been completed by his competent lieutenants. "Without vanity," wrote Orkney, "I think we did our pairts." [1] And so
had they all.

"The British troops at Blenheim," says Sergeant Millner,
"formed a lane wherein the prisoners stood all night, and
They on the Watch over the same."

[1] Athole Papers, *H.M.C.*, p. 62.

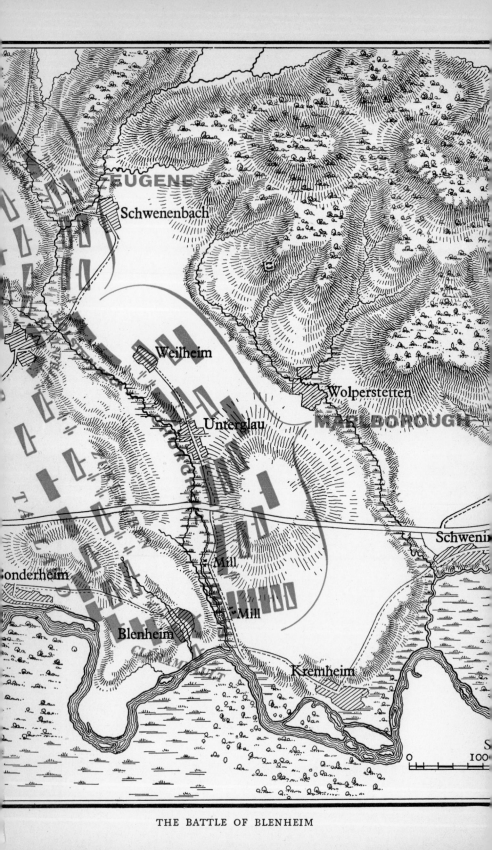

THE BATTLE OF BLENHEIM

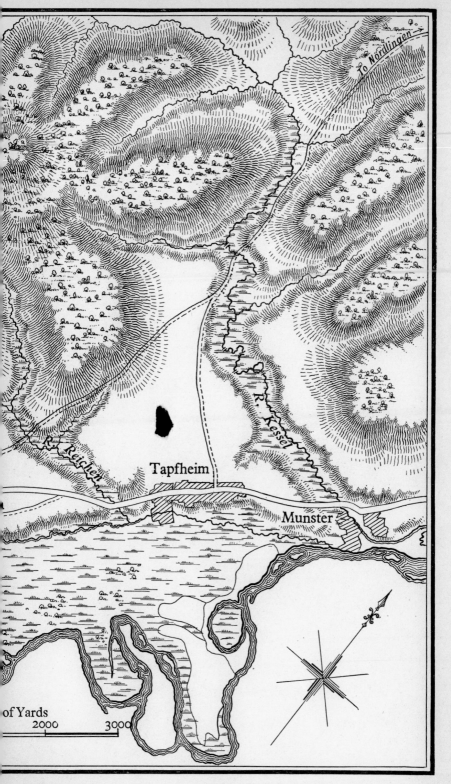

To Nördlingen

R. Kessel

R. Reichen

Tapfheim

Munster

of Yards
2000   3000

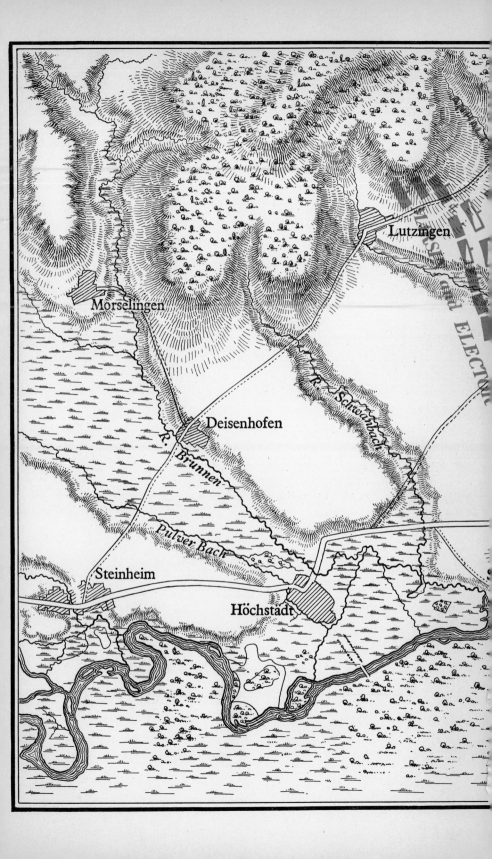

Lutzingen

Morselingen

Deisenhofen

R. Schwanbach

R. Brunnen

Pulver Bach

Steinheim

Höchstädt

ELECTOR

CHAPTER V

THE CONSEQUENCES OF VICTORY

1704, AUGUST

COLONEL PARKE rode fast across Europe, spreading the good tidings through the German and Dutch cities as he passed. On the morning of the 10th/21st he delivered his note to Sarah at St. James's, who sent him on with it at a gallop to Windsor. Queen Anne sat in the big bay-window of the long gallery overlooking the Terrace, and serious must have been her thoughts. Here, at the summit of England's war effort, many grievous pressures met in a sovereign's breast. It was but five days before that she had been forced to assent to the Security Act of the Scots Parliament with all the injury which it threatened to her island. She knew that far away in Germany Mr Freeman meant to strike some blow that should kill or cure. Rulers in constitutional states hear tales from many quarters, and the Queen understood only too well that the entire political system of her reign was under grave and pent-up challenge. She could read the stress of the times in Mr Montgomery's anxious eyes. With all her patient courage—and, let us add, Stuart obstinacy—she had sustained the men she trusted against the gathering antagonism of Parliament and society, and amid the growing degeneration of her affairs both at home and abroad.

A scarlet horseman has crossed the river: news of battle is in the air. They bring the weary messenger to her presence. He falls on his knee, but before he speaks she knows that all is well. He hands her Marlborough's note to Sarah, and tells her that with his own eyes he has seen the first army of France broken into flight and ruin, and the celebrated Marshal Tallard led off prisoner by the Duke's officers.

This was no regular dispatch. That would follow in a day or so. It was but a message to the Cockpit circle; but as the Queen read its pencilled lines she knew that something very great had happened to her country and to the world. It was the custom to give the messenger of victory five hundred guineas, but Colonel Parke, invited to name his reward, asked instead a miniature of the Queen. His request was granted, and in addition Anne gave him a thousand guineas in her relief and joy.

Meanwhile from Whitehall Godolphin spread the news throughout the town. The cannon of the Tower were fired; the bells were rung; copies of Marlborough's note, struck off upon the presses, passed from hand to hand. A wave of enthusiasm swept all classes. The streets were filled with cheering crowd. Bonfires and illuminations disputed the night. "Never were such demonstrations of joy since the laying of London stone." [1] Nor were these rejoicings unwarranted. Indeed, they arise from the smallest part of what had happened. Every one could understand that the Grand Monarch had had a drubbing, and that Marlborough had caught his famous general, old Tallard, the Ambassador, well known at St. James's, and packed him in his coach. But few could measure the consequences, and none could foresee how the fortunes of Britain would now broaden through the centuries.

The news of Blenheim came also to Versailles. A few days before the battle there had been a splendid evening fête at the Court. The most brilliant society in Europe was assembled, and the warm, delicious night favoured the festivities. Upon a triumphal car attended by warriors and nymphs the God of War was drawn past the daïs on which the Great King sat, and Louis XIV displayed a lively pleasure in accepting his dutiful salute. Then followed an allegorical representation of the state of Europe, in which all its rivers played their parts. The Thames, the Scheldt, the Rhine, the Meuse, the Neckar, and also the Danube made their submission to the assured pre-eminence of the Seine. The festival culminated in a prodigy of fireworks designed to bring

1 Trevelyan, *England under Queen Anne: Blenheim*, 397.

home to the numerous and exalted company a vivid picture of modern war.

An even more arresting topic occupied the Court. A dispute had arisen between two of the highest nobles upon their respective precedence. The historical argument ran back through the centuries, and raised at various stages some of the most delicate issues that had ever concerned a Board of Green Cloth. The whole Court was divided upon the question, and a solemn tribunal had been appointed to resolve it. The keen interest of the King in the matter was well known, and his calm suspension of judgment admired. The intriguing dilemma even interested the common people, and while the whole vast palace was thronged with courtier-notables, there was also a concourse upon its approaches. The imminence of the verdict kept all minds on tenterhooks. But one afternoon rumours began to spread of something ugly which had happened in Bavaria, and presently it was known that a courier from one of the armies in the field had been conducted by Chamillart to the King. They all had something else to talk about after that.

We must return to the Danube. Hare in his Journal says that as the night fell

His Grace gave orders about dressing the wounded men and putting them under cover. Then he made a separation of the French prisoners, which amounted to eleven or twelve thousand men. They had at least as many more killed and wounded. These prisoners, with their generals, being divided and disarmed were ordered to the adjacent villages in the rear of our Army, guarded by several squadrons of Horse Dragoons. The Author was commanded by General Churchill to go along with that part which was escorted by Colonel Wynne, to take a list of the French generals and other officers, and he humbly conceives it may not be thought improper or impertinent to recite this observation he made—viz., that after he had taken the generals names he went into a room where were at least 60 or 70 officers-subalterns, of which, some were blaming the conduct of their own Generals, others walking with their arms folded, others were laid down lamenting their hard fortune and complaining for want of refreshment, till at last, abandoning all reflections of this nature, their chief concern was for their King, abundance of these muttering and plainly saying, Oh que dira le Roy!

Sergeant Millner sets forth with careful pride the full tally of the slain, the wounded, and the captives.[1] The sergeant's

[1] Generals or noted Persons killed in the Field, or drowned in the Danube — 9

The Quantity of Thirty Squadrons rushed into the Danube and drowned, computed — 4400

Killed in the Time of the Battle, Officers included — 6000

Wounded or disabled therein, Officers included — 8000

Total killed and wounded, including the Thirty Squadrons drowned, and Ten Battalions cut in Pieces, with the Quantity of Twenty-two Battalions otherwise killed and wounded in the Action — 18409

Deserted in the Battle and precipitate Retreat, otherwise computed — 5000

Total killed or drowned, wounded and deserted — 23409

Note, That Three Generals of the aforesaid Nine were assuredly wounded, but no Account could be had of the other Six, whether killed in the Field, or drowned in the Danube; but certainly they were left in either of the twain; amongst which there was Four Marquises, Two Counts, and one Duke, whose Names I have here omitted.

Taken, Count Tallard, their Captain General, Four Lieutenant Generals, Six Major Generals, and Eight Brigadiers, Three other Colonels of Horse, Three of Dragoons, and Thirteen of Foot; most Counts, Marquises, Princes, Dukes and Barons, besides Three Marquises, and One Prince Captain of the Gen d'armes — 41

Besides all the Lieutenants, Colonels and Majors of the aforesaid Twenty-eight Battalions, and Twelve Squadrons of Dragoons, each computed to be compleat thereof — 64

Of Captains and subaltern Officers, computed accordingly — 1095

In the Twenty-eight Battalions of Centinels, &c. with some Stragglers, that fell into Blenheim — 2200

In the Twelve Squadrons, including also some Stragglers, and otherwise — 1800

Total of the whole killed or drowned, wounded, taken and deserted — 38609

By the several particular Accounts of the Enemies Loss, it appears that of the Sixty Thousand Men their Army consisted of before the Battle, there escaped but Twenty-one Thousand Three Hundred and Ninety One. Besides, there were several noted Persons and others taken by the other Allies, which I never found to insert herein.

The Enemy were industrious enough in concealing their particular Losses, but whether of these two Particulars it be, it matters not much; doubtless their Loss was very great in every Respect whatsoever; being conquered, beat and quite defeated; although Eight Thousand Men stronger than the Allies Army, besides being strongly posted with the Advantage of the Ground. . . .

Taken of War Utensils or Trophies, one Hundred Cannon, Twenty-four Mortars, One Hundred Seventy One Standards, One Hundred Twenty Nine Pair of Colours, catalogue of grisly spoils, although a little sanguine, has not been seriously challenged by the estimates of later times. The casualties of the allies were certainly not less than the 12,700 which he has recorded. Indeed, the later details of the British losses would seem to raise this figure considerably. The confederate army had lost by fire and steel nearly a quarter of its numbers. Six thousand lay dead upon the field, and the thirty-five or forty thousand hale men who stood to arms on August 14, worn out by their prodigious exertions and sleepless nights, had, besides their own six or seven thousand wounded and an equal number of the enemy wounded, twelve thousand prisoners on their hands: in all twenty-five thousand to tend or guard.

Considering that the whole impulse and vigour of the war emanated from Marlborough and Eugene, how generously they hazarded their lives and fortunes, and the immense personal contribution of their genius, it is remarkable that the negative, passive, or selfish elements which composed the mass of the alliance should have been so ready to criticize any shortcomings in those to whom they owed their salvation. But many who were incapable of even dreaming of the superb event which the two heroic men had produced were sharp enough soon to complain that the battle of Blenheim was not followed by a pursuit. The circumstances in which Marlborough decided not to renew the action against Marsin in the sunset of August 13 have already been described. But why, it was asked, were Marsin and the Elector not followed hotly in succeeding days? They had crossed the Danube at Lauingen on the 14th, burning the bridges behind them. On the 16th and 17th they were at Ulm, protected by the fortress. Was it not possible to overtake them there?

Seventeen Pair of Kettle Drums, Fifteen Pontons, Twenty-four Barrels, and Eight Casks of Silver, Thirty-four fine Coaches, Three Hundred loaded Mules, and Three Thousand Six Hundred Tents, standing and struck.

In the Confederates gaining this compleat, honourable, glorious, ever-renowned, memorable Conquest, and triumphant heroical Victory, over and against the proud and lofty French Army and Bavarians at Hochstat, August 2d. their Loss was computed Twelve Thousand Seven Hundred and Fifty-eight Men, killed and wounded, including Two Hundred and Seventy-four that were lost by Desertion, or otherwise taken moroding in the Time of our Army's Abode in Bavaria. . . .

The rapid movements before the battle and the sudden addition of thousands of prisoner-mouths above the pre-scribed population of the camp was paralysing. Bread was the imperious need. The Austrian Military History says revealingly:

> The commissariat of the Danube army, which till now had only been asked to supply the needs of the troops during a slow change of villages, had suddenly to call to life an organization which would probably have to follow the army to the Rhine almost at once. The principal lack was again money to buy what was required in Franconia and collect transport; while in the neighboring Bavaria the requisition commands found everything charred and devastated and the farms and monas-teries abandoned by the inhabitants. It was already a bitter revenge.[1]

This, added to the burden of the prisoners and the wounded, is an ample explanation. It was with difficulty indeed that the army moved forward on the 14th about four miles into a position opposite the Elector's old stronghold and bridge-heads, Lauingen and Dillingen. Here they remained for four days.

Lord Acton, in the exiguous but much-esteemed lectures which were almost all he gave to the world as the results of his life of study and capacious knowledge, said of the battle:

> Eugene at that moment was the most renowned commander in Europe. Marlborough was better known as a corrupt intriguer who owed his elevation to the influence of his wife at Court, who would disgrace himself for money, *who had sought favour at St Germains by betraying the expedition to Brest*. Blenheim altered the relative position of the two men in the eyes of the world. It was known that the day had been won not by the persistent slaughter of brave soldiers, but by an inspiration of genius exe-cuted under heavy fire with all the perfection of art. *In the midst of the struggle Marlborough had suddenly changed his order of battle, gathered his squadrons on a new line, and sent them against*

1 *Feldzüge*, vi, 530.

the French centre, with infantry supports. He did what Napoleon was vainly entreated to do in his last engagement. That is what suggested the simile of the angel, and what Addison meant by the words: "Rides on the whirlwind and directs the storm." The great Eugene had done well, as he always did. The Englishman had risen in a single day to the foremost rank of generals. And England rose with him.[1]

The reader who has persevered in this account will judge for himself the early sentences of this rare deliverance: but in his military comments the great mute student, though complimentary, is wrong. On the plainest reading of facts there was no "sudden change in Marlborough's order of battle," no "gathering of his squadrons on a new line." Marlborough's part throughout was to conquer the French right and centre. This he could only do by carrying the main body of his army across the Nebel between Blenheim and Oberglau and outfighting Tallard on the open plain. It would be a great help to him to capture Blenheim, and he assuredly bid high for the prize. But if he had taken Blenheim in the early afternoon he could never have moved the mass of his army through the village or across the water-meadows between it and the Danube. There would still have remained the task, so full of danger, of bringing his army across the Nebel and forming a line of battle beyond it. Short of the capture of Blenheim, nothing could help him more in this than the attracting into the village of the largest number of French infantry. For either purpose he must make the same kind of furious attack which he had led on the enemy's right at the Schellenberg. But the failure to storm the village required no alteration in his general plan. As we have seen, only one brigade of infantry and a few squadrons of cavalry were withdrawn from Cutts' command, and these used to wall off the enemy in Blenheim from interfering with the main advance, which once it began proved, as Marlborough had expected, irresistible. There was therefore no change of the plan, which, in fact, unfolded methodically, hardly modified at all by the convulsions of battle.

[1] *Lectures in Modern History,* p. 259.

The one great hazard which Marlborough was forced to
run was the crossing of the rivulet and its marshes. On this
his judgment and much else were staked. He achieved it by
the peculiar tactical arrangement of his lines of horse and
foot, which arose from his understanding of the new power
of firearms. It should not be assumed that Tallard could have
prevented the passage by attacking earlier with his whole
cavalry. He might well have worn them out against the fire
of the steady and well-trained infantry of Marlborough's
first line. Yet this operation and the passage of the Nebel
was at once the main, the most original, and the most dangerous part of the plan. When in the morning Eugene rode
off to attack the much larger numbers of Marsin's army, and
thought also of the task which his comrade must perform or
perish, he may well have felt that their burden had been
fairly divided.

Meanwhile the victors triumphed. A solemn thanksgiving
service was celebrated with joy-fire of musketry, and triple
discharges of cannon. Marlborough's bearing towards the
captives won general admiration. "Whereas Prince Eugene
was harsh," wrote Saint-Simon, "the Duke of Marlborough
treated them all, even the humblest, with the utmost attention, consideration, and politeness, and with a modesty perhaps
more distinguished than his victory." [1] . . . The rank and
file of the prisoners reserved to him received by his orders
every possible comfort and favour. Some of the interchanges
have been preserved:

> MARLBOROUGH: I am very sorry that such a cruel misfortune
> should have fallen upon a soldier for whom I have had the high-
> est regard.
> TALLARD: And I congratulate you on defeating the best sol-
> diers in the world.
> MARLBOROUGH: Your Lordship, I presume, excepts those who
> had the honour to beat them.[2]

All the Frenchmen of every rank showed the keenest

[1] Saint-Simon, *Mémoires*, iv, 130.
[2] *Histoire de Jean Churchill*, ii, 11 ; *The Lives of the Two Illustrious Generals*,
p. 73.

admiration for the Great Twin Captains, as they were already regarded, and clustered round them in curiosity. The soldierly bearing of a French private to whom Marlborough spoke drew from him the remark, "If the King of France had many men like you, he would soon be victorious." To which the soldier, somewhat unkindly to his superiors who stood around, rejoined, "It is not men like me he lacks, but a general like you." A trumpet was sent with a small escort to fetch Tallard's own coach from the enemy's lines, and every personal consideration was shown to him. Marlborough had known him well in London, and the Marshal's misfortunes commanded his sympathy in a peculiar degree. Not only was Tallard wounded, a captive, a discredited general, a broken man, but his son had been slain at his side. And Marlborough rendered him one act of real kindness. He enabled the ruined commander to give his own account of his conduct and of the battle promptly to Louis XIV. Tallard's friend the Marquis de Silly, also a prisoner, was on the 18th given two months' parole and a safe-conduct through Germany by the Duke's express direction.[1] No greater service could be rendered to a man in Tallard's position; and yet a cynic might observe that allied interests would be in no way prejudiced by any controversy that might arise between the Marshal who had been taken and the Marshal who had escaped.

John to Sarah

August 14

Before the battle was quite done yesterday I wrote to my dearest soul to let her know that I was well, and that God had blessed her majesty's arms with as great a victory as has ever been known; for prisoners I have the marshal de Tallard, and the greatest part of his general officers, above 8000 men, and near 1500 officers. In short, the army of M. de Tallard, which was that which I fought with, is quite ruined; that of the elector of Bavaria, and the marshal de Marsin, which prince Eugene fought against, I am afraid has not had much loss, for I can't find that he has many prisoners. As soon as the elector knew that monsieur

1 Marlborough to the Duke-Regent of Würtemberg, *Dispatches,* p. 147.

de Tallard was like to be beaten, he marched off, so that I came only time enough to see him retire. . . . I am so very much out of order with having been seventeen hours on horseback yesterday, and not having been able to sleep above three hours last night, that I can write to none of my friends. However I am so pleased with this action that I can't end my letter without being so vain as to tell my dearest soul that within the memory of man there has been no victory so great as this; and as I am sure you love me entirely well, you will be infinitely pleased with what has been done, upon my account as well as the great benefit the public will have. For had the success of prince Eugene been equal to his merit, we should in that day's action have made an end of the war.[1]

John to Sarah

STEINHEIM
August 18

I have been so very much out of order for these four or five days that I have been obliged to be let blood, which I hope will set me right; for I should be very much troubled not to be able to follow the blow we have given, which appears greater every day than another, for we have now above 11,000 prisoners. I have also this day a deputation from the town of Augsburg to let me know that the French were marched out of it yesterday morning, by which they have abandoned the country of Bavaria, so that the orders are already given for the putting a garrison into it. If we can be so lucky as to force them from Ulm, where they are now all together, *we shall certainly then drive them to the other side of the Rhine.*[2] After which we flatter ourselves that the world will think we have done all that could have been expected from us.

This day the whole army has returned their thanks to Almighty God for the late success, and I have done it with all my heart; for never victory was so complete, notwithstanding that they were stronger than we, and very advantageously posted. But believe me, my dear soul, there was an absolute necessity for the good of the common cause to make this venture, which God has so blessed. . . . My dearest life, if we could have another such a day as Wednesday last, I should then hope we might have

1 Coxe, ii, 6.
2 This shows that Marlborough never even contemplated an attempt to cut off the retreating army. He was in the grip of Supply.

such a peace as that I might enjoy the remaining part of my life with you.[1]

Every one could see, as Lediard says, that "the Face of Affairs was wholly changed."[2] The first decision of Marlborough and Eugene was to bring in the Margrave. There was no sense in besieging Ingolstadt when the whole of Bavaria must almost certainly fall into their hands by a treaty. Augsburg and Memmingen had already been abandoned by their French garrisons, and their deputations were at Marlborough's headquarters imploring government and protection. Ulm was obviously the first objective; and for that siege the cannon deployed before Inglostadt was required. Evidently the two captains had conscience-pricks about the Margrave, and were anxious to deprecate his jealousy and wrath. Above all, they must persuade him to relinquish the virgin fortress whose capture might have consoled him for absence from the victory. Their methods were elaborate. An officer was sent with letters making two requests. The first was that the Margrave should adjudicate the division of the prisoners, and especially the prisoners of note, between the two successful commanders; the second that he should march at once with all his troops and siege train to join them. The Margrave had received with incredulity the first accounts of the battle. As the tremendous facts and the new situation impressed themselves upon him amazement gave way to that bitter rancour which was thenceforward to hinder the allied cause, and make himself the butt of Europe. Still, on public grounds he was bound to rejoice. He could hardly repulse the compliment and implied superiority of rank of being arbiter upon the captives. Forthwith he assigned Marshal Tallard and his principal officers to Marlborough's share, and made an agreeable partition of the rest. In this mood he agreed to join his co-generals, and, leaving a dozen squadrons to blockade Ingolstadt, ascended the Danube by regular marches. The three generals were again united on the 25th.

Marshal Marsin and the defeated French made haste to

1 Coxe, ii, 8.   2 Lediard, i, 447.

quit Ulm. They left a garrison of nine weak French and Bavarian battalions in the fortress for the sole purpose of bargaining an honourable capitulation which would safeguard the future of the several thousand grievously wounded officers and men who could accompany them no farther. On the 20th they retreated to Tuttlingen, reduced to no more than sixteen thousand men. All the French had but one thought—to return to France. But for the Elector of Bavaria the question was more difficult.

On the night of the battle when he met d'Arco in the market-place of Leipheim (a village behind the field), he had cried out to him, "The devil take me if I know what to do now." Indeed hard choices lay before Max Emmanuel. Should he make peace with the Emperor and return chastened to his country, or should he cast in his lot as a soldier with France, and as a throneless prince with the Grand Monarch? Honour, frequently embarrassed, now pointed to Versailles; but his interest was more evenly divided. He sent to inquire from Marlborough whether the conditions which he had rejected before the battle were still open. He was answered that the accretions of territory could no longer be offered, but that if he would desert the French and furnish a contingent of eight thousand men, he should be restored to his dominions, and receive an annual subsidy from England and Holland. Marlborough, Eugene, and Wratislaw had only with the greatest difficulty procured the consent of the Emperor, now much stiffened, to such arrangements. These seemed large inducements for a man in the Elector's plight. Moreover, his wife, for whom he had developed another brief spell of romantic affection, made an effort to join him in Marsin's camp at Tuttlingen. Escorted by 14 squadrons of Bavarian horse, who perhaps would have been more useful in the battle, she quitted Munich with five children. The allied troops occupying Memmingen forced her to return to the city.

The spectacle which was next presented of the Elector refusing the favourable terms which were pressed upon him, separating himself from his country, from his family, and from his home, at the imperious call of honour, was impressive. In fact, however, the position was not so simple. As Vicar-General of the Spanish Netherlands, Max Emmanuel had another sphere of action in the North. All the Spanish troops in Belgium were subject to his orders. He could bring with him his own handful of Bavarians. He still believed that France was invincible; but if he were mistaken there was always another possibility. He might make an arrangement with the allies, and especially with the Dutch, to whom the independence of the barrier state was an idol. To come to terms with the Emperor about Bavaria at this juncture was certainly to sacrifice the interests he prized so dearly in Belgium: whereas a treaty with the Dutch about Belgium would naturally carry with it the restoration of his own Hereditary Lands. No one can prove that such considerations found any place in his mind. They were, however, certainly present at the council-table of Louis XIV. The King, while deeply touched by the Elector's misfortune, was surprised at the stern sacrifice of all that men hold dear which he had apparently so easily made at honour's call. Chivalric sentiment did not usually by itself, according to the long observation of the Great King, carry princes so far as that. As we shall see, the movements and conduct of the Elector in the Netherlands were watched with vigilance and suspicion from Versailles. Meanwhile some arrangement had to be made about Bavaria, and the Electress was empowered by her husband to treat with Wratislaw for an interim convention.

John to Sarah   SOFELINGEN
August 21

The poor electress has taken five of her children with her, and is following her husband, who seems to be abandoned to the French interest. Prince Eugene and I have offered him by a gentleman that is not yet returned that if he will join in the common cause against France, he shall be put in possession of his whole country, and receive from the queen and Holland 400,000 crowns yearly, for which he should only furnish the allies with 8000 men; but I take it for granted he is determined to go for France and abandon his own country to the rage of the Germans.[1]

1 Coxe, ii, 13.

John to Sarah

August 25

The elector of Bavaria has sent his wife and children back to Munich, and this morning by a trumpet has writ to me, and in it a letter to the electress open. It has made my heart ache, being very sensible how cruel it is to be separated from what one loves. I have sent it to her by a trumpet of my own, with assurances, that her answer shall be carefully delivered to the elector, for *I take pleasure in being easy when the service does not suffer by it.*[1]

The best—indeed, almost the only possible—route for Marsin and the defeated army lay through the Black Forest and by the tracks around Villingen along which Tallard had journeyed to his fate a few weeks before. They hoped that Villeroy as soon as he learned of the disaster would come to their assistance, and they hesitated to enter the forest-defiles of the mountains without hearing from him. They counted upon him not only for the protection of his army, but, what was even more vital, for the organization of the supplies without which they must have starved.

On August 17 Villeroy at Erlach was at length advancing against the Lines of Stollhofen in pursuance of the King's orders. That night the first reports reached him of an awful disaster upon the Danube. So far he had received no message from Marsin or from Versailles. What he heard was enough to arrest his movement. He waited in suspense during the next two days: but on the 19th, when Marsin's courier arrived, he resolved, without waiting for orders from Versailles, to march forthwith to the rescue of his defeated comrades. The decision does credit to his strategic comprehension. Only a Marshal enjoying his high favour would have dared to abandon the task so insistently prescribed by the King. Forthwith he set to work to bake bread and collect biscuit and transport, and marched with all his force along Tallard's old route towards Villingen. The fortress was still held by the Germans, but the neighbouring tracks were open. He arrived on the 23rd, and the next day the beaten army fell into his arms and upon his provision-

1 Coxe, ii, 13–14.

trains. They were a tragic remnant. The Elector had but three thousand Bavarians and Marsin thirteen thousand French. Their horses were devoured by the contagious disease which had already played so recognizable a part in the story. Their officers and men were infected with the

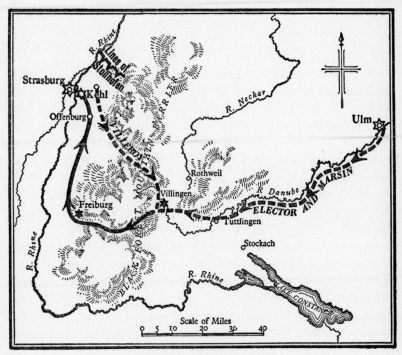

VILLEROY SUCCOURS MARSIN

not less dangerous virus of defeat and sense of hopeless inferiority which they had contracted upon the Höchstädt battlefield. Their despondency and lack of discipline spread throughout the ranks of their rescuers, and only a passionate wish to return to France held them all together. They marched by Freiburg, Hornberg, Offenburg, and Kehl, and crossed the Rhine at Strasburg on the last day of August.

Thus ended finally the design of Louis XIV against the Empire, and his far-reaching Bavarian intrigue. The sixteen thousand war-broken men who trudged across the Strasburg bridges represented the fragments of three powerful armies: first, the Bavarian army of 35 battalions and 55 squadrons; secondly, the army of Villars (afterwards of Marsin) of 60 squadrons and 50 battalions, together with Tallard's reinforcements, equal in themselves to 20 battalions; and, thirdly, Tallard's own army of 40 battalions and 50 squadrons. The total effort in the two campaigns could scarcely be measured by less than 150 battalions and 170 squadrons, or upward of a hundred and fifty thousand men. For all this and the vast ambitions and policies involved nothing remained but the dispirited sixteen thousand who gasped with relief when their weary feet touched again the soil of France. The Scarlet Caterpillar had not traversed the map of Europe in vain.

Blenheim is immortal as a battle not only because of the extraordinary severity of the fighting of all the troops on the field all day long, and the overwhelming character of the victory, but because it changed the political axis of the world. This only gradually became apparent. Even a month after all the facts were known, measured, and discounted, scarcely any one understood what transformations had been wrought. Until that August day the statesmen of every country must contemplate the prospect of the Elector of Bavaria supplanting the House of Hapsburg in the Imperial crown, with Munich instead of Vienna as the capital of Central Europe. Yet this Prince, should he become so bright a luminary, would be himself a planet only in the system of the Sun King. Spain and Italy would have their appointed orbits around the parent of light. The vast new regions opening beyond the oceans to the consciousness of man, those distant constellations, would shine with brightening gleams upon a French Monarchy of Europe and a dominant Gallican Church. The sullen and awkward Dutch and boorish English would perforce conform to the august design. Their recalcitrancy would be but the measure of their sufferings.

All this glittering fabric fell with a crash. From the moment when Louis XIV realized, as he was the first to realize, the new values and proportions which had been established on August 13, he decided to have done with war. Although long years of bloodshed lay before him, his object henceforward was only to find a convenient and dignified exit from the arena in which he had so long stalked triumphant. His ambition was no longer to gain a glorious dominion, but only to preserve the usurpations which he regarded as his lawful rights, and in the end this again was to shrink to no more than a desperate resolve to preserve the bedrock of France.

On the field of Blenheim also sank the fortunes of the House of Stuart. The collapse of the Grand Alliance and the hegemony of France in Europe must have brought with them so profound a disintegration of English political society that for perhaps a century at least vassalage under a French-imposed king might well have been our fate. However, a different tale was told by the good behaviour on August 13 of Cutts, Churchill, Orkney, Cadogan, Blood, Lumley, Ingoldsby, Rowe, many Captain Blackadders, and Parkers and Sergeant Millners, with their dauntless rank and file, marching onward behind the swords of Marlborough and Eugene.

The terror of the French armies was broken. Forty years of successful war, the invasion of so many countries, few and minor reverses, and these repaired by victory upon a hundred fields, had brought a renown before which, even while they still resisted, the most stubborn opponents bowed their heads. French generals and French troops believed themselves to be, and were largely accepted throughout the Continent as, a superior military order. All this was changed by the Danube battle. Here was defeat, naked, brutal, murderous; defeat in spite of numbers; defeat by manœuvre and defeat by force. The prolonged severity of the fighting and the extraordinary losses of the victors proved the reality of the test. But to all this was added the sting of disgrace and ridicule. A surrender in mass of the finest infantry of France, the most famous regiments disarmed wholesale on the battle-field, the shameful confusion and collapse of command in Blenheim village, the overthrow of the French cavalry front to front by sword against pistol, their flight while their comrades perished—all these hideous disillusionings had now to be faced. And with them also arose the red star of the island troops. Their discipline, their fighting energy, their readiness to endure extraordinary losses, the competence and team-play of their officers, the handiness of their cavalry and field artillery, their costly equipment and lavish feeding, their self-assured, unaffected disdain of foreigners, became the talk of Europe. There was a quality in their attacks upon the Schellenberg and the village of Blenheim, earnest, downright, and violent, which seemed to raise the fierceness of the war to a new degree. Few they were, but thenceforward they were marked men. Soon we shall see Louis XIV writing special instructions to his marshals that in any order of battle "the best troops should be placed opposite the English."

And their Chief! Here indeed was a portent. "The day at Höchstädt," wrote Napoleon's historian, "froze with horror the Party of the Two Crowns. Thenceforward the name of Marlborough became as it were a new power which entered into the confederacy and upheld it by a terror, the profound marks of which the passage of a century has not effaced." [1]

1 *Histoire de Jean Churchill,* ii, 1.

CHAPTER VI

THE RETURN TO THE RHINE

1704, September

AUGUST 1704 was glorious to the British arms by sea as well as by land. Rooke had entered the Mediterranean early in May with a superior Anglo-Dutch fleet. The French had, however, determined finally to abandon the Channel and the Narrow Seas, and the Comte de Toulouse had already sailed from Brest to join the Toulon squadron. Rooke's prime task was to prevent the junction of these forces. Beyond this he was to threaten the Spanish coasts so as to draw the enemy troops from resisting the invasion of Spain from Portugal, and finally he was to establish contact with the Duke of Savoy. In pursuance of these various instructions the Admiral had for three days in May demonstrated before Barcelona, landed marines, bombarded the town, and tested the feeling of the inhabitants. The fortress appeared impregnable, but the temper of the people was found most favourable to the Austrian claimant and, as usual, sharply opposed to the rest of Spain. Rooke failed after strenuous efforts to prevent the junction of the Brest fleet and the Toulon squadron, and for the moment the superiority passed to the French. But in the middle of June he was joined in Lagos Bay by reinforcements under Sir Cloudesley Shovell and was once again the stronger. Efforts were now made by Methuen from Lisbon to induce Rooke to make another attempt upon Cadiz, but the admiral had had enough of Cadiz and, forced to act against his natural inclinations, he resolved in July to attack Gibraltar. This endeavour was crowned with great and unexpected success. The bombardment began on the 21st. While the forts were engaged by the fleet the Prince of Hesse, who was the life and soul of all these amphibious operations, landed on the isthmus and cut the fortress from the mainland, and an English captain, Edward

131

Whittaker, apparently upon his own suggestion, landed upon the Mole and captured the silenced batteries. On July 24/August 4 the governor capitulated. The losses of the fleet were equal to the whole strength of the garrison, which was no more than three hundred men.

Gibraltar was at that time only a roadstead, and until the new moles were built a generation later could afford no permanent base for the fleet. But the magnificent aspect of the Rock and its position at the gateway of the Mediterranean were already strongly stamped upon the minds of both Louis XIV and Marlborough. The Great King sent the most urgent orders for its immediate recapture, and Marlborough as soon as this news reached him wrote that nothing should be grudged in its defence. Under imperative orders from Versailles the whole French fleet came forth to offer battle. On Sunday, August 13/24, the main fleets met before Malaga to fight the only general sea action of the war. Several detachments had weakened the Anglo-Dutch forces, and although Rooke ranged fifty-three ships in the line against fifty French, he could not be deemed the stronger. His ammunition had been depleted by the bombardment of Gibraltar; a thousand of his marines were ashore in garrison there, and his ships had been nearly six months from their home dockyards. Their bottoms were foul and their tackle in disrepair. The French fleet, on the other hand, was in perfect order.

In these circumstances the battle was long and bloody. All day from eleven in the morning till seven at night it raged in calm water with little attempt at manœuvre. The fleets lay in closest action and cannonade, each enduring heavy losses and fighting with extreme stubbornness. As the evening approached both the van and the rear of the French line (*i.e.*, the right and left wings of their line of battle) recoiled, although their centre, says Rooke, "did their duty very heartily and with great bravery." The victorious squadrons of Shovell at one end of the line and Callenburgh at the other could not press their advantage, and night fell with both fleets in the condition of which Shovell says "by the time one is beaten . . . the other is glad that the enemy has left him."

In this sea battle the English lost more men killed than at Blenheim, and the casualties in the combined Anglo-Dutch fleet were nearly three thousand. Their shortage of ammunition caused the allied admirals the gravest anxiety for the morrow; but when daylight came the French, whose losses in men were even greater, had disappeared. No ships were sunk or captured on either side. The Comte de Toulouse re-entered Toulon claiming a victory for France. But, says the French historian candidly, the victory was one in which the vanquished, in default of laurels, gathered the fruits.[1] Never again in the War of the Spanish Succession did the French Navy challenge a general action. The capture of Gibraltar was therefore sealed by Neptune, and the allied command of the Mediterranean finally recognized. These were far-reaching events.

When Louis XIV realized that Gibraltar could not be recovered by naval action, he ordered the concentration of an army for a siege of Gibraltar upon the greatest scale. The besieging forces, which ultimately amounted to fifty thousand men, were drawn from all parts of the peninsula. The land defence of Spain was fatally weakened and disorganized, and the monarchy of Philip V lay open to the invaders. This grave decision did not commend itself to Berwick. Indeed, he carried his opposition to the abandonment of the front against Portugal to such a point that Marshal Tessé was sent to replace him. That he was right on military grounds cannot be disputed. The physical consequences of the loss of Gibraltar were overrated by the leaders of the Two Crowns; but the measures which they took to regain it proved the extraordinary moral significance which the Rock had acquired. No diversion could have been more effective, and no prize was more enduring.

Meanwhile the position of the Duke of Savoy had become desperate. The plans prepared for his punishment in the winter of 1703 came into full operation in the spring. La Feuillade and Vendôme beset him from different quarters, and one by one the remaining fortresses of Piedmont were reduced.

1 Charles Bourel de la Roncière, *Histoire de la Marine Française*, vi (1932), 368.

The Emperor was incapable of sending any effective aid to his new ally, and the Sea Powers had other plans. Although his army of about thirty thousand men, opposed by double their numbers, defended themselves and their strongholds upon the whole with admirable constancy, the end of the campaign saw Victor Amadeus, with the remnants of his State, penned around Turin. But the strategic consequences of Blenheim and of Malaga revived his fortunes. On land the central power of France reeled under the stroke of the English general; at sea the command of the Mediterranean had fallen into the hands of the Admiralty. Although no actual succour in troops came to the hard-pressed Prince, the long arms of England, reaching deep into Central Europe and into the inland sea, now began to relieve him from the fierce pressures under which he was sinking. Could he but endure beyond the winter, all might be retrieved.

As a part of the attack upon the Duke of Savoy which Louis XIV had planned for 1704, a new policy had been adopted in the Cevennes. Up to this point the rebels had been treated with merciless severity. But now the atrocities with which de Broglie had blackened the countryside were replaced by the deft force and conciliation of Marshal Villars. Thither went this good servant of France to repair the loss of favour and repute he had suffered from his friction with the Elector of Bavaria. He pacified or suppressed during 1704 the revolt of the Camisards. Their most audacious leader, Cavalier, was corrupted, like Benedict Arnold in the War of American Independence, by a high command in the French Army, and after various almost comical transitions died in 1740 as George II's Governor of Jersey. The formidable character of the rebellion gradually faded. The dauntless and implacable were slowly run down and destroyed. Thus while their future strength upon the Mediterranean seaboard was compromised, the French position seemed for the time being locally restored.

After Blenheim there were still three months left of the campaigning season. Marlborough had no doubts how to use them. He wished to take Ulm, and neutralize and pacify the rest of Bavaria by a treaty. Having thus completely mastered the Danube valley and freed the Empire from all immediate danger, he proposed without a day's delay, except for supplies, to carry the entire army of the confederacy to the Rhine and thence to the Moselle. There he would establish the strongest possible forces in winter quarters for an advance towards Paris in the spring. Meanwhile he urged the Emperor directly and through Wratislaw to send substantial and speedy aid to the Duke of Savoy, and above all to make terms, involving some kind of Federal Home Rule, with the Hungarian insurgents. But the victory had seated the Emperor securely upon his ancient throne. He saw no reason to give in the days of regained strength what he had denied even in his worst straits and weakness. He and the proud incapables who surrounded him resented the interference of an English Parliamentary Government and a Dutch Republic in the domestic concerns of the Holy Roman Empire. All these Western ideas of constitutional right and self-determination for subject nationalities were subversive of the very foundations of his House. He was grateful to Marlborough for the deliverance he had brought; but he was also grateful to that Providence without whose blessing men's noblest efforts are vain, and whose strong arm required no reward but praise, for which the Church made regular provision. Moreover, the Emperor felt that he himself had contributed to the success of the allied army. Had he not prescribed the three days of solemn intercession on the very eve of the Danube cannonade?

This affords the occasion for mentioning a minor episode upon which there is a large mass of correspondence. On June 15, when Marlborough was marching to the Danube, Wratislaw had conveyed to him a proposal from the Emperor to create him a sovereign prince of the Empire. He was to have a principality and a vote in the College or Diet of the Reich. There is no doubt that the Duke desired the proffered title. It would give him an altogether different position in the army and among the princes and notables who served under his orders. But besides this he was personally attracted by the idea of becoming a prince with the rank of Highness and inclusion in the charmed circle of Europe. It may be thought a pity that so great a man had such weaknesses. We must make him some allowances for the times in which he lived. These were not the days when such distinctions were disdained by men of mark, nor when serving democracy for its own sake was for all public personages a full reward.

Marlborough handled this matter with his usual art of having a solid and becoming reason at every stage for getting what he wanted. He wrote to Sarah and Godolphin acquainting them with the Emperor's offer, and dwelling on the embarrassment which would be caused to the public service if he were called upon to refuse it.

"I know you wish the Queen and me so well," he told Sarah,

> that you would be glad that nothing should be done that might do either of us hurt. Therefore my opinion of the matter is that there can be no inconvenience in allowing Count Wratislaw's master to write to the Queen and ask her to consent for the doing of this and then to bring the letter to the Cabinet council.[1]

He added, "I am very clear in my own opinion that if anything of this be to be done, it will have a much better grace for me when the business of the war is over." The Emperor, however, on June 20 had signed a rescript instructing Wratislaw through his Minister in London, Hoffmann, to seek the sanction of the Queen. Harley as Secretary of State took him to Windsor at the end of July, when Hoffmann stated that Marlborough had replied that "his ambition was limited to the Queen's favours." Sarah, as Marlborough had foreseen, was even more opposed to this elevation than she had been to the dukedom. To her titles were the toys of fools, and religion too often only the mask for hypocrites. Anne, disregarding Sarah's rather scornful smiles, gave her consent with evident pleasure, and there for the time the matter had rested.

[1] Coxe, i, 342.

But now after Blenheim there is a letter from Wratislaw to the Emperor of August 22.

> . . . Marlborough came to me yesterday and asked me to write that if you were still most graciously inclined to raise him to the rank of Prince of the Empire, he considers that after this victory would be the right time. It was also for Your Majesty to name what territory or title he should have and bear.[1]

In his recuperation of spiritual health the Emperor began to see difficulties which had not previously occurred to him in creating Marlborough a prince of the Empire. Where was he to find the land for a principality? The Imperial estates were none too large. How was he to procure a seat for this English soldier in the supreme Diet of the Reich? Such dignities and status ought not lightly to be bestowed upon new people. The Duke had certainly rendered distinguished service to the house of Hapsburg, and was besides, by all accounts, a man of good appearance and manners. Still, he was by birth only a small country gentleman in an island where even the highest nobility were said to be uncouth. True, as Emperor he himself had authorized Hoffmann to obtain the sanction of Queen Anne for such a reward, and had allowed Wratislaw to press its acceptance upon Marlborough. But he had, he confessed to himself, at that time been gravely harassed by the public dangers, and had hardly been able to measure so great a departure from custom with the precision which was incumbent upon him. However, he felt personally committed at least to the honorific grant, and trusted that, if promptly made, it might suffice. He wrote back on August 28 a most gracious letter to Marlborough, addressing him as "Most Illustrious Cousin and most dear Prince."

> I do with pleasure salute by these titles Your Dilection, whom I have freely and of my own accord admitted among the Princes of the Holy Roman Empire, not so much in consideration of your noble Family, as upon account of your Personal Merit, and your great Deserts towards me, my August House, and the Holy Roman Empire. I have desired that this public monument of

[1] *Feldzüge*, vi, 866.

137

honour, the greatest there is in Germany, which I have so justly conferred on you should remain. . . .

These victories are so great, especially that near Höchstädt, past ages never having seen the like victory obtained over the French. . . .[1]

But Marlborough had no mind to be treated in this way. He wanted no empty title. He must have the principality and the vote. Without these the honour would become a source of merriment in every Court. He made all this plain in due course.

Marlborough to Godolphin

WEISSEMBERG,
September 22

Two days ago the count de Wratislaw gave me a letter from the emperor, in which he acquaints me with having made me a prince of the empire. I am very much surprised, and so I told him, that such a step should be taken before I had the least notice. Besides, this was not the method in which it ought to be done, for the notice ought to be sent to the several princes of the empire; and the lands from whence I was to take my title to be named to them; for that I could not have a seat in the diet till I was master of an imperial fief in the empire. He said it was right, and that he would write to the emperor, and not own to any body that he has given me the letter. However, I send you a copy, but desire nobody may see it but Mr. Secretary; for I believe the emperor must write another to me.[2]

Wratislaw's correspondence with the Emperor upon this topic is instructive and diverting. Through it we can see the suave, steady pressure which was put upon him by Marlborough, who all the time in his letters to Godolphin and Sarah was representing himself almost as the victim of inappropriate rewards. After dwelling on the services which the Duke had rendered, to which he bluntly declared the salvation of the Imperial throne was due, Wratislaw wrote, "This man will be indispensable to your Majesty for many years to come. It would be the greatest error in State policy to offend him." The lands must be found and the seat and

1 Lediard, i, 419.   2 Coxe, ii, 23.

vote in the Diet must be presented to the princes as an irre-
vocable decision. The lack of precedent would in itself make
the compliment adequate to the action. "I can assure your
Majesty," wrote the sagacious, if cynical, Envoy, "that King
Louis XIV would gladly give this man the finest province
in France to have his aid." Thus pressed, the Emperor
exerted himself to overcome the difficulties. Though
nothing was settled for many months to come, an estate
about fifteen miles square was eventually carved out from
the Imperial lands in Swabia to form the principality of
Mindelheim.[1]

At the conference on August 25 the Margrave pronounced
for the siege of Landau as an indispensable preliminary to
any campaign on the Moselle. There was much to be said
for this; the Germans were all set upon it, and Marlborough
did not seriously resist them. He knew they would never be
willing to run risks upon the Moselle till they had Landau
again in their hands. The strategic value of the place is
apparent, and its capture by the allies in 1702 and recapture
by the French in 1703 made it a trophy. It was agreed to
concentrate upon the Rhine by Philippsburg. General Thüngen, with the siege train and fifteen thousand men, was left
to reduce Ulm. With him stayed Wratislaw to negotiate the
neutrality of Bavaria; and Marlborough and Eugene tarried
for a few days, hoping for a speedy result.

On August 25 the allied forces began their march for the
Rhine. For the convenience of supply the three generals
moved by separate routes through Würtemberg. The English
and the Danes regained at Gross Heppach the road by which
they had come, and on the 31st were overtaken at Mondels-
heim by Marlborough. For a second time the redcoats were
welcomed in these German towns, and surely they might feel
that this time the tributes were deserved. In June they had
come as rescuers: in August they returned as victors. They
had certainly made good their untactful promise "to lend

1 Klopp devotes twice as much space to this example of Marlborough's pettiness as to the battle of Blenheim.

spirit to the Empire and spurs to the French." Joy, gratitude, and jubilation hailed their homeward path. But little more than half of them were there to tread it.

The concentration of the allies along the Rhine in the Philippsburg area was effected smoothly and punctually. Marlborough and Eugene arrived together, and the Margrave a few days later. Eugene had collected all the troops which had hitherto guarded the Lines of Stollhofen. At this stage it was only the enemy who would have need of defensive systems. The open field belonged to the allies. Marlborough summoned the heavy artillery furnished by the Landgrave of Hesse, which he had been forced to leave at Mannheim and had used as a feint on his original march. The total strength of the confederates on the Upper Rhine now amounted to 92 battalions and 181 squadrons. At this late period in the campaign all the units on both sides were much reduced in numbers. "Above one half of our battalions," wrote Marlborough (September 8) to Godolphin, "are extremely weak, so that if we come to action I intend to make the fourteen English battalions but seven, and to do the same thing to the Danes and Hessians, which will bring our battalions to seventy-eight." The numerical and moral superiority of the confederates was, however, not disputable. During the 6th, 7th, and 8th, after personal reconnaissances by Marlborough and Eugene, the army crossed the two floating bridges which had been thrown by Philippsburg, and drew out on a seven-mile front before the Queich river, along which lay the French main forces.

Louis XIV behaved with fortitude and dignity in the hour of misfortune. He made no reproaches and uttered no lamentations. He warmly commended Marshal Villeroy for spontaneously going to the relief of Marsin. He approved Marsin's conduct and comforted him. He wrote magnanimously to the Elector, declaring that he felt more sorrow for that unlucky prince than for his own troubles. His only comment upon Tallard was "I grieve for Marshal Tallard, and I feel deeply his pain at the loss of his son." Upon the military situation his outlook was broad. He wished indeed that the campaign were at an end. But worse must be expected from the strength and elation of the enemy. A defensive was imposed upon the northern French armies till the longed-for day of winter quarters arrived. Meanwhile the strength of the confederate forces was plainly gathering about Philippsburg, and the report was received that Marlborough in great strength was marching thither with winged foot-steps (*à tire-d'aile*). In the midst of this Marsin had hurt his leg and was laid up at Strasburg. Villeroy had himself to hasten with every available man to the defence of the Queich. Here he fortified all the crossings with entrenchments and palisades. By extreme efforts enough troops were gathered to raise his army to upward of 85 battalions and 112 squadrons, which

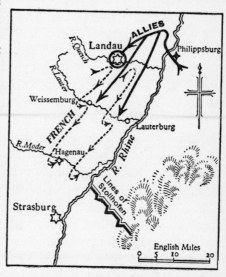

VILLEROY ABANDONS LANDAU

seemed adequate to hold so good a position. But the after-effects of Blenheim were destructive to all these expectations.

Early on September 9 Marlborough, Eugene, and the Margrave marched south against the Queich with all their forces in battle array, resolved to force the passages by general battle on the following day. Villeroy felt himself unequal, in the despondent mood of the army, by which he was himself affected, to meet the attack. He ordered a retreat of twenty miles to the next tributary of the Rhine, the Lauter. The alacrity with which this command was obeyed exposed to the confederates the remarkable disorder of the French. Marlborough followed them with the united army, and Villeroy thereupon retired another twenty miles to Hagenau and the line of the Moder. The Duke, to whom

141

another battle would have been most welcome, was both disappointed and surprised by the Marshal's timidity. "If they had not been the most frightened people in the world," he wrote to Godolphin, "they would never have quitted these two posts [positions]." "I should never have believed," wrote Chamillart to Marsin on September 19,

> that the consequences of the day of Höchstädt would be so disastrous as they now show themselves to be; so much so that now, only a month later, the enemy terrify Alsace and have it in their own choice to besiege this place or that, as they judge proper. This change is very perturbing and alarming for those unaccustomed to such great upheavals. God grant that we get out of it at no greater cost that we have already borne.[1]

Landau was now isolated and exposed. The Margrave undertook the siege, and Marlborough and Eugene covered him along the Lauter. For greater convenience in supply one of the floating bridges at Philippsburg was towed upstream, and established close behind the junction of the Queich and the Rhine. The fortress of Landau contained a garrison and nine battalions under a resolute governor, Laubanie, and before retreating Villeroy had thrown into it a mass of munitions and twelve months' victuals. In the preceding year it had yielded to a French siege in thirty days, and it was therefore hoped that the same allowance would now be sufficient. If so there would still be time for Marlborough to develop his projects upon the Moselle. But the Imperial army was found deficient in all the apparatus of a first-class siege. It was said of them that they "undertake sieges without cannon, ammunition or engineers with as much assurance as they did a war without money, credit or troops."[2] Besides this a singular lethargy seemed to have overcome the Margrave, whose foot, bruised at the Schellenberg, had begun to trouble him; and the progress of the works was judged by all observers to be unaccountably and unwarrantably slow.

The King of the Romans, an agreeable youth inspired

1 Röder, ii, 85.   2 Cowper Papers, *H.M.C.*, iii, 48.

by the keenest admiration for Marlborough, now arrived in great state from Vienna to take nominal command of the operations. Although this was a formality, it aggravated the Margrave's already festering internal griefs. He saw, with an irritation he scarcely troubled to conceal, that his reputation was eclipsed by the glory of Marlborough and Eugene. He had been kept out of Blenheim; he had been recalled from Ingolstadt; and now an obsequious world would ascribe the honours of the capture of Landau to the heir to the Imperial throne. As the poet fulsomely sang of the young King:

> What tides of Glory to his Bosom ran,
> Clasped in th' Embraces of the GODLIKE MAN.

The Margrave could hardly be expected to see Marlborough in so rosy a light. He resented both the domination and the bland dissembling of the English upstart, whom he conceived he had saved from disaster at the Schellenberg, and who had shown no gratitude even for that. Well, let him wait upon the siege, and wait also for his preposterous campaign on the Moselle. Imagine opening new operations at this season of the year! Was the man's ambition insatiable? Thus, we suppose, not without much evidence, did the Margrave chew his bitter cud.

General Thüngen's batteries had opened upon Ulm on September 8. The governor beat the chamade on the 10th, and the next day was allowed to march out with the honours of war. The Bavarians dispersed to their homes. Sickness and desertion were such that only nine hundred Frenchmen reached the Rhine. A great supply of munitions, including two hundred and fifty cannon and twelve hundred barrels of powder, fell to the captors; and the whole attacking force, with its much-needed siege train, set out for the Rhine and Landau.

John to Sarah   WEISSEMBOURG
Sept. 15, 1704

* I had sealed my letter to you before I received the express of Ulm's being surrendered, which place is of very great consequence, for whilst we have it the French will never think of returning into that country, and besides it helps us to 20 regiments of foot, and as many of horse, for the better carrying on of the siege of Landau. I have had millions of letters from all parts of the world since this battle, but having heard nothing from 21 [?] and 146 [?], I should be glad to know if they are in London. I am going with Prince Eugene to dine with Prince Louis, in order to press him to open the trenches; for should this siege last long it would make it very difficult for me to execute what I have very much at my heart which is taking winter quarters on the Moselle; for I think that would put the Allies in a condition of opening the next campaign with great advantage; and tho I wish from my soul to stay at home with you, I should be glad to take any pains that might make it easy to my successor to succeed against France. . . .

John to Sarah

WEISSEMBOURG
Octr. 6, 1704

* I did intend to have gone to Landau yesterday, but the weather being ill, and the Army being in some difficulty for forage, I put off my going till tomorrow. The great mind I have to put the Army into winter quarters that I might think of coming to my dear soul, makes me believe the siege of Landau goes on very slowly. The duke Regent of Wirtemberg has given me eight horses and a callash, which I have not seen, but by the description I believe you will like it. I have ordered them into Holland, and if you please it shall be brought to England with me; for I have already here two sets of coach horses which will not be proper for England.

Marlborough's health, never robust, was seriously affected by the stresses through which he had passed. His shining armour of serenity was heavy to wear. Within was a highly sensitive nervous organism whose concealed fires consumed itself. In his hours of depression he longed to resign his command, and wrote to Sarah almost as if his retirement were already arranged. Though prolonged intense strain did not exhaust his impulse, it deranged his system. A sense of pressure in the head followed what he calls "the heating of his blood." Two days after Blenheim he had had to be bled. This now-discredited old-world remedy always seems to have relieved him. "Ever since the battle," he wrote to Godolphin (August 17), "I have been so employed about our own wounded men and the prisoners, that I have not one hour's quiet, which has so disordered me, that if I were in London I should be in my bed in a high fever."

And again (August 23):

> I am suffered to have so little time to myself that I have a continual fever on my spirits, which makes me very weak; but when I go from hence, I am resolved to go in my coach till I come to the Rhine, which I do not doubt will restore me to perfect health. Nothing but my zeal for her majesty's service could have enabled me to have gone through the fatigues I have had for the last three months; and I am but too sure when I shall have the happiness of seeing you, you will find me ten years older than when I left England. I do not say this to complain, for I esteem myself very happy if I can make any return for her majesty's goodness to me and mine.[1]

In the middle of September he was "so uneasy with a cold fit of an ague" that he could neither read Godolphin's letter nor write in reply.

On October 10 to Sarah:

> For thousands of reasons I wish myself with you. Besides I think if I were with you quietly at the lodge, I should have more health, for I am at this time so very lean, that it is extreme uneasy to me, so that your care must nurse me this winter, or I shall certainly be in a consumption. I am very sorry to hear you have so often returns of your illness, and I do with all my heart thank you for the resolution you have taken of letting the physicians try to cure you, which I hope in God they will, and that you may live many years after me, which both by my age and constitution you must do.[2]

Sarah was distressed by her husband's accounts of his health. She evidently urged him to wind up the campaign and come home. When could there be a better moment than after so great a victory? Godolphin too was insistent. Parliament was meeting. The Captain-General's presence was necessary in England to use the full political effect of

---

1 Coxe, ii, 27. 2 *Ibid.*, 28.

his success while all were dazzled by it. The advantage of his return was not lost upon the practised statesman. The sound maxim, "Leave off a winner," occurred to the gambler of Newmarket and the Whitehall card-tables. Why worry about Landau, and still more about the Moselle? Enough had been done for the Germans. Let them go into winter quarters, as, indeed, they desired. Embark the Queen's troops at some handy place, and let the Rhine current bear them swiftly and easily back to Holland. Godolphin wrote to Harley:

> I am not very easy at their being so far engaged in the siege of Landau at this time of year; it may draw into length, and delay the Duke of Marlborough's coming over. Besides that, it may expose him to new hazards. All these, in my opinion, had been better prevented, and the Empire might have been contented with seeing the French gone back over the Rhine.
>
> The fears of France, as well as the desires of Holland, were that he should have brought his army down the Rhine in boats; and I must own, that for my own part I should have liked that measure better; but I can believe in him [Marlborough] against my own senses.[1]

To Godolphin's counsels Sarah artfully added descriptions of the improvements at Holywell which she knew would tempt the absent soldier, and, in no mood of spiteful gossip, but in pursuance of her strong, logical politics, she now began to play upon him in his tenderest spot. When he felt he had done well, he longed for the appreciation of his countrymen, and especially of those who had doubted or opposed him. He might justly hope that what had happened in Germany would soften their rage against him, or at least leave them confounded in argument. Evidence to the contrary wounded him deeply. Sarah therefore darkened her letters with the vicious comments of the Tory Opposition. His replies show that she wrote out for him the most disparaging, damaging, and mischievous criticisms which she heard; and she was a good judge of these. She was resolved to make a breach between him and the Tories.

1 Bath Papers, *H.M.C.*, i, 61.

John bared his breast to these assaults. His reaction was magnificent. On August 25 he wrote:

> I find by some of yours that I am very much obliged to 22 [probably Lord Rochester] and some of his friends, that take the action of Donauwörth [the Schellenberg] not to be a victory. I wish that and our last battle could have been obtained without the hazard of any but myself; his lordship then would not have complained. For this last action I will be answerable his friend the King of France will own the victory. It is not to be imagined with what precipitation they have quitted this country.[1]

GROSS-GARTACH
Sept. 2

> . . . I am sure we can never bless God enough for the success he has given us, it being much above our own expectations. But if those sort of gentlemen think there has not been enough done, I hope He will bless us with a farther success, which at last must bring us to happiness in spite of them, which shall be the prayers and endeavours of him that loves you dearly.[2]

Sarah had passed on an Opposition sneer about Blenheim: "It was true a great many men were killed or taken, but that to the French King was no more than to take a bucket of water out of a river." John replied:

> What 92 [unknown] says of a bucket of water; if they will allow us to draw one or two such buckets more, I should think we might then let the river run quietly, and not much apprehend its overflowing and destroying its neighbors, or be much concerned whether 17 [Nottingham] or 21 [?] were in or out of humour.[3]

On October 20, in the last thrust of the campaign, Sarah extorted from him a justly famous letter:

> I do assure you as for myself, my pretending to be of no party is not designed to get favor, or to deceive anybody, for I am very little concerned what any party thinks of me; I know them both so well that if my quiet depended upon either of them, I should be most miserable, as I find happiness is not to be had in this world, which I did flatter myself might have been enjoyed in a retired life. *I will endeavour to leave a good name*

1 Coxe, ii, 43.   2 *Ibid,*   3 *Ibid.,* 44.

*behind me in countries that have hardly any blessing but that of
not knowing the detested names of whig and tory.*[1]

But side by side with all this despondency, physical and
political—the shadow of brilliant success—a supreme desire

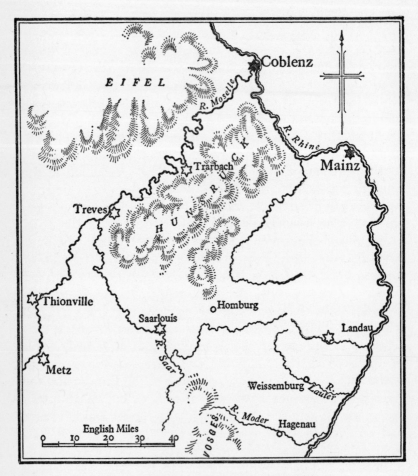

THE MOSELLE PATH OF INVASION

to bring the war to a victorious end by the surest and speediest
means possessed the general who was constantly accused of
prolonging it for his own advantage. After the capture of

1 Coxe, ii, 45.

Gibraltar and the battle of Malaga the combined Anglo-Dutch fleet might well control the Mediterranean. By this means the Italian front could be effectually restored to an activity which would exact exhaustive efforts from the French. For this purpose the Duke of Savoy must be strongly reinforced, both overland from the Empire and from the sea, by troops and naval action. The highest possible pressure must similarly be exerted along the front in Flanders. With these two wings rigorously engaging the enemy's strength, the conditions would be created for the main advance of the confederate centre by Thionville and Metz towards Paris. An army of a hundred thousand men must be concentrated on the Moselle, based principally on Coblenz, at the very opening of the new campaign. He must have forty thousand Germans, twenty thousand Dutch, and his own forty thousand in the Queen's pay ready to take the field by April, so as to have the full year's fighting before him and reach the result. Considerable forces must winter upon the Moselle, with the command of the river behind them. He must have Trarbach; he must have Trèves, and he must have Saarlouis. This structure of fortresses and magazines, held in force during the winter and filled continually with supplies, would be the foundation from which he could move in the spring as the first step upon Thionville. There was no surprising novelty in such a conception. In fact, so far as the Moselle was concerned, it was the plan which the Margrave had proposed at the end of 1703. But for the first time the rescue of the Empire and the ascendancy, as might have been hoped, of one mind in the allied war direction, together with the injury which France had received in 1704, the improved balance of forces, and the command of the Mediterranean, had made it feasible.

For this end every effort must be made. This was no time for triumph or repose. Was the war to drag on in costly, bloody gnawings around the frontiers of France until perhaps it died down in disastrous futility, until the Alliance, reforged on the anvil of Blenheim, broke again to pieces? For a thrust at the heart, the chance, the means, the time, and—might he not feel?—the man had now come. Beyond the battle-smoke of a terrible year he saw peace rising out of an otherwise endless warfare, and order emerging from chaos, with England the glorious deliverer at the summit.

On September 19 Louis XIV wrote a very fine and discerning letter to Villeroy. The Marshal had been much disquieted by the silence which his master had observed upon his hurried abandonment of the lines on the Queich and Lauter. This had lasted for no less than ten days. It must have been with relief that he read the generous, cheering message which reached him probably upon September 21.

> Raise yourself above the talk of the public. Do not look upon yourself as the victim of Höchstädt day. You have done your duty as a true man. You have taken the steps which you thought best for my interest. In disregard of a false pride which would have been ill-founded, you have been more concerned in preserving my army and my State than with your personal reputation. Nothing could convince me more of your devotion to me.[1]

The next day the King showed that he and his experts had penetrated Marlborough's future designs.

> I have reason to believe . . . four battalions are being sent from Overkirk's army to the Moselle. . . . It looks very much as if Monsieur de Marlborough will send at the same time cavalry, and perhaps even infantry to strengthen this corps to occupy Trèves if they can, and even to attack Trarbach in order to develop their plan and besiege Thionville at the beginning of the next campaign.[2]

This warning was written from Versailles on September 20, and it exactly embodied Marlborough's intentions.

We may be sure that Villeroy pondered deeply upon it. He had long conferences with Marsin, who lay crippled in Strasburg. Both Marshals decided that Marlborough would not be able to attack the Moselle before Landau had fallen, and all the troops fastened around it were released. They were therefore content to strengthen M. de Coigny, who

---

[1] Pelet, iv, 638. [2] *Ibid.*, 639.

commanded in the Moselle valley, to about three thousand horse, composed of their weakest squadrons. They must after all contemplate, at least as a possibility, that they would perhaps themselves be the objects of a major attack as soon as the fortress was taken. They could not tell what was happening at Landau, from which they were quite cut off.

The siege dragged on. "Our people," wrote Marlborough to Harley on October 6, "are advancing by the sap [*i.e.*, by sapping], in order to make a lodgment on the counterscarp. This method may save a few men, but will cost the more time, and, it may be, a great many more men in the end by sickness." [1] The cavalry captain Pope, writing a month later, expressed the common talk of the English regiments.

> The Prince of Baden is now sufficiently revenged for our robbing him of a share of the glory of the victory of Blenheim. He has spun out this siege till the left wing of the horse, to which that action was chiefly owing, is entirely ruined. We have not above twenty horses a troop left. [2]

At length Marlborough could watch this process no longer. It was not in his power to coerce or remove the Margrave. He determined to make a personal effort of his own. He was fairly sure the Marshals would not expect him to quit the main army before the capitulation of Landau. He therefore began from October 13 onward to build up secretly a force at Homburg, thirty-five miles to the westward. The defences of this place, as we have seen, had been recently dismantled by the French; and to Villeroy its occupation and repair might seem to be a natural precaution for the right flank of the confederate army covering the siege of Landau. On the 19th the Duke sent Colonel Blood with fourteen guns and four howitzers, escorted by 3 battalions, to this strong post. Twenty-two battalions marched thither on the 20th, 48 squadrons on the 21st, and he himself joined them on the 24th. This little army in its shrunken state amounted to twelve thousand men, but all lively. Eugene agreed to be left on the Lauter with no more than twenty-five thou-

---

[1] *Dispatches*, i, 497.   [2] November 8; Cowper Papers, *H.M.C.*, iii, 51.

sand men against Villeroy, twenty-seven miles away, with forty thousand.

On the 25th the Duke plunged into the wild Hunsrüch

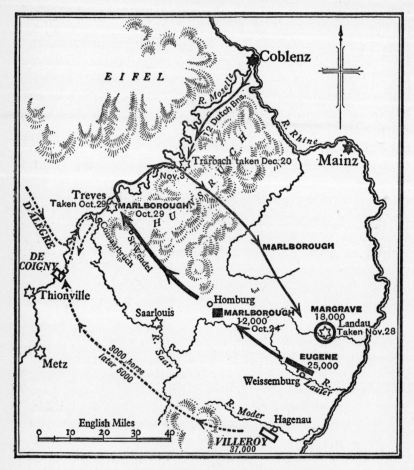

MARLBOROUGH SECURES THE MOSELLE

mountain region. In those days when roads were but tracks, and scarcely a dwelling pleaded with primeval solitudes, the march seemed forlorn and sombre to the troops. Marlborough with the horse reached St Wendel at the head of the passes on the 26th. But it was only with a hard struggle that the foot traversed the twenty miles in three days. He had to wait at St Wendel till they came up. He could not tell how many French he would find in the valley of the Moselle. His usually excellent information reported ten thousand reinforcements approaching Trèves, but there might be more. In his tent at St Wendel on October 26, while waiting for the rest of his force, he wrote several letters which lay bare his feelings and position with an attractive air of detachment. He was coming into contact with the unknown. He could receive no help. He was "very unwilling to be beaten at the end of this campaign," but he had not dared entrust this expedition, which might so easily miscarry, to any subordinate. No retreat was possible. Unless he could establish himself upon the Moselle and gather the Dutch troops now coming from Coblenz, he must "throw his cannon into some river"; for back they could never go. As when he marched out two years before on the heaths of Peer expecting to fight his first great battle, he seems to have wished to leave some record behind of his thoughts and reasonings.

John to Sarah　　CAMP AT ST WENDEL
October 26

I am got thus far in my way to the Moselle, after having marched through very terrible mountains. Had we any rain it would have been impossible to have got forward the cannon; and it is certain if the enemy are able to hinder us from taking winter quarters in this country [*i.e.*, on the Moselle], we must throw our cannon into some river, for to carry them back is impossible. I have been so desirous to make use of this fair weather, that I am here only with the horse; but as my march to-morrow will bring me within eight leagues of Trèves, and the enemy's troops being but five leagues from me, I must be obliged to stay for the foot, which will join me the next day.

This march and my own spleen have given me occasion to think how very unaccountable a creature man is, to be seeking for honour in so barren a country as this, when he is very sure that the greater part of mankind, and may justly fear that even his best friends, would be apt to think ill of him, should he have ill success. But I am endeavouring all I can to persuade myself that my happiness ought to depend upon my knowledge that I do

153

what I think is for the best. If I can succeed in the taking of Trèves, I shall not then stay above ten days longer in this country; for when I shall have given the necessary orders for the siege of Trarbach, I shall leave the execution of it to the Prince of Hesse, having promised the King of the Romans to be with him before the siege of Landau is ended.[1]

All went well. "We have had," wrote Cardonnel, who lost all his kit and baggage by a fire, "a most horrible march hither day and night, but I thank God it has had all the success we could desire."[2] Villeroy was not sure of Marlborough's movements till the 26th. He dispatched d'Alègre, a capable officer (Coigny having succumbed), with a reinforcement of five thousand men. They were within six miles of Trèves when Marlborough's vanguard, urged on by appeals from the inhabitants, came within sight of the ancient city. The handful of French in the fort fled without having time to burn the place as Marlborough, judging by his own severities in Bavaria, feared and expected. Instead of being a French fortress held by a skeleton force, Trèves now became a well-garrisoned confederate stronghold. Six thousand peasants were set to work night and day to repair the extensive but ruined fortifications, and they were covered by Marlborough's cavalry at Consaarbrück. The seizure and fortification of Trèves left the much more strongly defended fortress of Trarbach isolated and open to attack. The twelve Dutch battalions had now arrived from Holland. Marlborough could entrust the siege to the Prince of Hesse. He had to abandon his hopes of taking Saarlouis. Having neither the time nor the strength for this, he returned with his staff to Landau, the King of the Romans, and the Margrave. The campaign was now drained to the very dregs. Landau was not taken till November 28, and even so the garrison marched out under the honours of war. Laubanie, although blinded at the outset by a bomb, had made a fine defence of more than seventy days. The Margrave had to ascribe what there was of credit to the King of the Romans.

This winter effort of Marlborough's will-power deserves

1 Coxe, ii, 33.   2 Cardonnel to Watkins, Trèves, October 30; Add. MSS., 42176.

admiration. The whole feeling of the armies after Blenheim was that they had done their part for the year. Their commanders longed to parade their laurels before their countrymen, and to receive the tributes they had so well deserved. But Marlborough was deaf to all appeals, even the most seductive. He yielded neither to success nor exhaustion. He was dominated by his theme, or, as might be said, his duty. He was driven forward against longings for home and bodily discomfort by an overriding desire to achieve his purpose. His physical symptoms did not reduce his continuous output of hard work and thrustful energy, and ever he set himself new tasks and dared new hazards in his thorough, painstaking way. It is these moral and soldierly virtues which made Marlborough the greatest servant, who remained a servant, of any sovereign in history.

CHAPTER VII

THE CONQUERING HERO

1704-5, WINTER

THE labours of the year were not over. The campaign of 1705 which might end the war could not be fought without the vigorous and punctual aid of Prussia and the German states. The only chance of obtaining this was that the hero of Blenheim, now the cynosure of Europe, should in person visit the Courts of Prussia and Hanover. He was utterly weary. He wrote to Godolphin from Weissemburg:

> I think to begin my journey on Friday or Saturday next. I own that my heart aches at the thought of it, since I shall be forced to go above eight hundred miles before I get to The Hague, in the very worst time of the year; and, that which is worst of all, with very little hopes of succeeding.[1]

Eight hundred miles in the lumbering coach with its six horses and cavalry escort, splashing along the uneven roads in the depth of winter, interspersed by arduous ceremonial, by official festivities, and by intricate negotiations, before he could even reach The Hague and wait for a fair wind! "The ways have been so bad," he wrote to Sarah from Berlin (November 23), "I have been obliged to be every day 14 or 15 hours on the road, which makes my side very sore; but three or four days I shall stay here will make me able to go on."[2] He had a great welcome in Berlin. He was treated as the Prince he now was, and gazed upon as a marvel. The King was gratified by his visit, and by his tributes to the bravery of the Prussian troops.

But Marlborough's task was one from which, as he approached it, anyone might have recoiled. The northern war

---

[1] November 10; Coxe, ii, 59.   [2] *Ibid.*, 61.

had entered upon an extraordinary phase. In their fear of
Prussian domination both the Czar and the King of Saxony had
adopted the most desperate expedient open to statecraft. They
had deliberately courted defeat at the hands of Charles XII
so as to bring Prussia and Sweden face to face. Only a fortnight before Marlborough's arrival reinforcements were kept
back from the Saxon and Russian armies. Charles XII had
won his victory at Punitz, and Poland lay open to the Swedes.
Should Prussia intervene? This was the paramount question
in Berlin. The Prussian army was being rapidly recruited
and enlarged. Upon what fields would it seek fame and
booty? Patkul, the Livonian weaver of anti-Swedish coali-
tions, had hastened secretly to Berlin at the first news of
Marlborough's impending visit.

It was Marlborough's aim to prevent this vast extension of
the northern war, which by diverting German energies would
so seriously aid Louis XIV; and also to secure a large additional contingent of the Prussian Army to fight against France
in Italy. No wonder he thought it an unhopeful quest. The
language which he was authorized to use was hard. The best
account of his discourse is given in Frederick I's letter to
Augustus II, in which the Elector-King states that Marlborough went so far as to intimate that if Prussia stirred
up this new trouble she would *"be dealt with as Denmark had
been in 1700,"* when the English fleet had carried the Swedish
Army to the neighbourhood of Copenhagen. To prevent such
an ugly out-turn, Marlborough urged the Elector-King either
to disband his newly recruited troops or transfer them to the
Grand Alliance on favourable terms.

The rigour of such discussions must be apparent, and Marlborough had need to supplement the prestige which Blenheim
had given to the Maritime Powers with all his commanding
personal address and compulsive charm; and this was the
easier since the Elector-King and the General conversed easily
in French. It was fortunate that Frederick I was already
disgusted by the vacillations and suspected bad faith of the
Elector of Saxony. Marlborough caught Frederick I and his
Ministers at a most timely moment, when they were already

cooling from the projected triple alliance against the formidable Swede, and when the troops that had been raised in that intention might become superfluous. The Elector-King therefore hearkened to a voice which offered threats and bribes with equal smoothness, and set himself to make upon the best terms a bargain for farming out a part of the desirable Prussian Army. After his conversations with the King Marlborough was presented with proposals in fifteen articles. Declaring that these dealt with matters beyond the sphere in which he could presume to meddle, he would reply only in general terms. Nevertheless three days later he concluded in the Queen's name a treaty, to which he undertook that the States-General and the Empire would accede, whereby eight thousand Prussians would forthwith march to Piedmont to the help of the Duke of Savoy in return for an annual subsidy of two hundred thousand thalers from England, one hundred thousand from Holland, and bread-rations from the Empire.

John to Sarah

BERLIN
Nov. 27

I have been forced to stay here three days longer than I intended; but at last I have finished so far, that they have promised to sign the treaty for 8000 men for the duke of Savoy at 12 o'clock this day, at which time I shall have my coach ready; but shall not be able to get to Hanover till Monday night, and hope to finish what I have to do there by Wednesday night, so that I may set forward to Holland on Thursday. I am very well contented at the pains I have taken in coming hither, since it has obtained 8000 men for the speedy relief of the duke of Savoy, this being the only prince of the empire in condition to send any men. I hope Holland as well as her majesty will approve of what I have done, it being the only thing that in probability can save Savoy. It is not to be expressed the civilities and honours they have done me here, the ministers assuring me that no other body could have prevailed with the king. My next will be from Hanover, and then you must not expect to hear from me till I come to Holland.[1]

1 Coxe, ii, 62.

He set out from Berlin in a blaze of goodwill, with results far beyond his expectations or those of the Government he served. He had been greatly favoured, we now know, by unforeseeable events. But the effect produced upon the Courts of Europe was as if a magic wand waved in Berlin had changed the policy of the Prussian King, prevented the spread of the northern war, and turned the sharpened bayonets of Prussia from the shores of the Baltic to those of the Mediterranean. Without this succour the Italian front against France could not have been sustained during the year 1705. But Marlborough also deeply interested the King in his schemes along the Moselle. He carried away with him the King's gift of "a hat with a diamond button and loop and a diamond hatband valued at between twenty and thirty thousand crowns and two fine saddle-horses with rich furniture." [1]

The compliments and courtesies of Berlin were repeated in Hanover. He was received with the greatest honour. Here he trod the delicate ground of the succession to the British Crown, and he well knew that every step would be jealously scrutinized by both the great English parties and by Queen Anne. The Electress Sophia was now decidedly disposed to receiving an invitation to visit London. Marlborough knew that the Queen would resist and resent this while she had breath in her body. Therefore upon the main point he must chill the enthusiasm of his hosts. Instructed gossip at Versailles had spread about the rumour that the object of his visit was to prepare the way for the marriage of his youngest daughter with the Electoral Prince, afterwards King George II. Not only was there no foundation for this except the natural mischief-making of the enemy, but Marlborough must have known that the affections of the Electoral Prince were at this time being strongly directed by his grandmother, the Electress Sophia, towards the charming and gifted Caroline of Anspach, afterwards Queen 'Caroline the Illustrious,' and that their courtship had already begun.

The pre-eminent figure at the Court of Hanover in those

[1] Lediard, i, 464.

days was Leibnitz, the philosopher-mathematician, discoverer or inventor of the differential calculus. He was the honoured friend of the Electress, and his voluminous writings throw many intimate gleams upon the personages and thoughts of the Hanoverian circle. The historian Klopp, who in his own day faithfully served the last King of Hanover, also writes agreeably about this visit. He says:

> Marlborough for his part developed all the dazzling aspect of his personality. He showed towards the Electress a deference which surpassed all the customary forms of the German Courts. He refused to sit down in her presence even at a ball. The Electress invited him to take part in a game (of cards) so as to force him to sit down. In accordance with the English court custom he knelt and kissed her hand.

This procedure proved irresistible to the vigorous old lady whose homely candour and common sense had made her respected throughout Europe. She was at first prejudiced against Marlborough. We have seen her disparaging reference to "the great general Marlborough" in her letter to Leibnitz about the Schellenberg. Blenheim had effaced these impressions and contact with Marlborough transformed them. "Never," she wrote, "have I become acquainted with a man who knows how to move so easily, so freely, and so courteously. He is as skilled as a courtier as he is a brave general." [1] This comment travelled far.

Their conversation turned, of course, upon the Occasional Conformity Bill. Parliament had now met, and the progress of this measure was watched as narrowly and as anxiously in Europe as the movements of a most important army. Praiseworthy efforts were made by all the Courts, friendly and hostile, to understand why there was all this ferment in England about it, and what forces or causes the cryptic names of 'Tory' and 'Whig' meant. The nearest guess was that they stood for Anglican and Presbyterian. Marlborough did not attempt to explain the real differences. But he now declared himself plainly opposed to the Occasional Conformity Bill. This gave so much pleasure to the Electress

[1] Leibnitz, *Werke* (1873), ix, 112.

Sophia that she seems to have accepted without demur the intimation which he gradually conveyed that she ran no risk of being invited to England by Queen Anne. She declared him as sensible in politics as pleasant in manner, and presented him with a piece of tapestry. To this the reigning prince added a jewel reputed to be worth twenty-five thousand thalers, which we may be sure he accepted with grace and pleasure.

John to Sarah   HANOVER
                                                              Dec. 2, 1704

On my arrival here I found two of your dear letters, and could you know the true satisfaction I have when they are kind, you will ever make me happy. I shall go from hence on Thursday, so that on this day se'nnight I hope to write from The Hague, where I will make as little stay as the business will allow of. I have so much respect shewn me here that I have hardly time to write. The king of Prussia did me all the honour he could; and indeed I have met with more kindness and respect everywhere than I could have imagined. But by my letters from England I find that zeal and success is only [not even] capable of protecting me from the malice of villainous faction; so that if it were not for the great obligation I owe to the queen, nothing should persuade me evermore to stir out of England. We have the news here that Landau and Trarbach are taken, so that thanks be to God this campaign is ended, to the greatest advantage for the allies, that has been for a great while. I long extremely to be with you and the children, so that you may be sure I shall lose no time when the wind is fair.[1]

The city of Amsterdam had long been the focus of pro-French sentiment, and if its powerful magistracy had favoured Marlborough's appointment as Deputy Captain-General, it was, as we have seen, largely for the purpose of keeping the 'Royalist' office of War Lord in abeyance. But now the Amsterdammers wished to throw up their caps for Marlborough. They sent a special delegation to press him to visit their city, and received him with remarkable enthusiasm. On the 12th he reached The Hague. He had deceived the

1 Coxe, ii, 63.

States-General; he had purloined a part of their army; he had carried it far from the frontiers of Holland. Many sturdy Dutchmen lay by the Danube and the Upper Rhine. But his judgment had been right. He had stemmed the tide of adverse war; he had reconstituted the Grand Alliance in all its parts; he had saved the Empire; he had broken the military prestige of France. He was indeed their protector, and a champion worthy to hold—as deputy, of course—the military office of the great Stadtholders. The Grand Pensionary and seven Deputies received him on behalf of the Republic. He was presented with a basin and ewer of solid gold. The assembly listened with profound respect to his account of the general situation. The States of Holland immediately endorsed his Berlin treaty. All rejoiced that they had him safely back. They hoped and prayed that he would never go so far, nor run such risks again. They exulted in the past; they remained blind to the future. They did not understand that the destinies of Holland might be enlarged or restricted according as they used or spurned their new opportunities. Amid their blessings Marlborough sailed from Rotterdam to England, having been absent eight months, during which he had moulded Europe in a form which was not broken till the French Revolution.

Parliament had opened on October 29/November 9. The Queen's Speech extolled the triumphs of the year, and appealed for unity at home and for renewed and even greater exertions abroad. It had been thought better by the Ministers to make no special reference to Blenheim or to the Duke of Marlborough, but to leave it to Parliament themselves to fix and assign the credit. Accordingly in the House of Commons the Tory Party demonstrated their strength by joining the victory by the Danube with the naval battle of Malaga, which was dear to them because of the pronounced Toryism of Admiral Rooke. In the Lords, however, unstinted praise was bestowed upon Marlborough and his troops. No reference was made to Malaga in the Peers' Address. In debate it was argued that to couple a severe but apparently indecisive cannonade between the fleets with the battle of

Höchstädt was invidious and absurd. This criticism, though actually true, was put in a way that did less than justice to the work of the Navy or its commander. The Whig influence in the Lords enabled them to set their party view of strategy against that asserted by the Tories in the Commons. "We can never enough admire your wisdom and courage," they said to the Queen, "in sending that seasonable and necessary assistance to the Empire, and we cannot too much commend the secrecy and bravery with which your orders were executed."[1] Thus the session opened in the full rigour of the party game, to which the episodes of the widening world-war offered an exciting accompaniment and a succession of opportunities for debate.

Tory politicians found the victory of Blenheim hard to welcome. Not only did it crown with success the policy of Continental enterprises, but it had been gained by a General, also a kind of Prime Minister, who was well known to be lukewarm, if not indeed by now actually hostile, to the Occasional Conformity Bill. No doubt the success of the British arms and the allied cause was desirable and even necessary, but the party disadvantages resulting therefrom were obvious. The Tories were therefore torn between their relief and a good deal of uncontrollable pride as Englishmen, and their annoyance as partisans. In fact, there was much truth in Sarah's caustic remark that one would think from their demeanour that "the battle of Höchstädt had been gained over the Church of England and not over the French." The Tory chagrin was, however, restrained not only by their patriotism, but by a lively sense of the joy of the nation.

The estimates for the year guaranteed the still more vigorous prosecution of the war by land and sea. The Army was to be enlarged to fifty thousand men for Flanders and ten thousand for Portugal, and to be fully recruited. The Navy was raised from forty to forty-five thousand seamen, including marines available for landing purposes. All the subsidies to allies and for the hiring of mercenary troops at the joint expense of the Maritime Powers were continued. The expense

[1] *Parliamentary History*, vi, 356.

amounted to more than nine millions, three-quarters of which must be raised by taxation. The whole of this unprecedented supply was voted speedily and unanimously by the House of Commons.

Having thus discharged their unavoidable duty to their country, the Tory majority turned with relief to the serious realities of public life. On November 23 the Occasional Conformity Bill was reintroduced in the Commons and read a first time. And now the ex-Ministers Rochester and Nottingham revealed their designs. Incomparably the greatest source of revenue was the Land Tax, which alone yielded upward of four million pounds. Availing themselves of the precedent which the Lords were held to have admitted in 1702 when they reluctantly deferred to the Queen's wishes upon the grant to her husband, the Tory chiefs now proposed to tack the Occasional Conformity Bill to the Land Tax. Thus the Lords would have to choose between submitting to an odious measure or plunging the whole supply for the fleets and armies into hopeless confusion. This was indeed a fight with ball cartridge. Harley in his dual capacity as Speaker and as Secretary of State was well fitted and placed to advise the Queen's anxious Ministers. Members of all parties had access to him, and he did not refuse his guidance. Indeed, it was afterwards alleged that, looking several moves ahead, he had himself suggested to the Tory leaders the possibility of using the 'tack' with the intention of thereby drawing them into a trap.

If this were so, his artfulness was rewarded. The Tory Party was solid upon the Bill; but the tack split them from top to bottom. A large proportion of their members were not prepared to carry party warfare to a point where it challenged their country's safety and the honour of its arms. On November 28 the tack was rejected by a strong combination of Whigs and moderate Tories. The Ministry acted unitedly together. The military members supported them. Lord Cutts, who as an Irish peer could be elected to the Commons, has left a record of his feelings in a letter to a friend in Holland.

It is eight o'clock and I have just come from Parliament, where I have stayed until now without having eaten or drunk to-day. I have therefore only time to tell you that some persons have wanted to tack the Occasional Conformity Bill on to that relating to the Land Tax. We have had a great fight over that all day. I have spoken against it, without going into the merits of the Occasional Conformity Bill, and the assembly has listened to me with close attention. We won by a great majority, 251 to 134. That decision is of the utmost importance. For in the other event, if the proposal for tacking had been carried, the Money Bill would have been lost, the enmity between the two Houses would have become irreconcilable, and the Queen would have been forced to dissolve Parliament. The consequence of that would have been the collapse of the common cause against France.[1]

Untaught by this rebuff upon the tack, the embittered or devout Highflyers proceeded with the Bill, and it passed through the House of Commons by substantial majorities and reached the Lords in the last days of the year.

On December 14, in the midst of this furious party strife, Marlborough landed at Greenwich, and hastened to pay his duty to the Queen. He had brought with him to the Thames a shipload of thirty-six French officers of the highest distinction. At their head was Marshal Tallard; sixteen of them were generals; none was below the rank of lieutenant-colonel. He also deposited in the Tower all the standards and colours captured by his wing of the army at Blenheim.[2] The next day he repaired to the House of Lords, where he was solemnly thanked by the Lord Keeper in the name of the Peers. "Your Grace," said the Lord Keeper, "has not overthrown young, unskilful Generals, raw and undisciplined troops; but . . . has conquered the French and Bavarian armies; armies that were fully instructed in all the arts of war; select veteran troops, flushed with former victories,

1 Klopp, xi, 330.
2 The Dutch considered that a share of these trophies should have been assigned to them, and a committee of the States-General rebuked Hompesch for having handed over to the Duke's command the standards his squadrons had captured. But Marlborough as Commander-in-Chief claimed them all for himself and for England.

and commanded by Generals of great experience and bravery. . . .

"The Emperor is thereby relieved; the Empire itself freed from a dangerous Enemy, in the very bowels of it; the exorbitant power of France is checked, and, I hope, a happy step made towards reducing of that Monarch, within his due bounds, and securing the liberties of Europe.

"The honour of these glorious victories, great as they are (under the immediate blessing of Almighty God), is chiefly, if not alone, owing to Your Grace's conduct and valour.

"This is the unanimous voice of England, and all her Majesty's allies.

"This most honourable House is highly sensible of the great and signal services Your Grace has done her Majesty, this campaign, and of the immortal honour you have done the English Nation; and have commanded me to give you their thanks for the same."

Marlborough replied in three or four sentences. ". . . I must beg, on this occasion, to do right to all the officers and soldiers I had the honour of having under my command; next to the blessing of God, the good success of this campaign is owing to their extraordinary courage.

"I am very sure, it will be a great satisfaction, as well as encouragement to the whole army, to find their services so favourably accepted." [1]

He repeated this answer in somewhat different words to the Committee which tendered him the thanks of the House of Commons.

In the first days of the new year (January 3) all London crowded to a pageant the like of which England had never seen. A long procession of the household troops and footguards bore the captured standards and colours from the Tower to Westminster Hall amid the salutes of the 'great guns' and the cheers of the people. The thirty-four French standards were borne by the gentlemen of the Blues, and the hundred and twenty-eight French colours by the pikemen of the Guards. Through the city, down the Strand, along

1 Lediard, i, 470.

'the Pall-Mall,' before St James's Palace, through St James's Mews, they marched into the Park, where two salvos of forty cannon were fired. Queen Anne had let it be known that she would see them pass, and did so from Lord Fitzharding's lodgings in the Palace. These banners of mighty France, that nation of twenty millions, whom men in middle age could remember as England's disdainful paymaster, were received and set up in Westminster Hall for all to see. But more significant than this well-organized ceremonial was the temper of the masses who lined the route or thronged behind the procession. The foreign Ambassadors, bred in countries where Courts, nobles, and magnates counted for all, were struck by a manifestation of a national self-consciousness unique among the nations.[1] Here was a society which did not end with the powerful and the rich, which descended through every class of citizen down to the very poorest and most humble, all of whose hearts responded to the feeling that it was *their* victory, that *their* cause had triumphed, and that *their* England was growing great. Even while foreign observers cavilled with some reason that the London populace claimed for themselves a victory in which their troops had formed but a quarter of the army, they admired the integral force and comprehension of the vigorous islanders, who could quarrel so fiercely with one another and yet rejoice together in national glory.

Already, too, the City of London had risen upon the European scene as a financial and political entity. On January 6 the Lord Mayor and Aldermen entertained the Duke and his officers, together with Godolphin and the Queen's Ministers, at a banquet in the Goldsmiths' Hall. Marlborough rode in a royal carriage followed by a great train of other coaches containing the principal personages in the realm and the Ambassadors of all the allied and neutral states. Part of the expense of the new campaign was to be met by a sale of annuities yielding ten pounds a year for every hundred and fifty pounds of capital. Within two hours of the lists being opened the whole sum of nearly a million

1 Klopp, xi, 343.

pounds, impressive in those days, was subscribed by large numbers of persons eager to prove their confidence in the national cause at 6 2/3 per cent. In all the world at this time nothing could compare with these strong beginnings of nationalism and public credit. The destruction of the Armada had preserved the life of Britain: the charge at Blenheim opened to her the gateways of the modern world.

The antagonisms of political forces in England had brought a cool element into the welcome to which the victorious General was treated: but this quality of independence and restraint in a sense enhanced its significance. For now these estates and parties, this complex society, laid aside for the moment their feuds in order to do him honour beyond what any absolute monarch could bestow. The applause, the admiration, the gratitude of equals has a ring more true and more comforting than the favour of a prince, however mighty, however gracious. It was common ground among the whole society which then expressed the English nation that some magnificent and unprecedented reward should be bestowed upon the Duke of Marlborough, and the only question was what form it should take. Lords and Commons, Whigs and Tories, divided in so much else, joined with the Sovereign and her Ministers in this quest. Various benevolent schemes were mooted. At first there was an idea of clearing a large space in London for a square to bear his name, to set up statues of him and of the Sovereign under whom he had conquered, and to build him besides a fine house overlooking the scene. The wary Godolphin saw objections, and wrote to the still more wary Harley:

> I am not fond of the proposal of two statues, one for the Queen and th'other for the Duke of Marlborough. What merit soever a subject may have I am doubtful that may set him upon too near an equality with one upon the throne. My own opinion inclines most to an anniversary thanksgiving by Act of Parliament for so entire a victory, as the most public, the most decent, and the most permanent record of it to posterity, but if this be thought too much because it is upon a fact happening without the kingdom—whereas our precedents of anniversaries run

LORD TREASURER GODOLPHIN
From an engraving after the painting by Sir Godfrey Kneller
From a print at 10 Downing Street. By permission of the Office of Works

generally upon occasions at home—I must submit that to better judgments.[1]

One may here note the natural inclination of the Treasurer to turn to the best advantage those rewards which are inexpensive. Yet it would have been better for Marlborough's happiness and dignity if something like this had been done; for the course adopted was to lead him into many embarrassments and some humiliation. It was on all sides agreed that the gift should be, if possible, unanimous. The danger of one proposal being matched against another was avoided by framing the address of the House of Commons in general terms. Accordingly they solicited the Crown to consider proper means of perpetuating the memory of the great services performed by the Duke of Marlborough. The Queen replied, "I am very well pleased by this address, and will take it into my consideration and send you my thoughts upon it in a little time." Anne now gave full rein to the generosity which had been frustrated to her annoyance after the campaign in 1702. On February 17 she informed the Commons that in conformity with their address she proposed to convey to the Duke of Marlborough and his heirs the Royal Manor and Park of Woodstock, and desired "the assistance of the House upon this extraordinary occasion" for the purpose of clearing off various encumbrances upon the estate. The grant comprised about 15,000 acres, and was reported to be worth about £6000 a year.

The necessary Act was speedily passed without opposition. Its preamble contained a convenient epitome of Marlborough's military services up to this time:

. . . and that, in the first Year of Your Majesty's Reign, the said Duke of Marlborough did so well execute the Commission and Orders, which he received from Your Majesty, as Captain-General and Commander of Your Majesty's Forces, That he not only secured and extended the Frontiers of Holland, by taking the Towns and Fortresses of Venlo, Ruremond, Stevenwaert and Liege; but soon obliged the Enemy (who had been at the Gates of Nimeguen) to seek Shelter behind their Lines; And the next

1 Bath Papers, H.M.C., i, 63.

Campaign, by taking Bon, Huy and Limburg, added all the Country, between the Rhine and the Maese, to the Conquests of the preceding year. And that in the Memorable Year 1704, when your Majesty was generously pleased to take the Resolution of rescuing the Empire from that immediate Ruin, to which, by the Defection of the Elector of Bavaria, it was exposed, the Measures, which, by Your Majesty's Wisdom and Goodness, had been devised and concerted, were pursued by the said Duke, with the utmost Diligence, Secrecy and good Conduct, in leading the Forces of Your Majesty, and Your Allies, by a long and difficult march, to the Banks of the Danube, where the said Duke, immediately upon his Arrival, did attack and force the Bavarians (assisted by the French) in their strong Intrenchments at Schellenberg, passed the Danube, distressed the Country of Bavaria, and a second time fought the Enemies, who had ben reinforc'd by a Royal Army of the French King's best Troops, commanded by a Marshal of France; And, on the second day of August, 1704, after a bloody Battle, at or near Blenheim (altho' the Enemies had the Advantage of Number and Situation) did gain as Absolute and Glorious a Victory, as is recorded in the History of any Age; By which, Bavaria being entirely reduced, Ratisbon, Augsburg, Ulm, Memmingen, and other Imperial Towns being recover'd, the Liberty of the Diet, and the Peace of the Empire was restored, and Landau, Treves, and Trarbach being taken, the War is carried into the Dominions of France.[1]

At the same time the grant of five thousand a year upon the Civil List, which was valid only for the Queen's lifetime, was made permanent by Parliament. The Queen appointed him Colonel of the First Guards, in which he had originally received his commission; and finally she set herself to plan and build at her expense at Woodstock a splendid palace which, in memory of the victory, was to be called the Castle of Blenheim. She selected Sir John Vanbrugh as the architect, and interested herself keenly in the model which she had had constructed.

Marlborough was highly gratified by the splendid possessions which descended upon him. Although the pressure

1 Lediard, i, 467.

of great affairs absorbed almost the whole of his mind, his strength, and his time, he liked at odd moments to reflect upon his growing fortune and the princely setting in which his heirs and successors would dwell. He regarded the raising of his family to the first rank in England as second only in importance to raising England to the first place in Europe, and he saw no reason why these two processes should not be combined. His tireless industry and exertion, his profound sagacity and calculation, his constant readiness to stake not only his life, but all he had gathered in reputation and wealth, upon the hazards of war and of well-chosen battle, were faithfully offered in his country's service. But a time was to come when England needed for her guidance some high qualities beyond the constructive and acquisitive genius with which he was born, and when through the lack of these Queen, country, and servant were to taste griefs they had not deserved. The pursuit of power with the capacity and in the desire to exercise it worthily is among the noblest of human occupations. But Power is a goddess who admits no rival in her loves.

It should not, however, be supposed that such a moral was ever drawn by Marlborough. When to the favour and affection of the Queen there succeeded an aversion as strong and far less justified; when, stripped of his offices, he was the target of every calumny which a furious faction could hurl or an envious aristocracy applaud; when all that he had done was belittled and his victories contemned or written off as fully paid, he could still reflect that he had made his fortune, that he had founded his family, and that the stones of Blenheim Palace would weather the storms of a thousand years. Such were the stubborn consolations of this virtuous and valiant builder who built noble monuments beneath the stars.

CHAPTER VIII

THE MARGRAVE'S TOE

1705, SPRING

THE consequences of Blenheim governed the war in 1705. Louis XIV resolved to stand on the defensive upon all the fronts. Strenuous efforts were made during the winter to repair the losses of France in man-power and equipment. The regular troops were brought to full strength not only by compulsory recruitment, but by large drafts from the militia. The destruction of the cavalry, probably by the disease we now call glanders, was made good by enormous purchases of horses in Switzerland. Severe sacrifices were exacted in taxation, and the clergy alone were induced to contribute a free-will offering equal to six million pounds. To the astonishment of Europe the French armies in the spring were reported to be "more numerous and more brilliant" than ever. Actually, besides maintaining the war in Spain, the Great King was able to place in the field 100 battalions and 100 squadrons under Vendôme in Italy, and 200 battalions and 260 squadrons upon his northern frontiers. These latter were divided into three armies: 80 battalions and 100 squadrons commanded by Villeroy under the nominal orders of the Elector in Flanders; 70 battalions and 100 squadrons under Villars upon the Moselle; and 50 battalions and 60 squadrons in Alsace and upon the Upper Rhine. These Marshals were made aware that the entire forces in the north must be considered as a single group of armies, capable of reinforcing each other in accordance with the enemy's attack. To make this easy the lateral roads behind the front were brought into the best condition, and supplies were distributed along them, as well as in all the fortresses concerned. The Elector during the absence of Villeroy from Brussels had prepared a minor offensive along the Meuse, having for its object the recapture of Huy and Liége at the outset of the campaign. He was, however, told that he must await the development of the allied attack. This was expected along the Moselle, but no final opinion could be formed until the movements of the English were known. As these were now regarded as the best troops of the allies, it was thought that they would certainly be used for the main offensive. Accordingly it was upon them that the chief attention of the French headquarters was fixed.[1]

It was believed at Versailles that the Grand Alliance would be able to place sixty thousand men in Flanders under Overkirk, sixty thousand on the Moselle under Marlborough, thirty thousand on the Rhine under the Margrave, thirty thousand in Italy under Prince Eugene, and fifteen thousand in Portugal under Galway, in addition to the thirty thousand absorbed by the revolt in Hungary. Besides all these there were the forces of the Duke of Savoy and the King of Portugal, and the immense fleets by which England and Holland maintained what had now become the complete command of the seas. Actually, when the campaign opened, the confederates had, as we shall see, by no means achieved such totals. Nevertheless it may be broadly computed that the allies marshalled for 1705 field armies of nearly a quarter of a million men, and that the Two Crowns resisted them with about two hundred thousand. If we double these figures so as to comprise the garrisons, depots, and all the services in the rear, apart from the manufacture of munitions, we obtain a fair measure of the war effort which Europe now made, prodigious in proportion to its wealth and manhood and to its primitive organization.

Unity of command was imposed by Louis XIV upon the three French armies in the north. But Marlborough, although he tried to manage the whole war and to provide for every theatre, had in fact a lamentably defective control. He could, indeed, lead the dreaded English and the troops paid by the Queen where he pleased. But every movement of the Dutch Army must still be settled both beforehand with the States-General, and at the time with the Dutch Deputies and com-

1 Pelet, v, 14.

manders; and his influence upon the Imperial armies was exerted only through his correspondence with Wratislaw and Prince Eugene. Louis XIV was absolute Commander-in-Chief: Marlborough was only an informal chairman of a discordant committee. In this lies the explanation of the war in 1705. Moving painfully through obstructed channels and pulling many tangled strings, he was, however, able during the winter and early spring to prepare an allied front in the north, so as to leave himself a choice of action and impose uncertainty upon the French. Great magazines were established in the frontier fortresses of Trèves, Coblenz, Liége, and Maestricht, and large masses of horse and foot were gathered in Holland. Numerous flotillas of boats and barges were assembled and fitted which could carry all the material down the Scheldt for a siege of Antwerp, up the Meuse for a siege of Namur, up the Moselle for that of Thionville or Saarlouis, or along the Rhine towards Fort Louis, Kehl, or Old Brisach. He had no doubt himself which was the true line of advance.

While the siege of Landau had dragged on Marlborough had agreed with Eugene, and, as they both thought, with the Margrave too, upon the general plan. Marlborough had taken all the preliminary steps. He had recaptured Trèves and Trarbach, and put them in the strongest state of defence. He had made every arrangement in his power with the German princes and the Dutch agents to gather immense magazines in both those fortresses, and had obtained from all the German states concerned the promise that their contingents in the pay of the Sea Powers would be in readiness during April. He had himself visited the Courts of Berlin and Hanover. He had procured the assent of the Dutch Government and the reinforcement of the English army. Making allowances for the slowness of communication and the difficulties of supervision, he had reason to expect that he could take the field about the middle of May.

His plan was to stand upon the defensive in Flanders and on the Upper Rhine, and advance upon Saarlouis and Thionville, through Lorraine into France, with over ninety thousand men. These would be formed in two armies; the smaller, embodying the main war effort of the Empire, would operate under the Margrave from the area about Landau, westward towards the Saar; the larger he would

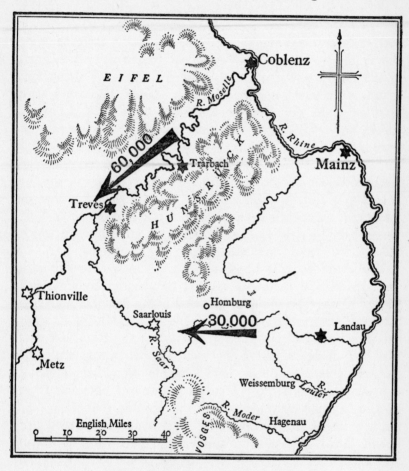

THE MOSELLE PLAN FOR 1705

lead himself, south-west up the Moselle. It was the essence of this plan that these two armies should work together within manœuvring distance, so that neither could be overwhelmed. The arrangements which he had made in Italy, and the action of the English fleet in the Gulf of Lyons, should enable Prince Eugene at least to hold the French in that theatre, if not, indeed, to press an advantage. Modern military opinion would endorse these conceptions.

The renewed desire of the Maritime Powers to mediate between the Emperor and his Hungarian subjects had thrust more weight on Stepney than the Ambassador could carry. He had espoused the policy of London and The Hague, already so irritating to Vienna, with an added ardour of his own. He had of necessity come into close touch with Rakoczy, and was on far better terms with the rebel leader than with the Court to which he was accredited. In all this he had the authority and support of the English Cabinet, whose orders he was obeying. The vexation of the Emperor and his Ministers, which could not be expressed to the English and Dutch Governments, broke upon the now hated figure of the Ambassador. It was easy to allege that his personal partisanship and tactlessness had become in itself an obstacle between the Empire and its allies. A demand was made for his recall.[1] Marlborough's headquarters in the field or office in Whitehall was the clearing-house for the ceaseless disputes which threatened to rend the Alliance. To him therefore Wratislaw and Eugene wrote appealing for the withdrawal of Stepney.

Marlborough behaved exactly as an experienced Foreign Secretary would do to-day. He had confidence in Stepney, agreed with the policy of which he was the exponent, and understood the trouble in which it must involve him. He thought, however, that more progress could be made if a new agent were appointed, and that the prospect of the recall of Stepney would smooth the mediation which England and Holland were determined to obtrude. He therefore wrote to Wratislaw from St James's on January 9, insisting upon the acceptance of mediation, declaring that if the Hungarians refused reasonable terms the Maritime Powers would join

---

[1] We may judge the feelings of the Emperor from imagining our own if in 1917 the French had proposed to send a Mission to mediate between Great Britain and Irish Home Rulers, in order to set free the forty thousand British troops garrisoning Ireland for service on the Western Front.

with the Empire in declaring them public enemies, promising
that Stepney would be withdrawn as soon as the Queen could
find another post suited to his rank and services, and request-
ing that he should be treated with all consideration meanwhile.
In order to be fair to Stepney, he sent him a copy of the
letter, adding:

> Neither must you take it amiss what you will find in relation
> to the sending another Minister to the Court at Vienna. You will
> see I have endeavoured to justify you from any blame they may
> pretend to lay at your door, and you may depend upon it that
> the Queen will have so just regard to your services as not to re-
> move you until her Majesty has provided otherwise for you,
> wherein you may be assured at all times of my good offices
> wherever they may be wanting.[1]

The Ambassador, inflamed by the local dispute, was so
angry that he forgot his duty. He wrote a bitter complaint
to his friend Count Harrach, an Austrian dignitary, declaring
that Wratislaw was seeking his undoing, and quoting letters
written by him to England—as he suggested, with the Emperor's authority—for that purpose. It was now Wratislaw's
turn to be aggrieved. His correspondence with Marlborough
was not only secret but sacred. He leaped to the conclusion
that Marlborough had shown his letters to Stepney. This
was quite untrue. Marlborough had never shown Stepney
Wratislaw's letters, but only one of his own replies; and this
in justice and candour to a public servant in a harassing position. Wratislaw's wrath had led him to declare that his personal relations with Marlborough must now end, and that
their correspondence in future would be purely formal. Marlborough's answer is a good example of the firmness and dignity with which he could now write.

St James's
February 9

I have received your letter with much surprise. . . . I in no
way approve the letter which Mr Stepney has written to Count
Harach, believing it to be altogether unfounded in its suggestions;
. . . and neither the Secretary of State nor anyone here can under-

1 *Dispatches,* i, 575.

stand how he ever felt entitled to write in such a manner; but I must also make it plain to you at the same time that I take it very ill that you should believe me capable of disclosing extracts from your letters. I had counted upon quite different treatment from you.

I see besides from all the rest of your letter that our correspondence is likely in the future to be very sterile, and as perhaps you have not kept a copy of what you have written, I send it you back in order that you may see the coldness with which you quit me [*la froideur avec laquelle vous me quittez*].[1]

To Stepney he was stern.

St James's
February 9

. . . By what I learn from the secretaries or otherwise, I can find no manner of reason for such proceedings on your part, especially since you have been often told by them as well as myself that her Majesty (to whom alone you are accountable) is entirely satisfied with all your transactions at the Court of Vienna; therefore as I now write to Count Wratislaw that I can no wise approve of your proceedings, as you will find by the enclosed copy, I should be glad for my own satisfaction that you would explain yourself a little further from whence it is you have all these reports. You see I have no reserve with you since I send you what I write to him, but must desire that neither this nor anything else you may have from me may be exposed.[2]

The Ambassador bowed to this rebuke, but Marlborough's breach with Wratislaw was an embarrassment not removed for many months. The sending of the Mission was accepted by the Emperor only under extreme duress; and in Vienna the strictures of Imperial policy in which the Parliament and the States-General freely indulged aroused a keen resentment. "I am amazed," protested Hoffmann to Harley, "that the continuance of the disorders in Hungary is ascribed only to the Emperor, and not attributed in part to the rebels, although the latter make or obstinately maintain demands to which no monarch in the world could agree."[3]

Marlborough reached The Hague in the early days of

---

1 *Dispatches,* i, 594.   2 *Ibid.,* 590.
3 Hoffmann's dispatch of February 6; Klopp, xi, 348.

April. He was evidently full of hope for the campaign, which he thought might carry him far on the road to Paris. As a prelude to taking the field he excelled himself in civilities to old friends and high personages on the enemy side. The return on parole of several gentlemen of fashion who had fallen into his hands at Blenheim afforded an occasion of an agreeable correspondence with Villeroy. He sent on April 15 by one of these indulged captives [1] a most obliging letter about the exchange of prisoners, and ended, "Some of my friends on my departure have begged me to procure a passport for Sieur Philippe du Ruel, one of our comedians, who is to go to Paris with his wife, Eleanor, and two other ladies in order to perfect his art under his old master." The Comte de Grammont, asking for the release of the Marquis de la Vallière, had sent him in December a snuff-box bearing a miniature of the Comtesse de Grammont. Marlborough had replied that he would value it in the same fashion as if she had given it to him herself: "You know me too discreet to show it to our ladies here." An old friend from the days of Charles II, the Duchess of Portsmouth (Louise de Kéroualle), had also written to him about a gentleman for whose lot she was concerned, and had asked him whether he could not procure her some of those liqueurs from Madeira and the Canaries from which Paris was now cut off by the English fleet. "As for sherry," he had written, "I am vexed that one cannot find any here since the war, but Palm wine and cider I shall not fail to send you the best through Brussels, as soon as I arrive in Holland." He now made good these promises. "The sight of the Marquis de la Vallière," he wrote on April 16 to the Comte de Grammont, "will convince you anew how much I defer to your commands, and how I endeavour by every means to deserve the snuff-box." To the Duchess of Portsmouth he wrote on the 27th:

I am delighted to tell you that the Queen has had the goodness at my request to allow M. de Hautfeuille to pay a visit to France.

[1] The Marquis de Monperous.

M. de Monperous has been good enough in leaving here to charge himself with a little present of Palm wine which I beg you to accept. I must indeed excuse myself for how little it is; but, since what is good is very rare just now in England on account of the war, I hope you will not take it ill that I have shared with you my campaign store [*ma provision de campagne*]. I hope that next year you will be better provided for here at home with us.[1]

At this time he met again his sister-in-law, the Countess of Tyrconnel, once "the fair Frances" of the Restoration Court. The account he gives of their talks shows the sense they had of being on opposite sides.

John to Sarah

HAGUE
April 21, 1705

* Now that you have settled everything with the builders, I am desirous you would take the first opportunity of sending me the draught Van brook [Vanbrugh] promised me.

I am uncertain as yet when I shall leave this place, everything being in a good deal of disorder, and the Generals here being desirous of keeping more troops than is for the Service. I have been again with your sister, who was very full of expressions of your goodness and my civilities, but not one word of Pollatiques, which I am extreme glad of, so that if I were to stay here I should see her often without having any constraint. I know not what your correspondence will be able to do, but I can get no Tee that is fit to be drunk. The picture of the battle that is in my closet, I desire may be sent by my Ld. Orkney or my brother or Lt. G. Ingoldsby, the first that shall come; for the painter asks fifty pounds for it, and it is not worth ten pounds. They must give it when they come here to Mr Stanhope.

These were but the lighter touches in a scene which at once became sombre and vexatious in the last degree. The letter ends:

I am like a sick body that turns from one side of the bed to the

1 *Dispatches*, ii, 17.

other; for I would fain be gone from hence, in hopes to find more quiet in the Army. God only knows what ease I may have when I come there. I am only sure that I can never be happy till I am with my dearest Soul.

Everything was behindhand at The Hague and on the Rhine, and everybody in the worst of moods. Marlborough with great labour obtained the consent of the Dutch Government to the concentration of the main army of the Sea Powers round Trèves, and of the second army at Maestricht. He found in the Dutch command an attitude of jealousy and envy towards himself and his astonishing success. Slangenberg headed the opposition. He claimed that his seniority and exploits entitled him to receive orders only direct from the Dutch Government. The Duke, to conciliate him, paid him in person a visit of ceremony, and in this considerate manner handed him the written order of the States-General to proceed to Maestricht. But Slangenberg, unmollified, objected even to receiving the order of his own Government from the Commander-in-Chief under whom he was to serve. He complained formally to his Government of the slight to which he had been subjected by receiving from the mouth of the Deputy Captain-General directions which should only have reached him through Ministerial channels. He added a demand for a substantial sum of money, which he alleged was due to him for his equipment, and asked also that he should be forthwith appointed governor of Maestricht. It took time and labour to dispose of these pretensions, and when they were dismissed the hero of Eckeren took the field in the utmost ill-humour.

As early as February 6 the Duke had written decisively to Prince Eugene at Vienna. He expressed his disquiet at the lack of care in making the necessary preparations in the Imperial army which was reported to him from all quarters. He asked for an exact statement at the earliest moment of the artillery and powder which the Empire would supply and of the strength of the Margrave's army. He requested that the fortifications of Landau should be repaired forthwith to prevent the field army being weakened by having to find a large garrison. Lastly he spoke of

> the necessity that the two armies should act in concert on the Moselle and that they should be able to aid each other as the need required. In that case we may be sure that as we advance towards Thionville the enemy will draw their last man out of Alsace to oppose us . . .; instead of which if the two armies act separately and are not near enough to support each other *it will only cost a stroke of the pen to France to throw her whole force on one or the other*, thus bringing about its ruin or at least rupturing all our plans.[1]

In consequence of Prince Eugene's advocacy the Emperor on February 25 called on the Margrave for his plan of campaign, but gave him at the same time the strongest hint that the two armies should work together. However, Prince Louis, at Rastadt, had formed a different plan. In his view it would be a mistake to concentrate so much force upon a central thrust. It would be better for Marlborough to work along the Moselle, while he would separately advance up the Rhine towards Hagenau and threaten Alsace. He wrote to Vienna a considerable memorandum upon the advantages of disconnected over connected operations. But all this discussion took time, and meanwhile the Margrave adhered to his view. He was building himself "a noble palace with beautiful gardens" at Rastadt. He did not wish to run the slightest risk of opening Würtemberg, Swabia, and Baden to French raids. He dwelt upon the importance of preserving the confederate conquests in Alsace. He was in his heart determined not to serve under Marlborough, or even with him—for that, according to his experience, was the same thing. His antagonism to Prince Eugene in the councils of the Empire continued; but it was dwarfed by his jealousy, now nakedly exposed to Europe, of the laurels which Marlborough had gained at Blenheim. Besides all this, the wound in his foot which he had sustained at the Schellenberg, though slight at the moment, had become troublesome. It broke out again, was no doubt infected, and often became inflamed. Thus

1 *Dispatches*, i, 591.

Prince Louis developed a resistance, expert, moral, and physical, to the great campaign which proved invincible. In those days, when every objection took at least a week to be answered, such a wealth of reasoning or pretext could not be overcome. On May 5 the Emperor Leopold died. He was succeeded by his son Joseph. This prince was extremely well disposed to Marlborough and an ardent admirer of his military qualities. There were therefore good hopes of support from Vienna.

After sending a succession of emissaries to the Margrave Marlborough had at length arranged a meeting with him at Kreuznach on May 20. Prince Louis now sent word that his leg was painful, and that he could not leave Rastadt. Marlborough, who had hoped to join his army at Trèves on the 21st, was forced, on the contrary, to journey up the Rhine to see his colleague. He travelled sixty miles a day, and on the 22nd was received by Prince Louis, who found himself well enough to spend the first afternoon conducting his guest round his unfinished palace, upon which many workmen and gardeners were engaged.[1] The Margrave had by now received definite orders from Vienna to co-operate with Marlborough, and he expressed his willingness to do so, but at the same time he unfolded the lamentable weakness and ill-equipment of his command. Marlborough had been entitled to expect the aid of an Imperial army of 50 battalions and 80 squadrons. He had for some time realized that this would not be forthcoming. All the recruits from the Hereditary Lands had been sent to Prince Eugene in Italy, and the Imperial regiments on the Rhine stood at little more than half their strength. A great part of the military effort of the Empire was absorbed in Hungary; even some Prussian battalions in the pay of the Sea Powers, which were due to join the army in Trèves, were still detained in Bavaria. Artillery, food, ammunition, and horses were all woefully scarce. In sending a field-state of the Imperial forces to Godolphin on May 4 Marlborough had written, "You see what a miserable thing a German army is."[2]

1 Lamberty, iii, 469.   2 Coxe, ii, 97.

The Margrave now made the most of his weakness. It was evident that the plan of working in two armies must be abandoned. One army alone must be formed at Trèves. The Margrave promised to join it. He could only bring 20 battalions and 40 squadrons, or less than half what had been prescribed in the winter. Of these only 12 battalions and 28 squadrons could reach the rendezvous by June 10—the rest must follow as they were ready. But the Margrave agreed formally, and in writing, to lead these forces himself to join Marlborough upon that day. With this the Duke had to be content.

Marlborough paid a flying visit to the Lines of Stollhofen. Cardonnel, who was tired after his hundred and twenty miles' drive, had to spend all day on horseback in a forty miles' 'ramble' round the celebrated fortifications, on which work was ceaselessly proceeding. They went within cannon-shot of Fort Louis, and within three leagues of Strasburg. "From the mountains we clambered up, we could plainly discern the Black Forest, and the mountains of Switzerland. . . . The Prince," he says, "was pretty well when we arrived yesterday in the afternoon, but he kept his bed most part of this day for his lameness." [1] After a week of ceaseless travel Marlborough arrived at Trèves on May 26.

His whole plan depended upon a certain speed of execution. He could not keep his army, with its mass of cavalry, stationary in any place for long. The herbage that year was scanty, and the delays had given Villars time to denude the Moselle valley and to fortify his position. The magazines at Trèves were but half full. Before leaving for England in the previous winter the Duke had arranged contracts with trustworthy agents for this essential supply; but after his departure the Dutch had accepted a lower tender from a commissary of less repute. This worthy had failed in his undertakings and, conscious of his guilt or neglect, now deserted to the enemy. The seven thousand Palatine mercenaries were already three weeks late, and still ten days distant. The twelve thousand Prussians were more than a week behind them. The

1 *Dispatches*, ii, 51.

troops under Marlborough's command, and in the pay of the Sea Powers, which were assembled round Trèves, were in excellent spirit and condition, well furnished, well disciplined, and eager to fight. In all, they amounted to 83 battalions and 94 squadrons, or about sixty thousand men. The delay had eaten up the local supplies, and even this partly formed army must now either advance or retire. It could not wait at Trèves for the Elector. Twenty-five miles to the southward lay Villars, with 100 battalions and 160 squadrons or nearly seventy thousand men.[1] The positions which he had taken up at Sierck, between the Moselle and the wooded heights of Caldaoven, were naturally strong, well prepared, and connected by military roads with the fortress of Saarlouis. To approach and draw up before them it was necessary to cross both the Moselle and the Saar, and traverse two long, dangerous defiles in the plain, at the farther end of which stood the enemy's army. "The greatest difficulty," Marlborough had written to the Elector of Hanover, "will be to debouch from Trèves."

Moreover, strategic success depended upon Marlborough being able to make the Moselle attack so dominant upon the enemy that they would have to draw reinforcements both from Flanders and from the Rhine, and so remove any danger of attack in those theatres. If he were able to deal Villars a heavy blow, Villeroy in Flanders would be paralysed. If he were able to invest Saarlouis, the fertile land of Lorraine would nourish the largest armies. The Duke of Lorraine, though nominally neutral and sending envoys to both headquarters, was at heart friendly to the allies, and his people generally shared his feelings. With one hundred thousand men it would have been easy to reach this vantage ground, and thenceforward the whole campaign would have been governed therefrom. But to move through the dangerous gorges with little more than half that number, with the chance of being brought to a standstill, even if not defeated, was a very hardy project. Prudence should have counselled Marl-

---

[1] Various estimates are given. I have come to the conclusion that Boyer (iv, Appendix xiv) is preferable.

borough to abandon his design. Almost every element in it had already miscarried. The breakdown of the Empire, the reluctance of the Margrave, the tardiness of the Palatine and Prussian contingents, the half-filled magazines, and lastly the failure of the various Electors along the Rhine to supply the three thousand draught-horses needed to draw the siege artillery, provided ample justification. But Marlborough's unrelenting will-power and his confidence in himself and his own proved army led him into a most daring perseverance. He determined to traverse the defiles and confront Villars. He hoped that his very weakness might be made the means of victory by tempting the Frenchman to a battle.

Marlborough to Godolphin

TREVES
June 2, 1705

* What I have always believed proves true, that the Germans would not be able to act till the middle of June; for till that time I shall not have the Imperialists nor the Prussians with me. However, forage is so very scarce here that I shall be obliged in five days to march, so that if Marshal Villars has power to venture a battle, he may have it. Though I want one-third of the troops that are to compose this army, I depend so much upon the goodness of these I have here that, with the blessing of God, I do not doubt of good success.

He adds a point about the Irish in the French service whom it was always hoped to bring over. His care not to break military faith with anyone is noteworthy.

I hope by the next post to send you my thoughts upon what ought to be done concerning the Irish Regts.; for I would be sure to perform what I shall have leave to promise them; for I think the power that is sent me may give them hopes of more than will be performed. . . .

You are certainly very much in the right, that *there ought to be a man of quality sent to this new Emperor,* who has assured me that he will do all he can to quiet the troubles in Hungary; and I verily believe he intends it, being very desirous of carrying the war with vigour against France; but his Ministers and Court are all in factions, which I fear will make it hard for him to execute his good designs.

At two o'clock on the morning of June 3 the Duke began his advance. By daylight his whole army was concentrated at Consaarbrück, having crossed both the rivers, and after a short rest marched in two columns over the hills which stood between them and Sierck. Marlborough followed the Roman road along the ridge, while the second column threaded the valley under his protection. At six in the evening both the columns began to deploy on a broad front in the plain of Sierck. The troops had marched nearly twenty-one miles across uneven ground, and now was the moment for Villars to fight the battle which Marlborough courted. But such was the impression which Blenheim had produced upon the

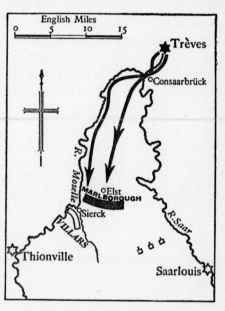

THE ADVANCE TO SIERCK

French High Command, and such was the surprise of this arrival, that as soon as the heads of Marlborough's columns and detachments were seen emerging at numerous points from the hills all the enemy advance troops, including a powerful corps before Sierck, hastily retreated into their fortified position, with a loss of some hundreds of prisoners, and the weary English and Dutch infantry lay upon their arms in battle order, unmolested through the night.

The next fortnight was terrible. Villars wisely refused battle. No supplies of any kind could be found in the district. Everything for man and horse must be brought

187

through the defiles from Trèves by convoys requiring strong escort, until the communications could be picketed, and the seven fords of the Moselle properly guarded. Marlborough had sent Cadogan, his Quartermaster-General, far back to appeal to the Margrave to come on. He seems to have managed the supplies himself. There are more than a dozen of his letters in the dispatches about bread and forage.[1] The movement of barges from Coblenz to Trèves, and of convoys thereafter, the distribution of bakers, and the activities of the bakeries both for bread and biscuit, at the front and at the base, claimed the first place in his thoughts. "We are in a country," he wrote to d'Almelo on June 6, "where nothing can be found, and should we lack bread even for one day we shall be ruined." He had also to provide for the large reinforcements of the Palatines and the Prussians which were drawing near, and must have in Trèves an ample reserve for contingencies. He therefore drew forward supplies to Trèves by every means through his contractor, Vanderkaa. In the meanwhile he held himself ready for battle at any moment. And almost daily he sent trusted officers back to the Margrave, and to Prussia and to the Rhine Princes, to hasten the fulfilment of their promises.

While he watched for a chance to spring he maintained an agreeable correspondence with Villars. On June 5 he asked for the return of stragglers from Churchill's command cut off in the march through Luxemburg, "as I know you find no pleasure in the sufferings of these good fellows." He promised to do the same by him with equal numbers. Villars replied the same day with profuse apologies for the extreme

---

1 "Send forward all possible grain and forage from Mainz and Coblenz. Send also with the utmost diligence the biscuit to Trèves, for I shall soon have need of it. Make it known to the vivandiers that they can come to the army and travel in perfect safety, and encourage them as much as you can, for we are in a country where we find nothing. . . .

"Send forward the biscuit as fast as it can be cooked to Trèves, but keep it strictly there, and distribute none without my orders. I shall send the fifty bakers to Saarburg, and the same number will come under escort to-morrow into Trèves. If you require more, you have only to let me know. . . .

"Set every one to work, for I shall soon have need of six days' bread in advance." (*Dispatches*, ii, 74.)

curiosity which had forced him to open some intercepted letters
addressed to Marlborough, which he sent on "well sealed." [1]
Marlborough responded with gifts. "M. de Marlborough
has sent me," wrote Villars to Chamillart June 10, "a quantity
of liqueurs of England, of Palm wine and cider; one could not
receive greater civilities. I have paid him back as much as
was possible. We shall
see how our serious busi-
ness will settle itself." [2]

Marlborough fixed his
headquarters in the castle
of Elst, high on the hills
opposite Villars' position,
and from here surveyed
the situation and the
scene. "I am placed," he
wrote to Eugene on June
11, "so that by a slight
movement and without
any obstacle I can come
between the enemy and
Saarlouis, to which we
aspire to lay siege." [3] But
nothing could be done
without the siege train
which lay at Trarbach,

THE MARGRAVE'S CIRCUIT

and for which the draught-horses were lacking. Whether his
measures to obtain these had been at fault we cannot pronounce. Already at the end of April he seems to have
counted upon them, and therefore presumably had ordered
them some time before. The Palatines had arrived on the
5th, but were mostly required for the communications. The
Prussians still lagged on the road. The Würtembergers and
Westphalians were only now approaching. As for the Margrave, he had never meant to come. He started as agreed
with about nine thousand men from Landau towards the

1 *Mémoires du Maréchal de Villars*, ii, 341.
2 Villars to Chamillart, June 10; Pelet, v, 451.   3 *Dispatches*, ii, 92.

end of May. Instead of marching across to Trèves by Homburg and St Wendel along the route which Marlborough had traversed in the winter, he made a détour of sixty miles by Kreuznach which secured another five days' delay. When Cadogan had ridden through Birkenfelt on the 15th even his cavalry were still two marches away. The Quartermaster-General found the longed-for reinforcements at Kreuznach. But the Margrave was no longer in command. By the advice of his doctors he had repaired to Schlangenbad, a rest by whose waters it was hoped would allay the undoubted inflammation of his wound. The Comte de Frise, who was now in command, manifested no zeal. He moved sluggishly forward. It was certain he would not arrive, if he could help it, before the 20th. But meanwhile what had been happening elsewhere?

Marsin from the Rhine had already reinforced Villars by a larger force than the Margrave had promised to bring. But even more serious news came from Flanders. Villeroy had taken the offensive. On May 21 he advanced upon Huy, and laid siege to this small but significant place. Overkirk, who was but half his strength, was forced back into his entrenched camp under the walls of Maestricht. Villeroy entered the town of Liége on the 18th, and planted heavy batteries against the citadel. From the moment when the French offensive began the Dutch demanded 30 battalions and 30 squadrons from Marlborough for the defence of the Meuse. Deputies were sent, and finally Hompesch, with the most insistent commands and appeals. It is important to notice the threat with which the Dutch backed their demand. It was a threat to make a separate peace.

Marlborough had foreseen such a development. Before leaving Trèves he had hinted to the States-General that he would not be averse from receiving a request to return. This he had done to secure himself a good reason before Parliament and the Alliance for abandoning his plan, if he should find himself unable to execute it. Now real emergency had arisen on the Meuse, and only the prospect of immediate and decisive action against Villars could absolve him from neglecting it. He had stood for fifteen days in a position of extreme difficulty, and, as it seemed to Europe, of much danger; and during that period he had not been joined by a single soldier not in the pay of the Maritime Powers. Of these several important contingents were still absent, and a month late in their concentration. His plan had failed. The combination he had designed had broken down in respect of every factor not under his direct control. He had hoped against hope, unreasonably perhaps, that his forward movement and dangerous station would draw to him from all quarters the help on which he had counted. He had forced the hands of doubting and obstinate allies the year before, and had dragged them all to victory and safety at Blenheim. He had vainly counted on repeating this process. He now resolved to extricate himself while time remained. In the deepest vexation and distress he wrote to Godolphin and Sarah.

Marlborough to Godolphin　　ELST
June 12, 1705

＊We have no letters from England notwithstanding the wind has been constantly fair, by which we believe the boats are all on this side; we have every night very hard frosts, which does hurt both to our men and horses. This weather, joined with some wants, makes a great many men desert, so that I have by this post desired of Mr Secretary Harley that with as little noise as possible there might be orders given at the sea-ports for the securing such as shall return. I may assure you that no one thing—neither for the troops nor the subsistence of the Army— that was promised me has been performed. This, and the running over to the enemy [of] our Commissary that has had all the care of our magazine this winter, is the occasion of our having had some uneasinesses. If this can't be remedied, and we shall opiniatre the staying here, this army may be ruined without fighting. These considerations and the knowledge I have that it is in this place where we can do most hurt to France, vexes me so that I have made myself sick. I will say no more to you upon this disagreeable subject; but hope if the alarm from the Meuse ceases that our affairs here may mend. Nothing is capable of giving us so much ease but a battle, which I am

afraid the French will not venture. You will see by this letter
that I am tired out of my life, but whilst I have any, I am truly
yours . . .

John to Sarah

I think every minute that I have a thousand things to say, but
I am so disturbed by being disappointed of every thing that has
been promised me, and that I should have, before I am able to
do any thing considerable, that my head turns, so that when I sit
down to write, the business of the army hinders me. But you
may be assured that you are dearer to me than all the world besides.
You will see, by my letter to lord treasurer, the reasons I have
for undertaking the march I shall begin to-morrow. I want sleep
and quiet; for till I have that, I cannot say I am well, nor do
I believe I ever shall be at ease till I am with my dear life. If
I had known beforehand what I must have endured by relying
on the people of this country, no reasons should have persuaded
me to have undertaken this campaign. I will, by the help of God,
do my best, and then I must submit to what may happen. But
it is impossible to be quiet and not complain when there is all
the probability imaginable for a glorious campaign, to see it all
put in doubt by the negligence of princes, whose interest it is to
help us with all they have.

This moment is come lieutenant-general Hompesch, from
Monsieur d'Overkirk, to let me know, that if I do not immediately help them they are undone, which only serves to shew the
great apprehensions they are in; for it is impossible for me to
send troops to them sooner than I have already resolved; but since
they have so much fear at the army, I dread the consequences of
it at The Hague. I wish my letters that I wrote yesterday were
with them, for I then assured them I would venture everything
for their security. My dearest soul, pity me and love me.[1]

And in another letter to Godolphin:

I have for these last ten days been so troubled by the many
disappointments I have had that I think if it were possible to vex
me so for a fortnight longer it would make an end of me. In
short, I am weary of my life.[2]

After darkness had fallen on the 17th the confederate army
folded their tents and repassed the gorges under pouring rain

1 Coxe, ii, 120.   2 *Ibid.*, 121.

in a long night march. They were safely across the rivers by noon. Daylight informed Villars that the tented city he had watched for an exciting fortnight had disappeared. Later his trumpet returned to the French camp, bearing an astounding verbal message from Marlborough. "Tell Marshal Villars that I am in despair because the Margrave has broken his word, and that I can hold only him responsible for the breaking up of all our plans." [1] A less trustworthy account has added, "Be assured that my contempt of him does not equal my respect for you." [2] From Trèves the next morning Marlborough wrote to the Emperor and Wratislaw, as he had written from Elst on the 16th to the King of Prussia and all the German princes concerned in the fiasco, an explanation of his action, which was in fact a grievous reproach. In every case he repeated the statement that he had waited for fifteen days in the camp at Elst without any other troops but those in the pay of England and Holland joining him; and that the alarms which the enemy, through inaction on the Moselle, had been able to cause in Holland had compelled him to withdraw. And in each case he held out the hope that in five or six weeks, if all was in readiness, he might be able to return.

When Villars' account of Marlborough's message was received at Versailles together with the Marshal's jubilant dispatch, the Court asked, with some relish, "Since when was it customary for a hostile commander to make his excuses to his antagonist for not having been able to attack him?" But this curious proceeding had another object besides relieving Marlborough's personal and professional feelings. Versailles was the sounding-board of Europe, and he meant to use it and every other means to fasten his just complaint upon the Margrave for all to see and hear. He knew how serious would be the attacks to which he himself would be subjected by the Tory Opposition, and he meant deliberately to invite the English people, at that moment in the throes of a general election, to pronounce between him and the foreign general who had tripped him up. He knew the English people

[1] *Mémoires de Villars*, ii, 347.   [2] *Histoire de Jean Churchill*, ii, 83.

and its politics well enough to be sure what the answer would be. Lord Treasurer Godolphin and Mr Speaker Secretary of State Harley, vying with one another, thrust forward the same suggestion, and only their most secure and audacious opponents dared to take the part of this German incompetent, or worse, with a pain in his toe, against the victor of Blenheim. This was rough work, and cannot be admired in any age whose popular elections are conducted with restraint, with good taste, and without appeals to prejudice.

The position of England in the Grand Alliance was now so strong through her wealth, her energy, the bravery of her troops, and the genius of her commander, that the rebuke to her allies was not in effect injurious, but, indeed, salutary. Historical justice, however, compels us to inquire whether the Margrave's conduct deserved it. It was freely alleged that his illness was a pretence, and about this there was contradictory evidence. Although Prince Louis undoubtedly died two years later from the septic reactions of his slight but unmanageable wound, he was able after this time to conduct two campaigns. He could superintend the building of his palace and the laying out of his gardens in his leisure. He was able at intervals often to make long rides and journeys. But one of Marlborough's English officers, who was with him when he handed over his command and retired to Schlangenbad, got near enough to see his foot when the bandages were removed for the doctors to examine it. He wrote to Marlborough that the leg was much inflamed, and that the doctors were all agreed that immediate rest was imperative. The Prince of Baden was neither traitor nor malingerer.

But this by no means disposes of the charge against him —apart from his general inadequacy—of ill-will and bad faith. Without quitting his bed at Rastadt he could have given the orders which would have brought his troops to Trèves by June 10. After all previous delays he had promised in writing they should start upon May 27.[1] The distance from Landau to Trèves by the road which Marlborough had

1 *Dispatches,* ii, 52.

MARSHAL VILLARS
From an engraving after the painting by Hyacinthe Rigaud
British Museum

traversed in October was only about sixty-five miles. It was safe and easy for a force unencumbered with cannon, and moving towards its supplies. Twenty-three days later these troops were still little more than half-way round the circuitous route their general had selected, which in itself was only 125 miles in length. They had actually made no more than seventy miles in three weeks, or an average of little more than three miles a day. And this while the army to whose help they were going was awaiting them outnumbered and in danger of both battle and starvation! Nothing could palliate this, and Wratislaw assured Marlborough that the Emperor would have dismissed the Margrave "but for his connexions and influence, not only as the reigning Prince of Baden, but throughout the Circles of Swabia and Franconia."

At Trèves Marlborough made the dispositions which the new situation required. The abandonment of the Moselle offensive released the full force of hostile pressure on both the Meuse and the Upper Rhine. It was necessary immediately to strengthen the Margrave. Marlborough had requested the Comte de Frise to meet him at Trèves to concert arrangements. But that officer, not wishing to face him, sent excuses. The Duke nevertheless ordered the splendid Prussian corps to join the Margrave. He left Count d'Aubach with the seven thousand Palatines to garrison the fortress of Trèves and guard its still vastly important magazines. He allowed his own troops an indispensable two days' rest to recover from the night march and the privations of Sierck, and to replenish their wagons and equip themselves for their new task. On the 20th he plunged into the wooded mountainous region, then almost a wilderness, which lies between the Moselle and the Meuse. He marched in several columns with all possible speed. On the 23rd he was at Prüm, on the 25th at Duren, and on the 27th at Maestricht. Frantic messages met him from the Dutch at every stage. He declared he would arrive in time to save the citadel of Liége "if its Governor did his duty." To make sure of being in time, and if possible of capturing the French siege train, he again adopted the expedient he had used before the Schellenberg, and ordered his brother to select a hundred men from every battalion to form a special force to act with the cavalry. The whole army was exhorted to make the greatest efforts. They responded nobly, it being understood that Villeroy might be caught and brought to battle. For ten days they averaged about eleven miles a day, though not without much suffering and some loss of life. At Hanef on July 2 the confederate armies united, and Marlborough was at the head of 104 battalions and 168 squadrons. But the rumours of his approach had ended the siege of Liége. On the 25th, while he was still at Duren, Villeroy dismantled his batteries and retreated within the Lines of Brabant. The measures to recapture Huy were at once set on foot. Thus the situation in Flanders was speedily restored.

MARLBOROUGH RETURNS TO THE MEUSE

Marlborough had received bad news at Maestricht. Count d'Aubach with his seven thousand Palatines had been left in charge of Trèves and the magazines collected there. These were still highly important. Without the slightest attack this officer on June 26 evacuated the city. After destroying the mass of costly material he fell back on Trarbach, where the siege train and ordnance stores had fortunately been deposited. It was not until two days after he had quitted Trèves in this shameful manner that Villars, hearing the news, sent a detachment of four hundred men to occupy the abandoned forts. Marlborough's anger at this abominable behaviour was keen. For a month his letters bear its traces. No explanation was ever vouchsafed to him by Count d'Aubach, nor was there, it seems, any effectual means by which this general, although in the pay of the Sea Powers, could be brought before a military tribunal. Months afterwards we find him still in command, and Marlborough compelled to correspond with him. However, by his letters Marlborough had blasted his reputation throughout Germany, and at the close of the campaign d'Aubach disappeared from the scene. The loss of Trèves and its stores ended all chances of Marlborough's return to the Moselle. He never returned there in any of the campaigns, and the surest road to Paris was never trodden by the allied armies.

We must not imagine when we survey this ill-starred episode that Marlborough's hard-bitten professional critics were always wrong about his operations. A solid case can be set forth against his attempt upon the Moselle. No doubt it was the true road into France, and if he could have planted his armies in unravaged Lorraine the highest prizes were within reach. But before he left Trèves he must have known that nearly all the conditions which would render such a movement possible were lacking. He required not only an army or armies of a hundred thousand men, but also to be able to make a speedy advance into the fertile regions. He could not hope to maintain armies of the size required for more than a few weeks in denuded districts upon any magazines which could have been created. But with less than these numbers the great thrust at the heart of France would not become dominant. It would be brought to a stop, and then immediately diversions would begin. Yet he persisted. To use his own phrasing, he "opiniatred" the matter. He tried to compel events beyond any fortune that men may hope from the gods. A battle at heavy odds with all the penalties of defeat at their highest and the rewards of victory severely curtailed was the most he could have expected at Sierck. This was all he sought, and even this he was denied.

Then we see a fresh aspect of his ingenious mind. He

prepares his retreat. He also prepares his reasons for a retreat. He feeds the Dutch with the very arguments he had so often tried to eradicate from their minds. He thrusts forward on this bleak adventure armed with the certainty of a recall, which he can use the moment that he needs it, to make his case to Parliament and to Europe. He does not scruple to launch a hard propaganda because he could not force men—and, we must add, facts and figures—to his high military purpose. He fastens the odium of failure where it was indeed not ill-deserved, but where it had little bearing. His Moselle plan required a very much greater development of supplies, transport, and comradeship than the Grand Alliance could produce. He ran the gravest risks on the chance that Villars would accept a battle, which was in itself a crowning risk. He extricated himself from all entanglements with extreme adroitness, and had an answer on every point to his critics. He also brought the army back safely, and in time to chase Villeroy from the Meuse. But it cannot be denied that many weeks of precious time and immense resources gathered with difficulty were fruitlessly expended in order to convince him that he could not realize his bright strategic dream. Still, in every war some one at the summit of intellect and authority has to try, and try very hard.

Marlborough had no need to offer excuses to the States-General for his failure upon the Moselle. They had nothing but gratitude to utter for his swift return. Yet their thanks were wounding. "How often," said the Dutchmen in effect, "have we begged Your Grace not to go so far from home to help these unworthy and ungrateful allies? Did we not warn you they would fail you? Never let yourself be put in such an unfair position again. Stay here with us and we shall all be safe, so long as we do not fight any battles. After all, you have a splendid army, and there are many fine fortresses to take." This absolute stultification of all Marlborough's conceptions of war only increased the bitterness of his disappointment. He wrote and spoke openly of his resolve to resign his command and quit the service. But of course at this time there was no chance of his being indulged. Such language

198

expressed his feelings, and at the same time strengthened his power. He still hoped "some accident," by which he meant a battle, might enable him to rescue the campaign from failure. But further tribulations were in store. He was to find that he had exchanged the delays and excuses of the Margrave for the open insolence and mutinous obstruction of Slangenberg. He had been deserted in Germany: he was to be fettered in Holland.

CHAPTER IX

THE LINES OF BRABANT

1705, Summer

THE famous Lines of Brabant covering the sixty miles from Antwerp to Namur have been frequently mentioned in this account. Then as now the best military opinion accorded only a secondary value to such systems of defence. The obstacles of ramparts, dammed-up streams, entanglements of felled trees, palisades with forts and redoubts at intervals, could easily be traversed, if no one was there to defend them. They were therefore only regarded as affording a series of carefully considered fortified battle-grounds upon which the defending army could meet its presumably stronger assailants. For this purpose all the side-ways roads behind the lines were carefully developed; food, forage, and ammunition were stored under guard in strong-holds at convenient intervals; and as the lines, following the course of the river Demer, curved outward towards the enemy, it seemed probable that with proper dispositions the defending army would arrive and man the ramparts before any large force could attack them. If so they would have a very great advantage. The method of the assailants was, of course, to deceive the enemy by feints into sending his field army in one direction while they themselves marched under the cover of night in the other.

There had not been any difficulty in making minor surprise attacks upon portions of the lines, and we have seen how Spaar at the beginning of 1703 and Overkirk during the winter of 1704 had without much loss made themselves masters for a time of sections of the defences. In 1704, while Marlborough was on the march to the Danube, Overkirk had been disconcerted by the ease with which a portion of his own army had penetrated the lines south of Merdorp, and had made haste under the orders of the

200

Republic to abandon such audacious gains. But the intention to carry the main army across the defences not only made surprise more difficult, but was tantamount to seeking battle either during or after the passage of the barrier. The Dutch had always shrunk from this as partaking of the nature of gambling with armies and contrary to their methods of warfare.

Marlborough, chafing over his disappointment on the Moselle, saw in forcing the lines the only means now open to rescue the whole campaign from failure. He saw no insuperable difficulty in the operation. There were a dozen ways of doing it—here or there; and as he was above all things anxious to fight a battle, about which he also felt confident, he was not alarmed by the risk. According to the principles which had gained acceptance during so many years of war, an army attacking under these conditions ought to have had substantial superiority over the whole force of the enemy. In fact he was somewhat weaker, having 92 battalions and 160 squadrons to Villeroy's 100 battalions and 147 squadrons, or say seventy thousand men in the open against seventy-three thousand behind their defences. This did not deter him. He had studied the country and the lines profoundly over many years, and their aspect was to him an open book. He therefore in the first days of July formed a plan nicely conceived in times and distances and garnished with the appropriate feints and deceptions whereby the lines could be forced. The novel feature, apart from his being numerically weaker, was his selection of the point to be attacked. Instead of seeking the weakest part of the defences, he chose one of the strongest. He argued to himself that because it was the strongest it would be the least considered, and probably defended by the fewest covering troops. He would feint therefore at a weak part of the lines, to which the enemy would have to hurry their main forces, and then by a very long night march in the opposite direction his men would assault the earthworks where the defenders were but few.

His greatest difficulties, as usual, were presented by his

own friends. The Government and States-General of the Republic cherished and admired him, but they trembled at his reckless and ruthless habit of mind. He seemed constantly to leave a great deal to chance. They felt that almost all his exploits would have ended badly if events had taken a slightly different turn. There was no general then alive except Eugene —and even Eugene was judged more correct—who appeared to trouble so little about taking what any experienced officer knew was a very dangerous course. It is marvellous indeed that during all these ten campaigns he was never made to pay any forfeit. He certainly ought to have been punished scores of times for his unprofessional temerity. The Dutch felt in their bones that they were always in jeopardy when they rode with him. It was only after Ramillies that they gave up thinking about it, and forgot for a while to clutch at the reins or the brake.

But with the generals of their army other complications appeared. Slangenberg, the hero of Eckeren, veteran of forty years of war, hated Marlborough as a foreigner, as a rival, and as a man. He had formed a low opinion of his tactics at Blenheim. He would not bow to the imposture of their success. No experienced, well-trained commander would have attempted such an operation. It was his duty and should be his care to prevent any such hare-brained gambling with the army that guarded the frontiers of Holland. Besides this he was personally annoyed by the fact that the Duke's brother, General Churchill, had through accelerated English promotion become senior to him as General of Foot. Finally, he had a poor opinion of Overkirk, whom he thought too old for active service, too subservient to Marlborough's insidious influence, and personally obnoxious because he held the chief command which another might better have discharged.

For all these reasons it was not deemed expedient to make Slangenberg privy to the design. Indeed, Marlborough seemed inclined to deal only with the Veldt-Marshal Overkirk as responsible chief of the Dutch army. At the council of war the plan of forcing the lines was not presented in the form in which he intended to carry it out. The proposal put forward was that the attack should be made on the weaker sector between the Mehaigne and Namur. The Dutch generals pointed out that they must expect to find the main French army behind the fortifications. They were all opposed to such a costly attempt. But Marlborough persisted, and Overkirk seemed to be with him; and after several days of confrontation rather than discussion the Council agreed to a manœuvre for forcing the lines, provided that no undue risks were run, and that no battle was fought without a further council of war, if peradventure the enemy should be found in force at the point of attack. Marlborough, impassive, inscrutable, endured this protracted ordeal, and accepted the grudged and limited authority offered to him. Since he had come back from the Moselle he had not merged the armies into one as had been the custom in the earlier campaigns before he went to Blenheim. On the contrary, he seemed bent on keeping all the English and the Queen's troops separate in his own hand, and he dealt with the Dutch army only through Overkirk, who seemed to Slangenberg and other brave Dutch officers willing to be his tool or his dupe. In fact Overkirk had become increasingly silent; yet it was he to whom above all the malcontents looked to lead a revolt.

Marlborough now acted. He had a twofold plan: he had to deceive both the Dutch, excepting Overkirk, and the French. Ten miles in front of Villeroy's lines northward and away to the confederate right lay the well-known and convenient camping ground of Saint-Trond. The allied troops who had been besieging Huy arrived on the 16th. Marlborough had let it be believed that he would pretend to be occupying Saint-Trond and then move southward across the Mehaigne river to attack the weakest point of the lines on the sector between that river and Namur. Slangenberg and his colleagues did not believe that Villeroy would be deceived. They predicted that he would ignore any feint at Saint-Trond and concentrate his army in the trenches between the Mehaigne and Namur. And they were right. Early in the morning of July 17 Overkirk, with the whole of the Dutch army, crossed the Mehaigne and began his southward march. His patrols and advance parties pressed far

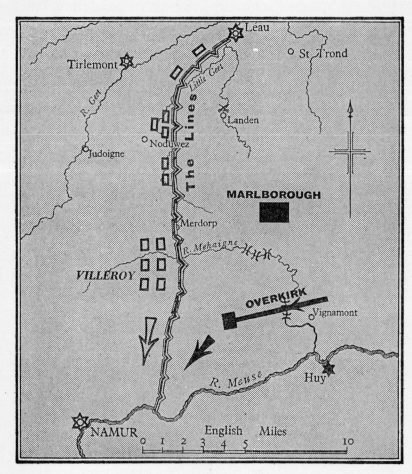

DUSK

on ahead even to the verge of the lines. Overkirk had passed the river by four bridges, but the French scouts and watchers from the lines reported that no fewer than eleven bridges in all were being constructed. Thus it was concluded that Marlborough's army would cross rapidly during the night, and that the whole force would advance together to the attack on the 18th. Villeroy therefore with the utmost speed concentrated forty thousand men upon the threatened front. Overkirk camped after a short march about six miles distant from the lines. The fact that the allied armies were divided by the Mehaigne led Slangenberg to make a written protest that the Dutch were being exposed to grave danger. To meet this criticism and for other purposes Marlborough built no fewer than twenty bridges across this little river, until, in the words of Orkney, "it was all one, as if there were no river." The last thing seen as darkness fell was Overkirk's dragoons marching southward beyond the Mehaigne towards Namur. It seemed almost certain that there could be no surprise, that the lines would be fully guarded, and that therefore the promised council of war would be able to forbid the battle. But when the stars shone in the sky and night's curtains fell upon the undulating plains sudden orders, equally unexpected by friend and foe, were issued. The Dutch broke camp and their columns were turned to the right-about. They counter-marched to the north. They recrossed the Mehaigne very swiftly by the numerous bridges. Whereas during the day there had seemed to be no hurry, and they had only moved four miles beyond the river before halting, now in the night the march was pressed with the utmost severity. Overkirk was evidently carrying out a definite plan. Argument was useless. Councils of war were impossible. Every general was with his command, and no collective representations could be made. On, then, through the night toiled and trudged the sturdy troops. Whither—no man knew.

They were not the only troops who were moving north. At four in the afternoon Marlborough had ordered his whole army to be ready to march, the baggage to be assembled by six. These preparations disquieted the field Deputies. They were, however, assured that only a reconnaissance was intended. At seven Count Noyelles, with twenty battalions and thirty-eight squadrons, started upon the road which leads through Landen to Saint-Trond. Six hundred pioneers with their tools and bridging-material were attached to the advance guard. Great pains had been taken about the numerous guides, and Noyelles and his principal officers knew the country well. As the making of fascines would have aggravated the suspicions of the enemy, each trooper carried

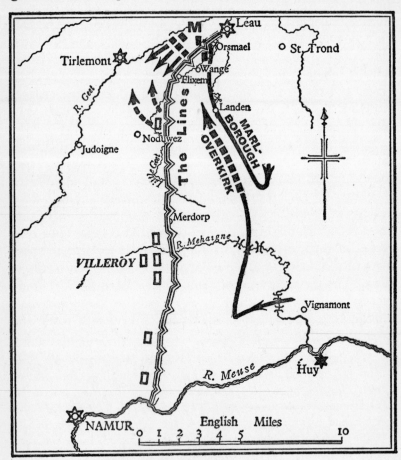

DARKNESS

instead a truss of hay which might either serve to cross a marshy stream or as forage for a long march. Marlborough himself started at ten with the rest of his army. The whole of the confederates were thus marching steadily towards Landen through a very dark night.

Marshal Villeroy did not lack vigilance. He was aware

that the allies were on the move. He remained, however, in total uncertainty. Numerous conflicting rumours had reached him. The most trustworthy pointed to a general attack the next day upon his lines south of Merdorp, and for this he was well prepared. Even when reports came in during the night that allied horse were moving northwards he concluded that their objective was Saint-Trond. Meanwhile he enjoined a strict alertness along the whole front. All his infantry and cavalry with their general officers slept on their arms at the head of their camps. Constant patrols were ordered out, especially from the posts on the left. He himself passed the night at Merdorp.

In spite of all precautions Noyelles' corps had much difficulty in finding its way through the black night. They toiled and stumbled across the battlefield of Landen, where thousands of skeletons had long lain unburied. They were nearly two hours late in reaching Landen itself. Up to this point their aim might well have been Saint-Trond. But now Noyelles in three separate columns marched towards the passages of the little Geet, behind which ran the French fortifications. The distance was but three miles. Lord Orkney commanded the van of Marlborough's infantry. "Though we had all the best guides that could be had," he wrote while the event was hot upon his mind,

> Count Noyelle lost his way at least two hours in the night, as also the first line, which I led, and the second line also. However Noyelle, by peep of day, came near to Orsmael, where the Geet runs before their line. There appeared a camp upon the right and left of the place. However he marched down to the bridge, where the enemy had a small guard, which made but very little resistance. We got some men on the other side; but these bridges were so bad that hardly above one man could go over abreast, and in some places one foot man and a horse-man passed over together. However, though the passages were very bad, people scrambled over them strangely. My Lord sent me word to make what haste I could with the line [*i.e.*, his troops]; and, though I had lost my way, I got up before the bridges were empty of the horse.[1]

[1] "Letters of the First Lord Orkney," *English Historical Review*, April 1904, p. 312.

In fact Noyelles broke into the entrenchments at three points—at Elixem, Wangé, and Orsmael. The Little Geet here is but a marshy stream three or four yards wide. Storm-

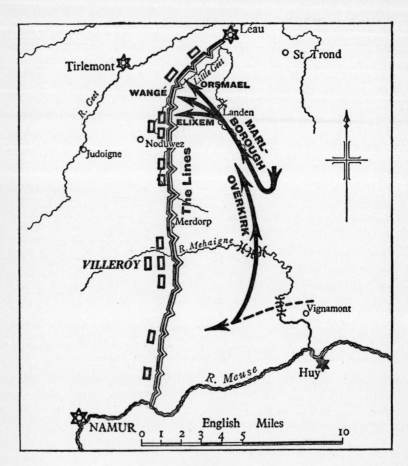

DAWN

ing parties of grenadiers waded through the water or rushed the stone bridge at Elixem. The French posts, suddenly aware of overwhelming numbers swarming upon them through the morning mists, fell back amid a splutter of firing. The three dragoon regiments in Orsmael fled at full speed into the fortress of Léau without even giving an effective alarm.

There is no moment in war more thrilling than a surprise attack at dawn. The confederate pioneers threw themselves diligently into bridge-making; but the infantry would not await their efforts. They knew too much about the war not to realize how precious was every moment. In their ranks were veteran officers and sergeants who had fought at Landen twelve years before. It had been the talk of the camp for weeks that the lines would cost ten thousand men. Here were the lines empty and undefended. To the impulse of adventure was added the sharp spur of self-preservation. Everywhere, forgetting eighteenth-century drill, they splashed through the Geet, scrambled up the bank, down into the miry ditch beyond, and hand and foot up the ramparts of the bugbear lines. From 4 A.M. onward they were pouring into the fortifications and forming up in good order on the farther side. Every house and every hedge they seized or lined. By five o'clock at least six thousand men were inside the French position. Meanwhile bridges and passages had multiplied behind them, and Noyelles' horse, almost equal to two modern cavalry divisions, were passed over. Behind the Geet the ground rises into fine open, down-like country, stretching to Tirlemont, perhaps fifty feet higher than the river-bed. Between Elixem and Tirlemont they had formed between half-past five and six a double line of horse at right angles to the entrenchments, facing south and with their left upon their ever-growing infantry. And now the enemy appeared in force.

Orkney, approaching the bridges in his turn with the Guards and the infantry of the first line, says:

> By the time I came to the river, I could see two good lines of the enemy, very well formed, coming down upon our people, a line of foot following them. We were in very good condition to receive them, and we outwinged them, and still more troops coming over the pass. As I got over the foot guards, I saw the shock begin.[1]

The French had reason to complain of the way in which

1 "Letters of the First Lord Orkney," *loc. cit.*

their outposts served them. Small posts cannot resist armies; but at least they are expected to cry "Alarm." It was not till after five o'clock that d'Alègre, only three miles south of Elixem, learned what was happening. He mounted thirty-three squadrons of Bavarian, Spanish, Cologne, and French cavalry, and sent for the eleven infantry battalions under Caraman, who were four miles farther off. By six all these troops were moving forward. With them hastened ten guns of a new design. These were the triple-barrelled guns which could either fire three cannon-balls in quick succession or three at once. High hopes and much mystery had enveloped this invention, the last word in modern artillery. By half-past six collision was imminent.

Towards Tirlemont from the Geet there run two sunken roads. The northern, near Elixem, which can be seen unaltered to this day, is a remarkably deep ravine with sides so steep that anyone would hesitate even to lead a horse up and down them. The hostile cavalry halted on their own side of this obstacle. They were already galled by fire from the houses, roads, and hedges by the Geet. The leading brigade of allied infantry advanced and seized the sunken road, and by their volleys forced the enemy to draw back out of shot. It happened, or Marlborough had arranged, that the sixteen squadrons that had first come across comprised the whole of the British cavalry. These, shielded by the infantry, either crossed the sunken road where it was practicable, or else, coming round where the road shallowed into the upland, continually stretched out to their right towards Tirlemont.

Let us salute these famous regiments of the British Army as they draw out in line on this summer morning. On the right, the Scots Greys; next the Royal Irish Dragoons (later called the 5th Lancers); next the King's Dragoon Guards; the 5th Dragoon Guards; the 7th Dragoon Guards; then the Carabiniers (6th Dragoon Guards); and finally the 3rd Dragoon Guards. Such is the array.

The matter stood thus when Marlborough, a little before seven, came on the scene. He saw before him two lines of hostile cavalry and, more than a mile away, Caraman's infantry deploying. He resolved to attack the horse while they were still separated from their foot. He had now already on the ground over fifty squadrons, but not more than half of these were clear of the sunken road or prolonging the line towards Tirlemont. He rode to the right centre of the line

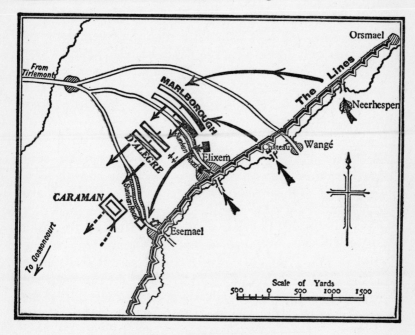

ELIXEM

and ordered the charge. All the English cavalry, with the Scots Greys on the extreme right, rode forward upon the enemy in echelon at a trot which it is believed, in parts of the line at least, broke into a gallop. The Bavarians were magnificent to see. They were nearly all cuirassier regiments. The Reverend Dr Hare at his master's side wrote two days afterwards, "There was in the plain on the other side about twenty-five squadrons of the enemy, many of them Bavarians and all in armour." [1] Between their squadrons appeared the triple-barrelled guns, which opened a remarkably rapid fire.

[1] Hare Papers, H.M.C., p. 202.

But the result was never for a moment in doubt. The Bavarians where they met the shock were overthrown, and for the rest driven into flight. On the right the Scots Greys broke four squadrons without losing a single man. The guns were taken.

Marlborough led the charge himself. He rode with the front rank like a trooper. The routed horsemen made no bones about galloping across the second and much easier sunken road. Arrived here, the Duke again became a General. Caraman's division was close at hand in line of battle. The left of the English cavalry was checked by infantry in the hedges and ditches along the Geet. Five fresh squadrons, including the Cologne Life Guards, reinforced the enemy. They rallied and attempted a charge. There was a moment of confusion. But by now the second line of the allied horse had also come upon the scene. A second charge was delivered by both lines of the allied horse, certainly no faster than a trot. Marlborough again rode with the English squadrons. This time the rout of the enemy's cavalry was final. They galloped off the field, leaving their pursuers face to face with the musketry of Caraman's infantry, who had at length arrived. According to Orkney,

> My Lord Marlborough in person was everywhere, and escaped very narrowly; for a squadron, which he was at the head of, gave ground a little, though [it] soon came up again; and a fellow came to him and thought to have sabred him to the ground, and struck at him with that force, and, missing his stroke, he fell off his horse. I asked my Lord if it was so; he said it was absolutely so. See what a happy man he is.

And then, referring to the success:

> I believe this pleases him as much as Hogstet did. It is absolutely owing to him.[1]

There are several accounts of this incident. These say that a Bavarian officer, recognizing the Duke, rode out alone at him, and, rising in his stirrups to cut him down, lost his balance; or perhaps the two horses bumped each other: the

---

1 "Letters of the First Lord Orkney," *loc. cit.*

officer fell upon the ground and was made prisoner by Marlborough's trumpeter, or, it is also said, dispatched upon the spot. It was hurly-burly. Usually, of course, the Commander-in-Chief would be attended by half a dozen devoted aides. His campaigning sword, which the corps of Gentlemen-at-Arms now possesses, was not a weapon with which more than a formal thrust could have been made. In the confusion he was left for the moment well-nigh defenceless. Certainly he was lucky to escape the fate of gallant old Schomberg, who was killed this way at the ford of the Boyne.

It was now eight o'clock. Marlborough, with his retinue and staff again about him, could survey the scene. Practically his whole army was inside the lines and advancing southwards between the Little Geet and Tirlemont. Overkirk, with all the Dutch, was approaching the bridges and river-crossings, now good and numerous; but it would be at least two hours before they could form in order of battle. Where was Villeroy? That was the question. The upland ridge rose in a gentle slope, and tended to narrow to the southward. Beyond the skyline, two miles away, all was unknown. If the alarm had been promptly spread, the Marshal at Merdorp should have learned before six o'clock that the allies had forced the lines between Orsmael and Elixem. Merdorp was only seven miles away from the second sunken road. It might well be that forty thousand men were approaching just "on the other side of the hill." It was the peculiar quality of Marlborough that his moods of awful gambling sprang from cold calculation, and were followed by sudden sober caution. Certainly when all were aflame he now pulled up with a snap.

The remaining feature of this brilliant action was the retreat of Caraman. After the fight the French—by no means less prone than other races to require the highest conduct from allies—were vicious about the Bavarian cavalry. They spoke of them as inferior troops who had failed at the moment of trial, who had let themselves be chased from the field by the truculent English. But throughout Europe, as well as at Versailles, the conduct of Caraman's foot was admired.

Collecting the battalions which were involved in the infantry fight by the river, and keeping always a respectable order, he formed his eleven battalions into a large hollow square, and in this array made good his retreat from the field. This feat excited wonder at the time; and it is another proof of the increasing fire-power of disciplined infantry. The English cavalry leaders and, we may be sure, Lord John Hay, of the Scots Greys, believed they could break this square, and several squadrons attempted to do so independently. But Marlborough would have none of it. Neither would he advance his infantry, now nearly thirty thousand strong, very far, and only with precaution. We now know that the danger he apprehended did not exist. Villeroy did not hear the news at six: he did not hear it till eight. He and the Elector only got their army on the march about nine. Galloping on ahead to the field with their leading squadrons, they met the flying rabble to which the Bavarian horse had been reduced. The infantry of the French army were still two hours away.

Marlborough dealt separately in daring and in prudence. Sometimes he was over-daring and sometimes over-prudent; but they were separate states of mind, and he changed from one to the other in quite definite phases. Having ruptured the lines and routed the counter-attack, the thought that dominated his mind was to concentrate the whole confederate army upon the conquered ground. We can express his feelings in the characteristic phrases of the Cockpit circle. "The army must be gathered with all speed imaginable. Until then I shall be most uneasy." There is no doubt that upon the knowledge which he had this was the right decision; and yet in fact, if he had given way to the general ardour around him, he might have had a greater success. Perhaps this extraordinary quality of using audacity and circumspection as if they were tools to be picked up or laid down according to the job is the explanation of his never being entrapped in ten years of war. His mind was a weighing-machine for practical affairs as perfect as has ever been known. Infallibility is not for mortals. It is enough to say that no one could do more than he could or try harder and more continuously.

It is on this morning field of Elixem that we see him as he should be remembered. It was one of the very few moments in his life when he came in contact with spontaneous mass affection. As he rode up sword in hand to take his place in the cavalry charges, the troopers and their officers broke into loud acclamations, quite unusual to the military etiquette of those formal times. And afterwards, as he moved along the front of his army, the soldiers, mostly Blenheim men, cast discipline to the winds and hailed him everywhere with proud delight. Here were the dreaded lines pierced and broken so easily, and the enemy baffled and put to flight, not at the cost of thousands of poor soldiers, but by the sleight of a master-hand and by the Queen's troops alone; and here was Corporal John, who could do it every time if only he were set free, who was so careful of their food and pay and so just in his government of the army, who thought for all as their commander and fought in the scrimmage as a private man—surely for once they might show him what they felt! Yet these soldiers were judges of war, and many knew the country well. Amid their cheers were mingled the cries, "Now, On to Louvain," and "Over the Dyle."

It was ten o'clock before Overkirk's army was across the lines. Marlborough, returning from the pursuit of the determined Caraman, was greeted by Slangenberg with the remark, "This is nothing if we lie still here. We should march on Louvain or Parc." The Duke would have demanded no better. He had, however, already heard from Overkirk that his troops must camp at once. Considering that they had marched twenty-seven miles in the last thirty-one hours, no complaint could be made of this. Still, as Colonel Cranstoun, who commanded the Cameronians, wrote:

Those who know the army and what soldiers are know very well that upon occasions like this where even the common soldier is sensible of the reason of what he has to do, and especially of the joy and success of victory, soldiers with little entreaty will even outdo themselves, and march and fatigue double with cheerfulness what their officers would at other times compel them to.[1]

Marlborough replied to Slangenberg, "I am very glad . . . to find you are of my opinion, for this is my judgment of it too; I think we should march on, and I entreat you to go back and dispose your generals to it." Slangenberg, completely stultified by the event and furious at not having been a party to it, was only establishing somewhat cheaply a controversial position for the future. He rode off to Overkirk, but he never returned to Marlborough; and as the Dutch tents rose continuously upon the plain it became certain that they would not move that day.

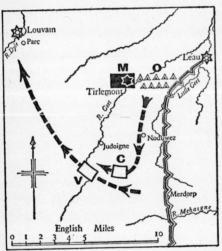

10 A.M.

A glance at the map will show that the confederates could have reached Louvain before Villeroy at any time on the 18th. They could probably have brought him to battle by marching towards Judoigne. The Elector, who waited and watched the scene from a distant eminence, realized to the full the plight of the French army, but

when he observed the first tents pitching, he cried out three or four times in a rapture, "*Grace à Dieu, Grace à ciel,*" and then ordered his own troops to march without obliging them to keep in order, and make the best of their way to Louvain. They marched and marched all the night long, and yet though our army did not budge till next morning, our advanced squadrons and even some of our infantry came time enough to interrupt the rear

1 Major Cranstoun's Letter, Portland Papers, *H.M.C.*, iv, 253.

of their army in crossing the river and to take some hundreds prisoners.[1]

That a fine opportunity had been lost, and whose was the fault, was long the subject of acrimonious discussion in the army between the two wings of the army. Marlborough's officers blamed the Dutch, who, already offended at having been tricked into forcing the lines and being absent from the action, retorted with venom. They and Marlborough's enemies said

> that the pleasure of writing letters with an account of that day's great success to the Emperor, the Queen, the States and others, and with [of] signing warrants for safeguards of which above two hundred were writ and signed that afternoon took *people* [meaning Marlborough] up so much that they forgot to pursue the advantages which were certainly in their hands.[2]

It certainly seems that Marlborough flagged. Perhaps he was exhausted by the night march, by the clash of the cavalry charges, and by the peculiar mental strain of having to deceive both the enemy and his allies and on this intricate tangle to hazard the forcing of the lines. The carnage of the Schellenberg was fresh in his mind. He must certainly have braced himself to lose seven or eight thousand men, probably not to be supported, possibly to be repulsed. What would the outcry have been then? What would the Dutch have said, and what the Tories? He knew himself for a hunted man with foes on every side, longing for their opportunity, if he should but stumble, to drag him down and trample upon him. Yet if the allied cause were not to fail he had to scheme and dare. Once again he had dared, and once again he had won. Can we wonder that for a while under the reaction he bent and relaxed? One must not expect too much of mortal man. The vivifying force that flowed from him so generously and through such wearying years had its intermissions. It was not impossible to wear him down and

---

[1] Major Cranstoun's letter, *loc. cit.* In fact nearly two thousand stragglers were captured on the 19th.
[2] *Ibid.*

drain the fountain dry. Another struggle with the Dutch, another forward bound with the army, another battle to be begun in the late afternoon—he had not got it in him. Let us discern his limitations as he paused and rested and thanked God that so far all was well.

If he had wielded the authority of Frederick the Great or Napoleon, or any of the commanders of armies in modern times, more than half his burden would have been lifted. Could he but have said to the generals who argued everything beforehand and criticized everything after: who had to be convinced, persuaded, wheedled, or even hoodwinked into every march and manœuvre, "Obey, or I will have you shot! Silence, or I will deprive you of your command!" it would be easy for us to fix his responsibility and blame. But at this time he had to work with and through at least twenty proud, jealous, competent or incompetent colleagues whom he had no effective power to discipline or punish. Cranstoun's very free-spoken letter shows the shrewd, instructed malice with which this crowd of professional rivals and critics could express themselves. It was for him to invent and urge, for them to cavil and oppose. It was for him to shoulder the responsibility. If disaster came, he by his rashness had caused it. If, in spite of all, there was success, why had he not turned it to better advantage? All the same, Marlborough had lost a chance.

An event of capital importance had, however, occurred. The piercing of the Lines of Brabant marked an important stage in the world war. The stalemate in the northern theatre was ended, and henceforward much might happen there. The French abandoned Aerschot and Diest. They left Léau to an inevitable and speedy fate. The battalion of Monluc which garrisoned Tirlemont surrendered at discretion. Fifty miles of the lines, including the technically important salient, passed into the power of the allies. From Aerschot to the purlieus of Namur the famous front which had so long scared off attack and guarded the whole of Belgium was left for the conquerors to demolish. The tide of war flowed thirty miles farther to the west. These

TAPESTRY OF THE LINES OF BRABANT

By permission of the Duke of Marlborough.

Photograph by permission of the Victoria and Albert Museum

gains far exceeded the material prizes of action. But several notable leaders of the enemy and all the cannon on the field were captured, and the French forces were weakened by perhaps five or six thousand men. Counts d'Alégre and Horn, both lieutenant-generals, were prisoners of the English. But most important of all were the moral effects. The French knew themselves beaten and outmanœuvred. All the difficulties of their defensive were worsened and multiplied, and the advantages of the assailants proportionately improved. The destruction of the Lines of Brabant was an event which Europe recognized had definitely altered conditions in the main theatre of the war.

Marlborough's letters tell the tale of the next few days: but they afford us also an insight into his nature which is rare in these chronicles of war and affairs. In seeking to observe a man who always maintained such a majestic façade, the moments of weakness are fruitful. There is no doubt that, what with fatigue and relief and the hope that he had the next move in his hands, he gave way to rejoicing. He had won a double victory over his Dutch friends and his French foes. "I was forced to cheat them into it," he wrote. "He dared not offer to persuade the Deputies of the States," wrote Hare, "*but perfectly bubbled them into it.*" As for the enemy, their discomfiture was patent. His own delight sparkles in his letters. Most of all was he thrilled with the admiration and cheers of his troops. There is a boyish ring about his letters to Sarah. He felt very young that day. He writes rugged, strong English, not unworthy of the Shakespeare that was his main education.

John to Sarah   TIRLEMONT
July 18, 1705

. . . It is impossible to say too much good of the troops that were with me, for never men fought better. Having marched all night, and taken a good deal of pains this day, my blood is so hot that I can hardly hold my pen; so that you will, my dearest life, excuse me if I say no more, but that I would not let you know my design of attacking the lines by the last post, fearing it might give you uneasiness; and now, my dearest soul, *my heart is so full of joy for this good success, that should I write more I should say a great many follies.*[1]

And two days later:

CAMP NEAR LOUVAIN
July 20

I was so pleased when I wrote my last, that if I had writ on I should have used expressions which afterwards I should have been ashamed of. *The kindness of the troops to me had transported me,* for I had none in this last action, but such as were with me last year; for M. Overkirk's army did not come till an hour after all was over. This was not their fault, for they could not come sooner; *but this gave occasion to the troops with me to make me very kind expressions, even in the heat of the action, which I own to you gives me great pleasure, and makes me resolve to endure anything for their sakes.*[2]

Marlborough to Godolphin

TIRLEMONT
July 18, 1705

. . . As I had in this action no troops with me but such as I brought from the Moselle, I believe the French will not care to fight with them again. This bearer will tell you that Monsieur Overkirk's army was not in the lines, till the whole action was over, *and that I was forced to cheat them into this action;* for they did not believe I would attack the lines, they being positive that the enemy were stronger than they [actually] were. But this is what must not be spoke of, for it would anger the Dutch, with whom I think, at this time, I am very well, for their Deputies made me the compliment this afternoon that if I had not been here the lines would not have been forced. I intend to march to-morrow towards Louvain, by which march I shall see what Monsieur de Villeroy will do. This day has given me a great deal of pleasure; however I think 500 pound is enough for the bearer.[3]

Marlborough to the Queen

CAMP NEAR LOUVAIN
July 23, 1705

MADAM,

I have had the honour of your majesty's letter of the 3d [14th], in which you are so extremely good, that I want words

---

[1] Coxe, ii, 143. [2] *Ibid.,* 146.
[3] *Ibid.,* 144. Marlborough evidently knew that Colonel Parke had received £1000 for carrying the Blenheim dispatch.

to express the sense I have of it; and as I am sure I would not only venture my life, but also sacrifice my quiet for you, so I beg you will believe that I shall never think myself master of taking any resolution till I have first obtained your majesty's leave. By my letters I have had from Holland, I find the Dutch are so pleased with the success we have had that I believe they will not now hearken to any proposals of peace without first acquainting your majesty. I do also hope that it may have some effect on the parties in England, for the advantage of your affairs, which I pray God may prosper as your own heart can desire, and then I am sure England must be happy.[1]

The effect produced upon Harley by the exploits of Elixem can be judged by the following letter, which should be remembered when we come to the later phases of their relationship.

Harley to Marlborough

July 28, 1705

Saturday col. Durel brought the good news of your grace's glorious action. . . .

You have, my lord, exceeded our very hopes or expectations, and no person could have done it but yourself. What I took the liberty to say to the queen upon this occasion is what I believe in my soul, that no subjects in the world have such a prince as the queen, and that no prince in the world hath such a subject as your grace.

Your friends and servants here cannot be without concern upon your grace's account when we hear *how much you expose* that precious life of yours *upon all occasions*,[2] and that you are not contented to do the part of a great general, but you condescend to take your share as a common soldier. I hope your lordship's unwearied care and unparalleled merit will in due time procure a lasting and sure peace for Europe, with repose and eternal renown to your grace.[3]

Meanwhile the operations had been checked. The rancours and reproaches that had arisen in the army were to wreck the rest of the campaign. It was evident that the next step was a left-handed movement across the Dyle. Swayed by the diverse emotions of the 18th, the Dutch

[1] Coxe, ii, 147.   [2] Harley's italics.   [3] Coxe, ii, 148-149.

generals made no objection to an attempt to force the passage of the river. All preparations were made for the 22nd. But now "great rains" descended, and "drowned all the meadows, by which we were to have marched to have gone over the Dyle."[1]

By the time the ground was dry again the resolution of the Council of War had also oozed away. By much patient pressure Marlborough obtained agreement to an attack upon the 29th. The plan was conventional. He threatened the French on the north side of Louvain, and then sought by a long night march to cross the Dyle on the south side. But the feint to the north proved singularly ineffectual. Villeroy was not at all deceived by it. On the contrary, his only response to Marlborough's demonstration against his left was to strengthen his right. Dark suspicion arose about this in Marlborough's circle. Several letters assert that the French Marshal had exceptionally good information where the effort would be made. Of course, if fifteen or twenty generals have all to sit for hours round a table for several days debating in committee a deadly plan of war, there is bound to be a leak. Each member of the Council has two or three confidants, and these again often have others to whom they talk. The camps were infested with eavesdroppers. But the assertions of Hare, Cardonnel, Orkney, and others hint more than mere inadvertence.

However this may be, on the 29th the movement began. Marlborough, with Overkirk on his left, marched by night to the fords of the Dyle, preceded by strong advance guards with new copper pontoons. At daybreak, both Heukelom from the Dutch and Oxenstiern from Marlborough's army passed the river. Heukelom made much ground and established himself strongly. Oxenstiern made a bridgehead. The French, as soon as they saw the movement, marched to oppose the passage. There is little doubt it could have been effected, but by ill luck the English missed their way in the darkness and were two hours late in coming upon the scene. Thus it was the Dutch who were up to

1 Marlborough to Godolphin; Coxe, ii, 152.

time and alone in a position to begin crossing the river at Neerysche. The easy success of Heukelom and the substantial lodgment which he had secured on the opposite bank should have encouraged them. But now Slangenberg led opinion at the Dutch headquarters against attempting the passage. Marlborough was in a weak position because the main part of his own army was still some distance away. He could not therefore commit the Dutch by making the passage on his own front. Cranstoun says:

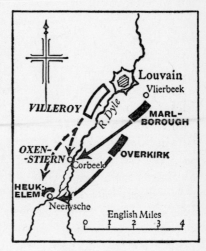

THE DYLE

Our people loitered and were in suspense as it were in laying the bridges, and indeed they say that where they did lay them, the ground on either side was impracticable for cavalry. . . . However, they were but laying the second bridge about break of day, when the Duke came there himself and being, as it is said, asked by Brigadier Ferguson, who commanded in that detachment as Brigadier under Oxenstiern, why we halted as if we should not march on, the Duke made him answer, grasping his hand, "Hold your tongue, you know nothing. I have given my word to do nothing without consent." [1]

He then rode the mile and a quarter to the Dutch headquarters, where the generals were gathered humming and hawing in a knot. Slangenberg immediately forced the issue. He accosted Marlborough with vehemence. He was heard to say, "Mon Dieu, my Lord, for God's sake, my Lord, don't . . ." and then drew him aside in voluble expostulation. Overkirk remained mute, but it was clear that negative views prevailed. The discussion, conducted with great formality, each

[1] Major Cranstoun's letter, Portland Papers, *H.M.C.*, iv, 254.

speaking in his turn, dragged on. Marlborough had at length to avert a disaster for which he would have been made responsible. All the time the French were marching on. Heukelom with six battalions was well advanced on the far side of the river. He must either be supported in an action which would develop into a battle, or he must be withdrawn. Marlborough demanded a decision. Would they support him or not? The Council was unable to reach a conclusion. There were so many to be consulted, each with due regard to his rank and consequence. The French vanguard was already in contact, and their cannon had begun to play. Marlborough therefore left the group of babbling officers and sent one of his own aides-de-camp to Heukelom with an order to retire across the bridges forthwith. Heukelom, who had fastened his twelve battalions well into the hedges and ditches and looked for a good success, protested. Marlborough repeated his order in the most peremptory form. Heukelom withdrew raging, but with scarcely any loss. Oxenstiern, who had been for some time under serious fire, was made to conform. The whole confederate army then retreated about six miles. Slangenberg could boast that he had prevented a disaster, and could anyhow feel sure that he had baulked the English interloper. Such was the fiasco of the Dyle.

The bewilderment produced in the army by these proofs of indecision is clearly apparent in contemporary accounts. Noyes wrote:

August 10

*. . . Our aforesaid detachment came to the river, and under the cover of our cannon, which did great execution, laid six bridges. Colonel Godfrey with the Grenadiers of the four English battalions, passed over, as did also twelve of the Dutch battalions and beat all before them, cleared all the hedges and enclosed meadows and the two villages, notwithstanding which Count Oxenstiern who commanded all the detachments ordered the remainder of them to halt, and those who now passed to return, and the Duke commanded the Copper boats to be taken up again, the reason of which is variously reported. Some said the States refused to expose their army any further; others that the ground was so morassy that our Horse could never have got over; 'tis allowed they were morassy where the Dutch had made their four bridges, but very good hard ground where the English had made their two. However, by this refusal of the Dutch General Officers the whole thing fell to the ground.[1]

One cannot feel that this was a good way to conduct war, or, indeed, any business that is liable to move rapidly. The eyes of Europe were upon Marlborough. Was he the greatest general of the age or only a lucky gambler? Was Blenheim an accident or a portent? Had he been a Royal Prince he would have been differently appraised. But an English Court favourite of humble origin must be judged severely. Here was his attempt to cross the Dyle mismanaged and a failure. He had marched out so boldly and then turned tail. He had wasted a fortnight of the campaigning season. Was not the man a fraud: and if so, said the Tories, was it not a public duty to expose him? All very annoying to the labouring Duke as he sat in his tent before Louvain and wondered how he could rescue order from confusion and action from futility. It is astonishing that he should have endured such prolonged and repeated vexations. There may have been greater Captains, but none was ever more plagued.

"I am now almost in despair," he wrote to Godolphin, "of having that advantage we ought to expect from our last success; for we have now been here nine days in sight of the enemy, the river Dyle only between us."

Hare says:

* Little did I imagine when I wrote last that a delay of twelve hours should have drawn after it one of so many days; much less that we should at the end of it miscarry and aim a blow we thought sure: who could have apprehended that an army which had overcome so successfully the greatest difficulties should have its progress stopped by a little rivulet? But Dyle they say in Scotch is devil, and so this paltry river has proved to us. . . . I believe I may add, it would have been done *if somebody had been away whose intolerable temper will let him know no Superior.* He cannot for-

[1] "Pocket Book of Dr Samuel Noyes" (MS.).

give the Duke the glory of passing the lines without letting him into the secret. . . .[1]

Godolphin, anxious to conciliate the Whig Junto without actually forcing one of them upon the Queen at her Council, had proposed to them that Sunderland should be the "man of quality" to be sent to mediate between the Emperor and the Hungarian rebels. This was no doubt a convenience to the Lord Treasurer, but the appointment created the worst impression at Vienna. It was arranged that the new envoy should visit his father-in-law on his way: and the interview was deemed indispensable to the public interest. He was to be warned not to irritate the Imperial Court, and to keep his Whig and Republican pedantry in proper restraint. He arrived at the camp just as the army was moving off into the night on their march to the Dyle. No dinner, no bed but the saddle! He must have made many grimaces. Hare says, ". . . He had jumped into all the hurry of the campaign at once. I believe twelve hours have given him enough of it."[2] Marlborough is jovial about this misfortune in the midst of his own vexations.

John to Sarah

MELDERT
July 30, 1705

✳ My Lord Sunderland came here last night, and I believe is spoyled for a soldier, not having leave to go to bed. I did verily believe we should have had a very considerable action this day; but by the backwardness of some of our friends and our misfortune of being two hours longer in our march than we ought to have been, the whole ended in a good deal of cannon and some small shot; but we lost very few men. If God intends us any more success, it must proceed from some occasion M. de Villeroy must give us. I am vexed, so that my heart is full, or I should not have been able to have said so much, I am so extremely tired.

The story of his personal encounter at Elixem spread with the tidings of that action. Although no generals in those

---

1 Meldert, July 30. Blenheim MSS.   2 *Loc. cit.*

THE THIRD EARL OF SUNDERLAND
By permission of Earl Spencer

days were respected who did not go into danger with their troops, it was unusual for commanders-in-chief to charge with the cavalry like Eugene. Sarah was naturally agitated by the accounts she received. We have only John's letter in reply.

John to Sarah

MELDERT
August 6, 1705

My dearest soul I love you so well, and have set my heart so entirely on ending my days in quiet with you, that you may be so far at ease as to be assured that I never venture myself but when I think the service of my queen and country requires it. Besides I am now at an age when I find no heat in my blood that gives me temptation to expose myself out of vanity; but as I would deserve and keep the kindness of this army, I must let them see that when I expose them, I would not exempt myself.[1]

When every excuse has been made for the failure to use the brilliant passage of the Lines of Brabant, a very definite residue of criticism remains. In the sphere of war Marlborough was a creature of fire. But on the afternoon of the 18th the fire sank to a genial glow at which he warmed himself, instead of emitting fresh flames to destroy the foe.

[1] Coxe, ii, 147.

CHAPTER X

THE UNFOUGHT WATERLOO

1705, AUGUST

OUR General resolved to make a final effort before the campaign ended. A peculiar quality of his manœuvres is the ease and exactness with which they can be explained to the lay reader. From the moment of his return to the Meuse, Villeroy, although slightly the stronger, had yielded him the initiative. He had used it to pierce and render useless the Lines of Brabant. All the more after that did he enjoy the right to move; all the more were the French obliged to wait on his movements. In a country studded with fortresses the concession or loss of the initiative imposed grievous disadvantages upon the defenders. They could not tell where they would be hit. Therefore they had to garrison all their threatened fortresses and weaken their field army accordingly; while on the other hand Marlborough, master of the proceedings, could gather nearly all his troops into a striking force. His new plan was to advance deeply and suddenly into the enemy's country, so as to menace equally and at once a number of important places, and then, when Villeroy had been forced to detach troops for these, to fall upon his weakened army and destroy it in a battle.

After being baulked by Slangenberg and the Deputies at the Dyle, he sought freedom to carry out a fresh design which he had formed. The detail of his plan was contrary to many of the accepted conventions. He baked at Meldert five days' bread, and ordered from Liége a convoy of six days' biscuit. He also brought from Liége a considerable siege train, including ten twenty-four pounders and sixteen mortars. To aid in the dispersion of the French he reinforced Baron Spaar on the sea-coast to the north with four battalions and directed him to raid the enemy country between Bruges and Ghent. He wrote to Godolphin:

THE UNFOUGHT WATERLOO

MELDERT
August 3, 1705

I have sent Lieutenant-General Hompesch once more to The Hague. . . . You will see that I have a mind to serve them if they please; but if they should not allow of what I propose, it is impossible to act offensively; for besides the danger of resolving everything that is to be done in a council of war, *which cannot be kept so secret, but that the enemy must know it time enough to prevent it, as we had the experience of in our last undertaking,* so monsieur Slangenberg, though he is a brave man, his temper is such that there is no taking measures with him. I am so tired that I cannot answer yours at this time.[1]

Hompesch returned with an absurd compromise. The field Deputies were instructed to permit the Captain-General to make two or three marches without summoning a council of war. At the same time Marlborough was not to bring the army to any serious engagement without the approval of both Overkirk and the Deputies.

In spite of these insensate restrictions, Marlborough determined to persevere. He hoped by his three free marches to create a situation in which either the enemy would make a battle inevitable, or his advantage over the enemy would be so obvious that even the Dutch could not deny him. On this basis therefore he decided to take this hampering chance over and above the deadly hazards of war. On August 13 the biscuit convoy reached Meldert from Liége. Marlborough had now acquired eleven days' manœuvring power in many directions without regard to his own communications. On the 15th he marched southward to Corbaix, with Overkirk keeping pace with him on his left. On the 16th he moved on to Genappe, crossing the headstreams of the Dyle. On the 17th he turned north along the Brussels road towards Waterloo. The three marches "in scorching hot weather"[2] totalled thirty-three miles.

Villeroy and the Elector, encamped between Louvain and Brussels, saw with astonishment this movement of the whole confederate army across and round their front. They had heard from sure sources that the convoy of biscuit had

---

1 Coxe, ii, 161.   2 Blackadder, p. 260.

been kept loaded on the wagons, and that Marlborough was carrying with him the batteries for besieging fortresses. They saw that he had let go his communications with Liége: these were now exposed to their attack if they cared to pay the price of battle. They preferred to await events. They must now be concerned for the safety of five fortresses,

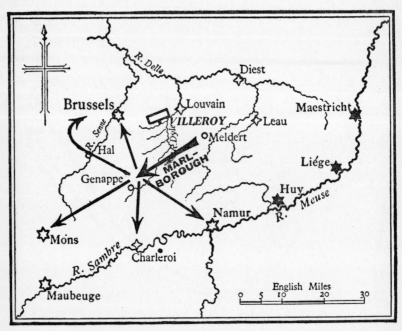

MARLBOROUGH THREATENS THE FORTRESSES

Namur, Charleroi, Mons, Ath, and above all the weakly defended Brussels. A report, based on the intercepted letter of a member of the States-General, had also reached them that Marlborough intended to pass the Senne at Hal and march right round them to the attack of Dendermonde, thus placing himself between them and Antwerp. Both Villeroy and—when they were informed—the main headquarters at Versailles were unable to understand the purpose and hardihood of such manœuvres. That a commander should be prepared to sever his communications and move so large an army encumbered by a siege train and heavy convoy across their front into

230

their fortress zone was a departure from every canon of the military art deserving the severest punishment. However, since Marlborough was known to be seeking a battle and they were not anxious to fight, they did not try to exact the forfeits which they conceived were their due. Instead, as he had

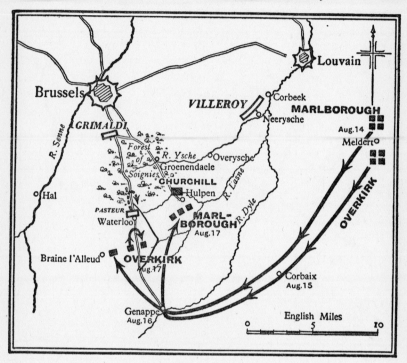

AUGUST 17

expected, they submitted to his will. They assigned a strong garrison to Louvain and detached Grimaldi with eighteen battalions, twelve squadrons, and ten guns to support a Colonel Pasteur, who with a small force was barring the road from Waterloo to Brussels. They moved their main army slightly to its right in order to be nearer Grimaldi. They still remained in their central position between Louvain and Brussels; but they were completely mystified about Marlborough's intentions, and the dispersion of their army was far advanced.

During the night of August 17-18 the confederate advance

231

guards were found to be still moving along both the roads to Brussels. Pasteur, though he returned during the night to his position at Waterloo, was roughly thrown back. When the morning of the 18th broke, the reports which reached the French command from all quarters convinced them that Marlborough was striking at Brussels with his whole force. The high road was crowded with his advancing infantry, while the French army was, it seemed, only to be 'amused' by a cavalry flank guard. This revelation of what they conceived to be Marlborough's true purpose confronted Villeroy and the Elector with a grievous dilemma. "I confess to Your Majesty," wrote the Elector of this moment,

> that the choice was very difficult, because a single false step drew with it the loss of the Low Countries, and I believe that for centuries there has not been a more thorny hour. To march to Brussels was to abandon the position which up to this time has saved Louvain and all Brabant; to stay in it was to lose Brussels, and by that the larger part of the country as well. To divide the army was impossible; for we should not have been strong enough for either purpose and by that we should have lost the army into the bargain; *and through being forced to guard so many open places at once there were already 27 battalions and 20 squadrons detached from Your Majesty's army:* delay also, even the slightest, would have lost all upon the instant. . . . It was necessary to choose . . . between the loss of Brussels or of Louvain, there being no middle course.[1]

They decided to sacrifice Louvain. About seven o'clock they prepared to march by their right to join Grimaldi, who was at the same time moved nearer to the main army while still covering both roads to Brussels.

This resolve was hardly taken when the whole scene was transformed. "The order was no sooner given," says the Elector, "than there appeared before our eyes a column of hostile infantry which we could well recognize to be the English, thus revealing from this moment that their main design was not against Brussels, for the English infantry came from that quarter."[2]

1 The Elector to Louis XIV, August 20; Pelet, v, 596.   2 *Ibid.*, 598.

These masses began to debouch upon the French right from the Forest of Soignies. Great numbers of the allied cavalry advanced towards the French centre beyond the Ysche stream between Overysche and Neerysche. Behind them heavy columns of infantry could be discerned. It was not Brussels, then, that Marlborough sought: it was BATTLE! They were about to be attacked; and for all their vigilance they were as much astonished as Tallard had been a year before, almost to a day, at Blenheim. Marlborough had, in fact, quitted the Brussels road during the night, and was rapidly building up a front to his right which continually grew along the French position.

All this was grave. But there was one factor they did not know, or could not measure. At 2 A.M. Marlborough had sent his brother Churchill with 20 battalions and 20 squadrons from Hulpen, where he had bivouacked, to march upon Groenendaele. This powerful detached corps found the roads obstructed by felled trees. They had nevertheless made good progress, and at ten o'clock were established across and beyond the Ysche near Groenendaele and in a position where they could turn not only the French right flank, but by persisting traverse his rear and assail his retreat on Brussels. Meanwhile Grimaldi remained tethered to the protection of the Brussels roads, and was as much out of the impending battle as Churchill was in it. This use of a large detached corps of manœuvre as an integral part of the main battle was hitherto unexampled in the European war.

"There was also a stratagem to be used," wrote Blackadder,

which, if it had taken effect, would probably have decided the battle in our favour. There were twenty battalions (ours was one), and horse conform[able], that were to march through a wood and post ourselves quietly in the wood till we should hear that the battle was fully joined. Then we were to come out and attack them in the rear. Accordingly we marched at three in the morning, and posted ourselves in the wood, where we stayed till three in the afternoon. General Churchill commanded us. . . .[1]

All the rest of the confederate forces were meanwhile

1 Blackadder, p. 262.

233

rapidly approaching and deploying. But let us see what were
the armies now, it seemed, to be matched together in decisive
conflict. With the reinforcement he had already received
from the Moselle, Villeroy had under his command 103 battalions and 147 squadrons. Of these he could now only marshal (including Grimaldi) 76 battalions and 127 squadrons.
All the rest had been drawn from him piecemeal by the
various pressures and anxieties we have described. Marlborough had, on the other hand, concentrated 100 battalions
and 162 squadrons; or more than four men to three for the
operation, and much more upon the actual front of his attack.
We have seen him eager to fight Villars with four men to five,
and victorious at Blenheim with ten men to eleven. Later
both at Ramillies and at Oudenarde he was slightly inferior.
Always he welcomed a trial on equal terms. This was the
only battle except the Schellenberg which he planned or
fought where he had a large superiority in numbers. His
combinations had been entirely successful. Every forecast he
had made of the psychological effect which his marches would
produce upon the enemy was vindicated. First he had compelled their strategical dispersion throughout the theatre of
war; and secondly their tactical dispersion on the chosen
battlefield. Not only had they been forced to weaken their
army to guard so many threatened points, but now, at the
moment of action, they were drawn out on a front larger than
their force could cover, their main position divided by a dangerous ravine, and with an important part of their army under
Grimaldi completely out of joint. Superiority of numbers,
the confusion visible in the French lines—troops moving forward, backward, now here, now there—the proximity of
the Dutch, and above all the death-dealing position in which
Churchill and his corps stood, all encouraged a just confidence. Marlborough had still eight days' food in his wagons
and could manœuvre or pursue with exceptional freedom.
It was with a glow of inward satisfaction that he began about
nine o'clock his customary close, personal reconnaissance of
the hostile front.

When Villeroy and the Elector understood that they were

about to be assaulted by the violent Duke at the head of a much larger army, their first impulse was to retreat to Brussels. Considering the dangers of combining a flank march and a rearguard action, they decided to fight it out. Forthwith they began to fortify the villages behind the Ysche and to

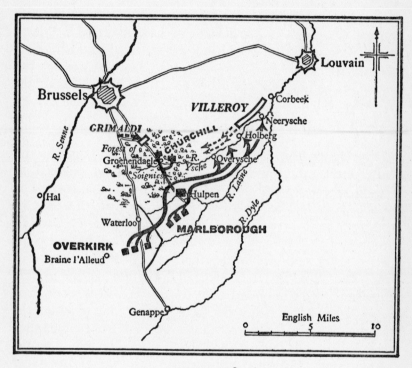

AUGUST 18

array their troops for a dire struggle. Marlborough meanwhile had discerned four practicable points of attack.[1] These are shown on the plan. Prying closely at one of them, he was fired upon by a battery, and when the cannon-balls sang through the air or smote the ground amid his staff, he remarked complacently, "These gentlemen do not choose to have this spot too narrowly inspected."

By the time he reached the end of the front Overkirk arrived, and Marlborough, bound first of all to convince him,

[1] Hare Papers, *H.M.C.*, p. 205.

took the old Dutchman over the dangerous ground. Overkirk agreed to fight. Thus the first condition of the States-General was established. Indeed, Marlborough had actually issued orders for his infantry to seize the weakly defended passage near Holberg, when he learned that his artillery had been delayed on the march, and forbore pending its arrival.

Hare's narrative already quoted gives a reason, perhaps of prejudice, for its delay.

> * The army was formed in line of battle and our artillery had been up at the same time *if the person* [Slangenberg] *who had so great a hand in the miscarriage of the last attempt had not resolved that this should succeed no better.* Notwithstanding the wheel baggage had been ordered to Wavre, and there had been the strictest directions that nothing should be suffered to break into the march of the train, this gentleman would bully the officer that commanded it, and broke their march to make way for his baggage, which made it four o'clock before the artillery could come up.[1]

The deployment of the army was steadily proceeding when, at about noon, Marlborough met the Field Deputies. He greeted them with confidence. "Gentlemen, I congratulate you on the prospect of a glorious victory." He invited their assent to an immediate attack. They curled up. "Your Highness will doubtless allow us to request the opinion of our generals." Although this demand was outside the resolution of the States-General, Marlborough had foreseen that it would be made. He bowed to it. Strong in the support of Overkirk, the Dutch Commander-in-Chief, and in the splendour of the opportunity, he braced himself for confrontation with subordinates. It was some time before they could be assembled on the high ground opposite Overysche. His words have been recorded by Dr. Hare, who was at his side. "Gentlemen, I have reconnoitred the ground, and made dispositions for an attack. I am convinced that conscientiously, and as men of honour, we cannot now retire without an action. Should we neglect this opportunity, we must be responsible before God and man. You see the confusion which pervades the ranks of the enemy, and their embarrassment at our

1 Hare's letter of August 20. Blenheim MSS.

manœuvres. I leave you to judge whether we should attack to-day or wait till to-morrow. It is indeed late, but you must consider that by throwing up entrenchments during the night, the enemy will render their position far more difficult to force."

There was a sullen murmur, and then Slangenberg—"that beast Slangenberg," as Hare calls him—broke out, "Since I have been led to this place without any previous communication of the design, I will give no other opinion than that the passage at Overysche is impracticable. However, I am ready to obey the orders which I may receive." Marlborough fastened on the last sentence. "I am happy to have under my command an officer of your courage and skill, and I flatter myself that in a situation which requires instant decision you will start no difficulties." It is sometimes possible to induce a contumacious person to act by giving him charge of the action to which he objects. Accordingly Marlborough proposed to Slangenberg that he should himself direct the attack upon Overysche. Slangenberg was not to be cajoled. "Murder and massacre!" he muttered in audible tones. Of course it would be the Dutch who would be sacrificed. "No," replied Marlborough, "I will place two English battalions at the side of every Dutch one." This must have involved a considerable dislocation of the front. But Slangenberg only rejoined that he did not understand English. "German battalions then," replied the Captain-General. Slangenberg fell back upon his assertion that the attack was impracticable. "Then I will lead it myself," said Marlborough. "I will not send troops to dangers which I will not myself encounter."[1] To this there could be no answer.

He then appealed again to the Deputies. The Deputies turned obdurately away and formed a circle with the generals, where they all stood growling together for about two hours, while the French dug and the day wore on. There is hardly any picture like this in war annals. This cluster of men, shame-faced but stubborn, shifting from one leg to the other, shaking

1 *Ibid.*; Coxe, ii, 168.

their heads and repeating their arguments while their so-called Commander-in-Chief, humiliated, defied, stood or paced up and down a little way off, now breaking in with words of conciliation and then with words of wrath. But they all knew that if they talked long enough the matter would settle itself as they meant. And here surely Overkirk, from whom history will not withdraw a friendly regard, ought to have made his authority felt by his own Dutch officers. He had agreed to the attack. Should he not have said, "I have given my opinion to the field Deputies, and I cannot allow my officers to contradict me"? But Overkirk, though worth the lot, was old. He was alone among his fellow-countrymen. Faithful in thought and action, he lacked personal dominance. He subsided. If the Duke could not persuade them to it, who could?

The afternoon was now far advanced. Some of the generals had safeguarded themselves by saying that they could not pronounce a final opinion without inspecting the actual points of attack themselves. Slangenberg then proposed that a delegation should make a personal reconnaissance. It was agreed that Slangenberg, Salisch, and Tilly should compose it. The chance of the day was now gone. To-morrow the line of the Ysche would be a fortification. Still, Marlborough named three of his officers to accompany them. Count Noyelles could not trust himself to ride in courtesy with Slangenberg. But Bothmar and Starck complied. As they toured the line the Dutchmen dwelt at every point upon the dangers and difficulties of the attack. Slangenberg claimed that Starck admitted the position to be three times as strong as Höchstädt. But this is denied. Slangenberg then made the offensive remark that "the attack at Höchstädt had been regarded as an imprudence and censured as such by many." Upon this Marlborough's two officers without a word turned their horses and rode away. The remainder of the delegation returned to make their report. Slangenberg seems to have expected that Marlborough would be anxious to renew the argument with him. In this he was disappointed. ". . . And as we came to make our report to the

Veldt-Marshal, of what we had seen," he wrote in his justification, "and came into the road which was bordered on both sides by tall hedges behind which the Veldt-Marshal had camped, the Duke of Marlborough passed before us without speaking to us." [1] He added a reference to Overkirk which did himself harm in Holland when the account was published. "After that we came to the Veldt-Marshal, *whom we found sleeping in his coach*, to whom we made our report, and heard no more talk that night nor the following day of attacking the enemy." [2]

What followed is well told in Marlborough's letters. The first is written on the eve of the crisis, and conceals its imminence from his wife.

John to Sarah

LOWER WAVRE
August 17, 1705

We shall march again to-morrow; for we cannot stay longer in this country than the bread we bring with us will give us leave. I hope in a week or ten days I shall have more leisure than I have now, and then I am resolved to drink the Spa waters. I wish with all my heart those of Tunbridge may do you good; and then I am sure the first summer I am with you I shall desire to go thither with you, and then I believe the waters will do me good; for till I am pleased and at ease with you no waters nor any thing else will do me good.

August 19

When I had writ this far, I took the resolution of not letting the post go, believing I should have engaged the enemy yesterday, which I certainly had done if it had been in my power. But all the Dutch generals, except M. Overkirk, were against it, so that the Deputies would not consent to our engaging, notwithstanding we were in battle, within cannon-shot of the enemy; and I do assure you that our army were at least one-third stronger than theirs. We are now returning; for we cannot stay longer than the bread we have brought with us will give us leave. It is impossible to make the war with advantage at this rate. I have sent a copy of my letter to the States to lord treasurer. I should have

---

[1] Slangenberg to Fagel, August 27, 1705; Lamberty, iii, 487. [2] *Ibid.*
[3] Hare's letter. Blenheim MSS.

239

writ in a very angry style, but I was afraid it might have given the French an advantage.[1]

Marlborough to Godolphin   LOWER WAVRE
August 19, 1705

You will see by the enclosed to the States that after four days' march, I found the enemy encamped as I expected, so that I thought we should have had a very glorious day. But as the Deputies would not consent without first consulting the generals, who were all against it, except M. Overkirk, we have been obliged to retire from the enemy, notwithstanding we were at least one-third stronger than they, which I take to be very prejudicial to the common cause, and scandalous for the army. I think this will shew very plainly that it is next to impossible to act offensively with this army, so governed as they are; for when their general and I agree, as we did in this, that it shall be in the power of subaltern generals to hinder the execution, is against all discipline. This last action of the Dutch generals has given us great mortification; for the enemy will see very plainly that they have nothing to fear on this side, nor can I ever serve with them without losing the little reputation I have; for in most countries they think I have power in this army to do what I please. I beg you will give my duty to the queen, and assure her that if I had had the same power I had the last year I should have had a greater victory than that of Blenheim, in my opinion; for the French were so posted that if we had beat them they could not have got to Brussels.[2]

On the same day he sent his formal report to the States-General:

. . . Yesterday we were in motion before daybreak and after passing several defiles we came into fairly open country [*une assez grande campagne*] having found the enemy as we expected them between Overysche and Neerysche with the little stream of the Ysche before them. At noon or a little afterwards all our army was ranged in battle, and, having examined with M. Overkirk the four posts which I wished to attack, I flattered myself already, in view of the goodness and superiority of our troops, to be able soon to congratulate Their High Mightinesses upon a glorious victory. But at the last moment when nothing remained but to attack, it was not judged advisable to seek a decision [*pousser*

[1] Coxe, ii, 170.   [2] *Ibid.*, 176.

l'affaire]. . . . I am sure that the Deputies will explain to Your High Mightinesses the reasons which were presented to them on both sides, and at the same that they will do justice to M. Overkirk in stating that he shared my feeling that the occasion was too good to throw away. I submitted however, although with much regret.

He added a postscript of severe protest.

My heart is so full that I cannot refrain from representing on this occasion to Your High Mightinesses that I find myself here with far less authority than when I had the honour to command Their troops last year in Germany.[1]

Thus set the star of the Dutch Republic. It is vain to plead that nine months later, only a score of miles away, the victory of Ramillies destroyed Villeroy's army and regained Belgium, and that still the war went on. Time is inexorable. Had Marlborough won the unfought battle of Waterloo in August 1705, all the French power in the Netherlands would have been thereby annihilated. The French stood with their faces towards France, just as the Dutch looked towards Holland. In such a situation there could have been no recovery in the Low Countries for the defeated side. Marlborough would have acquired that supreme authority which he always lacked to plan the campaign of 1706. He would have been there to execute the great projects which we shall presently unfold, unless even better had presented themselves. The year of victory, 1706, might also have been the year of peace. But the Dutch wore out Fortune with their sluggish precautions. Six or seven separate times, for reasons which no instructed modern soldier would tolerate, they "feared their fate too much," and paralysed the genius which could have delivered them. Not all their courage, their sacrifices, and their dauntless constancy could appease the insulted gods. Long and bloody years of struggle lay before them. They were to see their cherished Blue Guards mown down under their own prince at Malplaquet. Their Deputies were even to beg Marlborough to fight a battle against his better judg-

1 *Dispatches,* ii, 223.

ment in 1711—and beg in vain. They were to exhaust their wealth in a seemingly interminable series of campaigns. Their sea-power and their share in the New World were to pass insensibly, but irresistibly and soon, to England. In the end Marlborough, serviceable, grand, helpful, would fall victim to the English parties, and England, now so fierce and ardent, would sicken of an endless war, desert her allies, and leave them to their fate. But if the valiant Republic, to whom Protestant civilization owes an inestimable debt, was to be deprived of its fruition in modern times, condemned for ever to be a minor Power while rivals grew so great, this was the fatal scene. Here by the cross-roads of bodeful Waterloo, as earlier upon the heaths of Peer, the destinies of Holland turned; and upon that milestone there may well be inscribed the not otherwise noticeable name of Slangenberg.

CHAPTER XI

THE MORTIFIED ADVENTURER

1705, SEPTEMBER

MARLBOROUGH'S wrath and protest caused widespread commotion. A long swell rolled across England. Marlborough knew that in fastening a reproach upon the Dutch he would find a ready response. The Whigs, the advocates of vigorous war, were bound to support it. The Tories marched up eager for a quarrel with those Continental obstructionists and shirkers for whom English citizens had sacrificed too much already. The Queen shared these sentiments with spontaneous warmth, and the Cabinet responded. Harley, as Secretary of State and Speaker, gave full vent to the national mood. For the Dutch formal processes were prepared. A nobleman of the highest standing should be sent as Envoy Extraordinary to the States to protest before the world at the treatment the Captain-General of the joint armies had received. Lord Pembroke was actually selected for this grave mission. The feelings of the magnates and legislators were voiced in rough form and to a most unusual degree, not only by the well-to-do citizens and country gentlefolk, but by the populace. Blenheim sunk throughout the year ever deeper into the national mind. Here was this accursed war which they must fight and which they must win or else be made "slaves and Papists." Here was their own English General who had the secret of victory, whose sword could deliver them from the toils. And here were these pinchbeck princes of Germany and money-grubbing burghers of Holland who would not allow him to strike the blow that would free them all from the heavy, harsh yoke. Gallas, accustomed to the eddies of Court intrigue, was astonished by contact with a national force not understood at all in Central Europe. "These people here," he reported to the

243

Emperor, "can be content with nothing but battle and blood-shed." [1] He had not the wit to add that this was because they wanted to win and end the war, and had a sound military instinct as to how it might be done. But what a contrast our country now presented, after four years of high taxation and onerous warfare, with the England of 1701! Then the only care of the Parliament was to abolish the armed forces, and to make it plain for all to see that England would never fight again in a Continental war. How King William would have marvelled and also rejoiced if he could have seen the vision of the pacifist island which four years of Marlborough had made consciously and unitedly the drill-sergeant of Europe!

Marlborough continued to express his disappointment in all quarters. He proclaimed his reproaches to the whole circle of the Alliance. To Godolphin he wrote (August 27):

> . . . I have reason to believe that Slangenberg has resolved to give all the hindrance he could to whatever should be proposed, so that you may see how the common cause is like to thrive, *when it is in the power of a roman catholic of his temper* to hinder whatever may be designed. This makes it impossible for me to serve with these people; for I take it for granted their constitution will not allow them to give us such power as for the good of the service I ought to have; so that the next year's project ought to be so made, as that the Dutch army in this country may be on the defensive, by which all the other armies may be put in a condition to act offensively.[2]

John to Sarah   TIRLEMONT
August 31, 1705

I have so many things that vex me that I am afraid the waters, which I think to begin to-morrow, will not do me much good. That I may be the more quiet during this siege of Léau, I have taken my quarters in this town, and will trouble myself with business as little as possible. My letters from The Hague tell me that the factions there are divided concerning the last disappointment I had. Those that are for a peace think their generals acted prudently; but the others are angry with them and their

---

1 Gallas's dispatch of August 4.   2 Coxe, ii, 177.

Deputies, so that it is with them as with us in England, they judge by parties. . . . But if it be possible they have more faction than we have, by which we may fear everything.

It is impossible for me to express how much I long for the end of this campaign, for I have no prospect of any thing considerable that can be done, unless the French will take heart and offer at something [*i.e.*, battle].[1]

Marlborough to Godolphin   TIRLEMONT
August 31, 1705

You do in yours complain of some things at home; but if you could know all I suffer here abroad, you would agree with me in begging of the queen that I might never more go out of England. . . . In Holland the people . . . *are of my side against their generals.* By this you may see how difficult a part I have to act, being obliged to take care that neither the French nor Dutch common people know how I am used; for it is most certain I have not the tenth part of the authority I had last year; and it is as certain that if I had had the power of fighting, with the blessing of God the French must have been beaten. By all this you will easily believe me that I shall make it my endeavour to be in England early. But if any misfortune should happen to the army after I were gone, I should never forgive myself; for, though I am used ill, the public must not suffer . . .[2]

On September 1 there arrived a letter from Harley expressing his sympathy. "The queen upon reading your grace's letter," he wrote, "ordered the lords immediately to be summoned; they were all of opinion to advise the queen to take notice of this to the States, in regard not only to the public service, but also what is due to your grace's great merit, to which such usage is very inconsistent."[3] He then explained the plan of Lord Pembroke's mission of protest. Marlborough saw in a moment that this would be regarded throughout Holland as a national insult. He was at the height of his vexation, but he kept his head even in anger. He rejected the proposal at once. He wrote:

From the knowledge and experience I have of these people, that while they are in such a ferment on this very occasion, and that

1 Coxe, ii, 182.   2 *Ibid.*, 183.   3 *Ibid.*, 178-179.

there are such divisions reigning amongst them, I can no ways think it for the public good or her majesty's service, as believing it might rather give an advantage to the French, and those that wish them well, or at least that are over-forward for a peace . . .[1]

On the same day (September 2) he wrote to Sarah, "But really my spirit is so broke, that whenever I can get from this employment, I must live quietly or die." [2]

Meanwhile the recriminations in the Army had risen to a dangerous height. Marlborough's letter of August 19 to the States-General, with its accusing postscript, was published even before it was considered by the Assembly. The disclosure was traced to the English Mission at The Hague, and there is little doubt that the Minister, Stanhope, had acted upon Marlborough's instructions. The anger of the British Government and the proposal to protest by a special envoy also became known throughout Holland. There was a crisis of public opinion, and for some days the preponderance was not clear. The peace party naturally took the side of the Dutch generals and Deputies, and the States-General gave prominence to peace talk as an effective counter to the grievances of their ally. Nevertheless, for a space Marlborough did not restrain the resentments which burned within him. Nor was this without a definite purpose. Slangenberg must go. If he remained with the army after what had happened the authority of the Captain-General was at an end. Unless an example were made it was vain to persevere in the campaign. Slangenberg was a national hero in Holland, and he had the whole weight of the Dutch generals and field Deputies on his side. For a fortnight the tension was extreme.

To be rid of Slangenberg Marlborough assigned to him the siege of Léau with fifteen battalions and as many squadrons. Slangenberg, apparently sure of his position, refused unless he were given thirty battalions. The duty was therefore entrusted to General Dedem. The fortress surrendered a week later as soon as the batteries were planted. The publication of Marlborough's protest drew from Slangenberg and

1 Coxe, ii, 180-181.   2 *Ibid.*, 184.

the Dutch Deputies lengthy explanations of their conduct, some of which were widely circulated. But now the voice of the Dutch people was heard from many quarters. They declared themselves on Marlborough's side and against their fellow-countryman. Rotterdam led the popular movement: Amsterdam, where the peace party at first was strong, underwent a swift change. The burghers beset the council house with demands "that more attention should be paid to the Duke of Marlborough's advice." Feeling was not less vehement at The Hague. Shrewsbury, who passed through Holland that winter, used that grim phrase which every functionary in the Republic understood only too well. He wrote that if Slangenberg had been seen in the streets he would have been "de-Witted." The storm grew among the masses of the common people, and the magnates bowed to it. Slangenberg, astonished and abashed, withdrew on the plea of ill-health to Maestricht and afterwards to Aix-la-Chapelle.

According to Cranstoun,

> General Churchill hearing that he [Slangenberg] spoke too freely and disrespectfully of his brother, and being informed that these [his] letters were detracting from the Duke's reputation, sent Brigadier Palmes to him to tell him that if these things were as he was informed, he expected to meet him and find satisfaction; and if it was otherwise, he expected he should show his letters to Mr Palmes.[1]

Palmes was the cavalryman who had done so well against the Gendarmerie at Blenheim, and was one of the younger officers whom Marlborough was advancing. Slangenberg showed him the letters and denied that he had ever spoken unbecomingly of the Duke, and on this the matter dropped. Here Slangenberg passes out of the story. He was never employed again in any military command. This closing incident shows, however, how acute the controversy had become among the armies. Cranstoun says, "The dryness grew to so great a height that it was like an open breach." One must admit that "dryness" is not a term which fails through excess.

[1] October 1, Portland Papers, *H.M.C.*, iv, 255.

We do not know precisely what assurances Marlborough received from Heinsius and the Dutch leaders. It is certain that up till September 9 he was still hot in his pursuit of Slangenberg. Cardonnel's bulletin of August 19 had contained the words:

> About noon our army was formed in order of battle, and my lord the Duke of Marlborough having with M. Overkirk visited the posts they resolved to attack, were accordingly giving orders to the troops to advance, with every prospect of success, but the Deputies and the States, having consulted with their other generals, would not give their consent so that it was given over.[1]

Upon the remonstrances of Vryberg, the Dutch Ambassador, this passage had been omitted from the *Gazette*, making the account entirely colourless. The following remarkable letter shows Marlborough's indignation at this suppression.

Marlborough to Godolphin TIRLEMONT
Sept. 9, 1705.

> After I had sealed this letter, Mr Cardonnel shewed me the Gazette, in which I think I am used very hardly. I send you the paper he wrote by that post, by which you will see what was left out, which I think the writer of the Gazette would not have ventured to have done if he had not had orders for it. If I had not had more regard for the public than for myself, I should have writ more plainly the truth, of the unreasonable disappointment I met with that day, which if I had, I am very confident the common people of Holland would have done me justice; but that would have given great advantage to the French, which was reason enough for me to avoid doing it. But I am much mortified to see that an English gazette has more care not to offend monsieur Vryberg than to do me justice. They have but to see this gazette in Holland, and they will have reason to lay aside any farther thoughts of making new regulations for the giving more authority to the general that shall command, which I hope her majesty will have so much goodness for me as to let it be some other person; for *I am very sure I must be madder than any body in Bedlam if I should be desirous of serving when I am sure that my enemies seek my destruction, and that my friends sacrifice my honour to their wisdom.*[2]

1 Bath Papers, *H.M.C.*, i, 75.   2 Coxe, ii, 186.

"The Duke of Marlborough," wrote Godolphin to Harley on receipt of this, "shows more concern and trouble than I have known him to do on almost any other occasion."[1] Profuse apologies were tendered by both Secretaries of State. But it was the departure and downfall of Slangenberg which appeased the injured commander. By September 14 he had evidently gained his point. He had appealed against the functionaries to the people. Satisfied upon the essential, he was among the first to be alarmed by the vehement response. No one saw more plainly than he the peril with which the passions he had been forced to unleash threatened the Grand Alliance. He could probably have withdrawn the British Army from the Continental war and returned home amid the plaudits of an angry and short-sighted nation. But this was the conclusion which he most feared and hated. He had tested his strength in England and found it superabundant. All this foreign talk of his being a rash general who had had a lucky fluke, and set his somewhat amateur opinions against the experts of European warfare, counted for nothing in his native land. Queen, Parliament, and people brushed it aside with an instinctive gesture. Slangenberg was gone. The Duke now exerted himself to allay the storm he had aroused. That wind had been felt in every allied Court from The Hague to Vienna. His authority prevailed. The Queen was soothed, the Cabinet was cooled, and Parliament and the people were allowed to simmer down.

In the midst of these trials Marlborough's poise was undisturbed. He would always go out of his way to do a kindness— "where the service does not suffer by it." With the world, he loved a lover.

Marlborough to Godolphin TIRLEMONT
Sept. 10

The enclosed is a letter from a young woman of quality that is in love with the Comte de Lyon.[2] He is at Litchfield. I am assured that it is a very virtuous love, and that when they can get their parents' consent, they are to be married. As I do from my

1 September 5, Bath Papers, *loc. cit.*
2 One of the Blenheim prisoners of war.

249

heart wish that nobody were unhappy, I own to you that this letter has made me wish him in France, so that if he might have leave for four months, without prejudice to her majesty's service, I should be glad of it; but if you think it should not be done, you will then be pleased not to speak to the queen of it.[1]

The Queen endeavoured to cheer her General. She wrote:

WINCHESTER
Sept. 6/17

I am very sorry to find, by your letters to lord treasurer, you are so very much in the spleen. I own all the disagreeable things you have met with this summer are a very just cause for it, and I am very much concerned for the uneasiness you are under; but yet I cannot help hoping, that for the good of your country and the sake of your friends, who cannot support themselves without you, you will be persuaded to banish your melancholy thoughts. . . .[2]

And Eugene, in a letter which arrived about the end of September, wrote:

TREVIGLIO
Sept. 13

I profit by this opportunity of assuring your highness of the interest I take in the success of your arms. It is extremely cruel that opinions so weak and discordant should have obstructed the progress of your operations, when you had every reason to expect so glorious a result. I speak to you as a sincere friend. You will never be able to perform any thing considerable with your army unless you are absolute, and I trust your highness will use your utmost efforts to gain that power in future. *I am not less desirous than yourself to be once more united with you in command.*[3]

The event turned gradually in Marlborough's favour. Pembroke's mission was abandoned by the Cabinet. The States wrote to their Deputies and generals:

. . . So as that their generals are not pleased, for they would now have their army fight. I am afraid there will not be an opportunity for it; but should an occasion offer, I do verily believe

1 Coxe ii, 188. 2 *Ibid.,* 189. 3 *Ibid.,* 190.

every body would consent to it, now that we have the happiness of not having Slangenberg, he being gone to Maestricht; and I do, with all my heart, pray to God that I may never be in an army with him.[1]

There is no doubt that the Dutch were deeply distressed. It was true that Louis XIV was busy with proposals for a separate peace. Terms most favourable to the Republic were offered. Barriers, securities, trade—lucrative trade—were laid before them. Why should they, the French whispered, exhaust themselves for this bloodthirsty island and for the vanity and ambition of a single man, risen from nothing, who wished to make awful experiments in war? But the cause held good. The Dutch were as much alarmed by the French blandishments as by the English anger. They, like Marlborough, realized that their road lay together. There had grown up around Marlborough a curious affiliation in Amsterdam. Those who would not deal with Heinsius would work for Heinsius' policy through him. Buys, the Pensionary of Amsterdam—so lately a leader of the peace faction—volunteered, and was eagerly chosen, to wait upon Marlborough in his camp and offer him satisfaction for the past and assurances for the future. There must be a reconciliation: after all, no one doubted that the Captain-General was the appointed guide. No one could express their affection and his worth to them. If only he did not demand such horrible and dangerous gambling warfare!

On the 21st Buys arrived at headquarters to express the regrets of the States-General. He promised that Marlborough should never be asked to serve the Republic again under the conditions of the last campaign. The obnoxious personalities should be removed. Trust would be reposed in the Commander-in-Chief.

"Pensioner Buys," Marlborough wrote to Godolphin (September 24), "has confirmed me in my opinion that the constitution of the States is such that they cannot take away the power the Deputies have had at all times in the army; for

<hr />

1 Marlborough to Godolphin, September 14; Coxe, ii, 191.

in the king's time they had the same authority, but he took care *to choose such men as always agreed to whatever he had a mind to.* Now this may, if they please, be put again in practice, but can never be done by a treaty. I have also underhand [confidential] assurances that they will never employ Slangenberg in the army where I may be. By the whole I find they would be very glad to content me, but, I am afraid, would be glad also to have it still in their power to hinder a battle, for they do seem to apprehend very much the consequences of such a venture." [1]

The care which Marlborough had taken to strengthen the Rhine secured the Margrave a substantial superiority over the French. Nevertheless Villars, reinforcing and later replacing Marsin, developed a vigorous campaign. He stormed Kron-Weissemburg and regained the line of the Lauter. He reoccupied Homburg and rebuilt its fortifications. The Margrave continued to nurse his foot, against which his debilitated constitution could make no headway, and to supervise the laying out of his gardens at Rastadt, the blooming of which he was never to see. Meanwhile his conduct was under critical review at Vienna. The new Emperor was almost resolved to face the grave embarrassments of removing him when, at the end of August, the ailing general made a vigorous effort to retrieve his reputation. With a superiority of nearly seven to five he advanced suddenly across the Lauter, and recaptured Hagenau and the whole line of the Moder. This exploit was worthy of his former career. It quashed the adverse proceedings on foot against him at the Imperial Court. Villars, arriving after the misfortune, drew out in full array and offered battle. But the Margrave was content with what had been achieved. He treated the French demonstrations with a contempt which Klopp assures us was well-founded, and rejoiced in the fact that, while the enemy were thus vaingloriously parading, a large provision train had been successfully received. The relative strengths of the opposing armies show the different standards by which Villars measured Marlborough and the Mar-

1 Coxe, ii, 192.

PENSIONARY BUYS OF AMSTERDAM
From an engraving after the painting by Constantin Netscher
By permission of ' s Rijks Prentenkabinet, Amsterdam

grave. At Sierck, although he was at least five to four, he had refused battle to Marlborough, but upon the Moder he challenged the Margrave with only six to seven. His bid was not accepted. Thus the campaign ended with a confederate success upon the Upper Rhine which was, however, inadequate to the forces employed.

It should be added that by orders from Berlin the powerful Prussian contingent was withdrawn from the Margrave's army on the eve of his attack on the lines of Hagenau, and that the Margrave considered this an evil turn which Marlborough had done him. The truth is that Marlborough, thinking that he might need the Prussians in Flanders and that they were being kept idle on the Upper Rhine, had suggested their transference to the north through Lord Raby at Berlin. The Margrave's sudden activity changed the situation, and Marlborough had the order rescinded almost as soon as it had been issued. The Prussians did not, however, take part in the attack at Hagenau, which succeeded in their absence. They rejoined the Margrave a few days later and were available for battle with Villars, had that offer been accepted. A study of the dates and orders shows that Marlborough acted in perfect good faith, but it is easy to understand why the Margrave had a grievance.

The forcing of the Lines of Brabant had produced a deep impression upon the Great King. He lost faith in a purely defensive policy. On July 21 he wrote Villeroy a letter which was afterwards to prove of the highest importance.

> Although I am convinced of your vigilance and the pains which you have taken to be carefully informed of the movements of the enemy, is it none the less most disagreeable to see them in the middle of the Low Countries masters of the lines and several important posts, and my army compelled to retire precipitately before them to avoid its entire defeat. . . . The disorder which has befallen you springs from the disposition of your army, which is consequent upon the great stretch of country you have to guard. I blame you in no way for what has happened; but, our affairs having definitely changed their character, we must forget a kind

of warfare which is suited neither to the genius of the nation nor to the army you command—at least as numerous as that of the enemy. . . . You should not in the future avoid them with too much care; you should make war as we have made it in the past; hold the field, take full advantage of the strength of the positions which you may occupy. Do not expose yourself to a general engagement without need, *but do not avoid it with too much precaution;* because if the enemy perceive this they will take advantage of it.[1]

The fiascos at the Dyle and before Brussels enabled Chamillart to reach a conclusion upon Marlborough's generalship. He wrote to Villeroy on September 6:

I shall not try much to conceal from you that I have only a mediocre opinion of the capacity of the Duke of Marlborough; his performance during this campaign destroys in my view the great impression which one had formed of him after the battle of Höchstädt, where the victory ought rather to be attributed to luck alone than to the capacity of the enemy generals; it is true that they knew how to profit by our bad dispositions. Send him back to England after the capture of Léau, and he will look in vain for his brilliant reception of last year.[2]

The Marshal did not feel so confident; nor did he avail himself of his new freedom during Marlborough's march around him towards Brussels. Both he and the Elector had dangled throughout on tenterhooks. They felt themselves being laid hold of by a strong, stealthy hand. Suddenly the grip had relaxed. The aggressive movements of the enemy had ceased. At the moment of crisis the allies had tamely withdrawn, and all their marches and countermarches resulted in nothing but a waste of their strength and of the remaining weeks of the campaign. The French leaders were, however, in little doubt about the cause. Marlborough had been frustrated by the Dutch. This was soon confirmed by the commotion which the episode excited in England and Holland, and by the talk of Europe. Villeroy felt that he had escaped so far by a miracle. He protested vehemently to Chamillart against sending any substantial

1 Pelet, v, 57.   2 *Ibid.,* 608.

reinforcements from his army to Villars. In his letter of September 30 he uses expressions which in boastful phrases reveal his secret fears.

> Would God that the King's interests could be served by my renouncement of command. I would reduce myself with pleasure to dwelling only in a flying camp [*camp volant*], so as to send all the troops to Marshal Villars; but I must point out to the King that the Duke of Marlborough *against every principle of war* wished again to attack the King's army in the last camp which we have just left. His journey to Turnhout was for the sole purpose of obtaining permission from the States. We have *an adventurer mortified with the scanty success of his campaign* who seeks only to stake all; he is within striking distance, in the same mood, and will be so to the last day of the campaign. *We have miraculously saved Flanders.* Would it be prudent to expose it to its fate, when it is only a question of waiting for twelve or fifteen days? . . .[1]

These painful words bring home to us the sense of domination and almost terror with which Marlborough had inspired the soul of his adversary. Villeroy felt himself face to face with a furious wild beast. True, it was caged by the Dutch veto, but it was tearing at the bars, and at any moment might break out in frightful strength and rage. Mercifully in another fortnight winter would come. The monster would have to hibernate. There would be a breathing-space. Meanwhile with a larger army, the first army of France, in an area fortified from end to end, he had "miraculously saved Flanders."

But the King in the tranquillity of Fontainebleau adhered to the robust views he had formed after the piercing of the lines; and his resolve reached its conclusion when a few months later Villeroy met the "mortified adventurer" on the field of Ramillies.

1 Pelet, v. 90.

This is the back of a map showing part of the Rhineland region, faintly visible through the paper. Readable place names (shown in mirror/reverse) include:

ENGLISH Guides
DERLAND
Venloo

Kaiserswerth

Dusseldorf

Weert

Cologne

Julich

Aix la Chapelle

Bonn

Coblentz

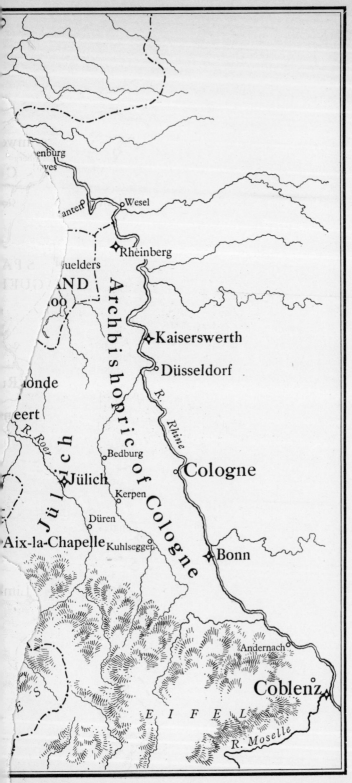

GENERAL MAP OF THE NETHERLANDS, ETC.

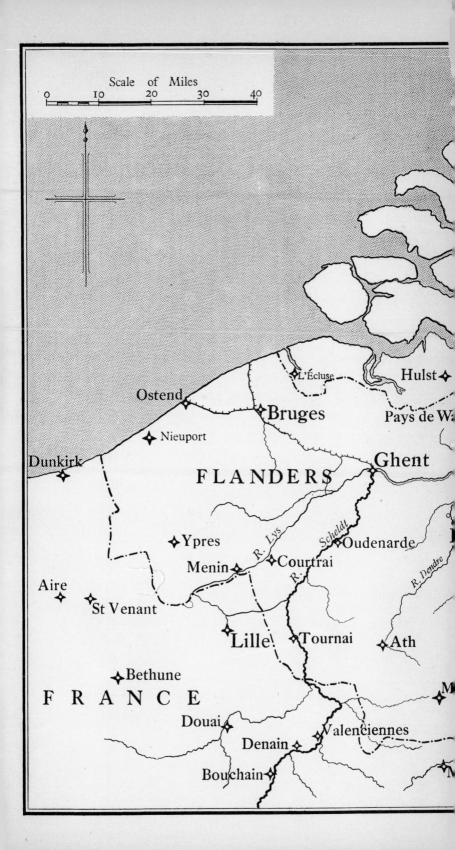

Scale of Miles

0   10   20   30   40

L'Écluse

Hulst

Ostend

Bruges

Pays de W

Nieuport

Ghent

Dunkirk

FLANDERS

Ypres

R. Lys

Scheldt

Oudenarde

R. Dendre

Menin

Courtrai

R.

Aire

St Venant

Lille

Tournai

Ath

M

Bethune

FRANCE

Douai

Valenciennes

Denain

Bouchain

Orkney
Islands

NORTH

SEA

rgh

UNITED
PROVINCES
Amsterdam
The
Hague
 ns

Brussels
Ostend
le

Luxemburg
ris
Thionville

ce

ons
its

Toulon

Christiania

NORWAY

DENMARK AND

Copenhagen

S W E D E N

Stockholm

BALTIC SEA

BALTIC SEA

Stralsund
Hamburg
Stettin

HANOVER
WOLFEN-
BÜTTEL
Cologne BRUNSWICK
Coblenz
Treves
Frankfurt

BRANDENBURG-
Berlin

SAXONY
Elbe
SILESIA

FINLAND

G. of Finland
Narva St Petersburg
ESTHONIA INGRIA

LIVONIA

COURLAND

Vilna

L I T H U A N I A

PRUSSIA

Pultusk
R.Vistula Warsaw

P O L A N D

R. Dnieper

Meuse
Mosel
Mainz
Mosel
Lorraine PALATINE
ALSACE
BADEN Nuremberg
Strasburg
WÜRTEMBERG
Ulm

Basle

SWITZERLAND

R.Rhone

FRANCHE
COMTE

SAVOY

Milan

Turin
PIEDMONT

Nice

Genoa

ra
Luxemburg

Munich
Innsbrück
Brenner
Pass
TYROL
Trent

LOMBARDY
Mantua
Parma
Luzzara
VENICE

Donauwörth
Ratisbon

BOHEMIA

A U S T R I A

Vienna

R.Danube Budapest

H U N G A R Y

TRANSYLVANIA

Cracow

R. Dniester

MOLDAVIA

WALLACHIA

Belgrade

R.Danube

R U S S I A

BLACK   SEA

Corsica

TUSCANY

PAPAL STATES

Rome

norca
Mahon

Sardinia

Naples

The   Two

Palermo

SICILY

Syracuse

TUNIS

Venice

ADRIATIC   SEA

NAP

Sicilies

SEA

T

U

R

ROUMELIA

Constantinople

K

E

Y

ÆGEAN

SEA

Malta

CRETE

CYPRUS

RANEAN   SEA

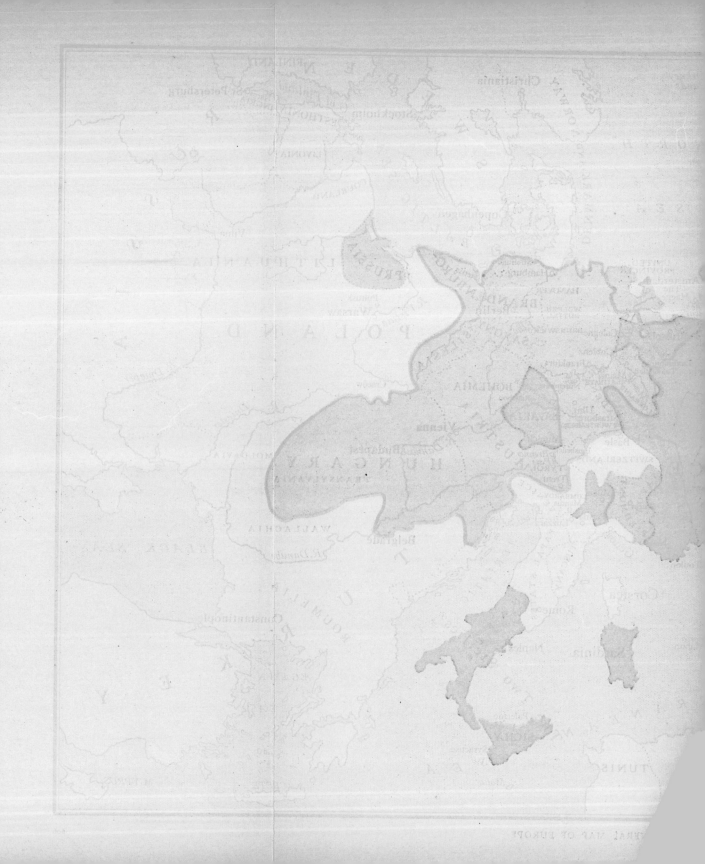

BIBLIOGRAPHY[1]

I. MANUSCRIPT SOURCES

The Public Record Office
  State Papers [S.P.]: Domestic (No. 18); Austria (No. 80); Holland
  (No. 84); French Transcripts (Tr. 3).

The British Museum
  Additional Manuscripts [Add. MSS.], 9092–9122 (Coxe Transcripts),
    17677, XX, YY, ZZ, AAA (Dutch Transcripts, L'Hermitage),
    28918 (Cardonnel to Ellis), 34518 (Blenheim Transcripts),
    42176 (Cardonnel to Watkins).

The Bodleian Library, Oxford
  Carte MSS., 208, 209 (Nairne Papers).

Le Ministère des Affaires Etrangères, Quai d'Orsai, Paris
  Correspondance politique, Angleterre.

Staatsarchiv, Vienna
  Grosse Politik.

The Huntington Library, San Marino, California
  Stowe MSS., 58 (Brydges Letters).

The Royal Archives, Windsor Castle
  The Stuart MSS. belonging to His Majesty the King.

Blenheim Palace, Woodstock
  Marlborough MSS. belonging to the Duke of Marlborough.

Althorp, Northamptonshire
  Spencer MSS. belonging to Earl Spencer.

Welbeck Abbey, Nottinghamshire
  Portland MSS. belonging to the Duke of Portland.
  Cadogan MSS. belonging to the Hon. Edward Cadogan, C.B., M.P.
  "The Pocket Book of Dr Samuel Noyes, Fellow of King's College,
    Cambridge" (Chaplain, 1st Battalion, Royal Scots (Orkney's))
    (April 20/May 1, 1705–November 2/13, 1706); belonging to
    Major H. Noyes.

---

[1] Abbreviations used in the footnotes are shown within square brackets in the bibliography. The dates indicate neither the first nor the current editions of works, but the editions consulted in writing this book. Dates in the footnotes are inserted on the same principle.

II. PRINTED SOURCES

AILESBURY, THOMAS BRUCE, EARL OF: *Memoirs*, vol. ii (Roxburghe Society, 1890).

BERWICK, JAMES FITZJAMES, DUKE OF: *Memoirs*, vol. i (English translation, 1779).

BLACKADDER, LIEUTENANT-COLONEL JOHN: *Diary* (1700–1728) (ed. A. Crichton, 1824).

BOYER, ABEL: *History of the Reign of Queen Anne digested into Annals*, vols. i–iv (1703–6).

BURNET, GILBERT: *History of His Own Time*, vol. v (1823).

CLARKE, REV. J. S.: *Life of James II*, vol. ii (1816).

DALTON, CHARLES: *British Army Lists and Commission Registers*, vols. iv–vi (1898–1904).

DANGEAU, PHILIPPE, MARQUIS DE: *Journal*, vols. ix, x (ed. Soulié, etc., 1857).

EUGENE, PRINCE OF SAVOY: *Feldzüge* (with correspondence printed as a supplement to each volume). Series I, vols. i–vii (Imperial General Staff, Vienna, 1876–81).

—— *Militärische Correspondenz* (ed. F. Heller, two vols., 1848).

HILL, RICHARD: *Diplomatic Correspondence* (July 1703–May 1706) (ed. W. Blackley, two vols., 1845).

KANE, BRIGADIER-GENERAL RICHARD: *Campaigns of King William and the Duke of Marlborough* (1735).

LA COLONIE, JEAN MARTIN DE: *The Chronicles of an Old Campaigner* (1692–1717) (translated W. C. Horsley, 1904).

LAMBERTY, G. DE: *Mémoires pour servir à l'histoire du XVIII siècle*, vols. ii, iii (1735).

LEIBNITZ, BARON G. W. VON: *Die Werke . . . durch die Munificenz des Königs von Hannover ermöglichte Ausgabe von O. Klopp*, vol. ix (1873).

LUDWIG WILHELM, MARKGRAF VON BADEN: *Kriegs- und Staatsschriften über den spanischen Erbfolgekrieg* (ed. P. Röder von Diersburg, two vols., 1850) [Röder].

LUTTRELL, NARCISSUS: *Brief Historical Relation of State Affairs*, vol. v (1857).

MACPHERSON, JAMES: *Original Papers containing the Secret History of Great Britain*, vol. i (1775).

MAFFEI, ALESSANDRO, MARQUIS: *Memorie del General Maffei* (Lieutenant-General in the Bavarian service) (1737).

MARLBOROUGH, JOHN CHURCHILL, DUKE OF: *Letters and Dispatches*, vols. i, ii (ed. Sir G. Murray, 1845).

MARLBOROUGH, SARAH, DUCHESS OF (and NATHANIEL HOOKE): *Account of the Conduct of the Dowager Duchess of Marlborough from her First Coming to Court to the Year 1710* (1742).

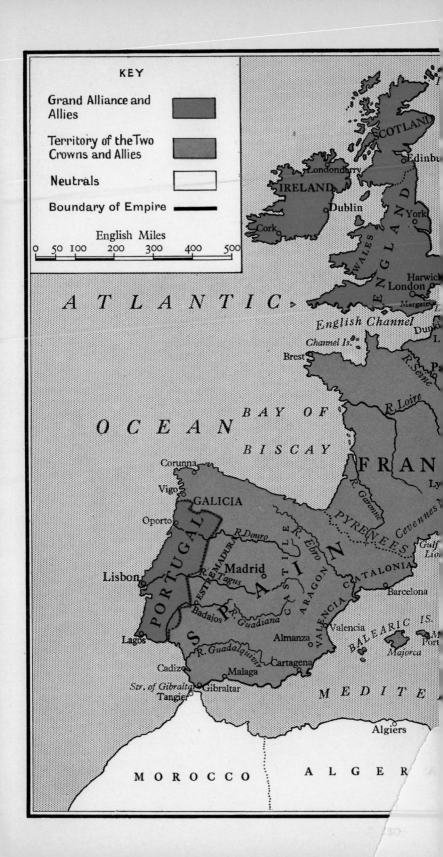

KEY

Grand Alliance and Allies

Territory of the Two Crowns and Allies

Neutrals

Boundary of Empire ━━━━

English Miles

0   50 100   200   300   400   500

ATLANTIC

OCEAN

SCOTLAND

Edinbu

Londonderry

IRELAND

Dublin

ENGLAND

York

WALES

London

Harwich

Cork

English Channel

Channel Is.

Dunki

Margate

Brest

BAY OF

BISCAY

R. Seine

R. Loire

FRAN

Ly

Corunna

Vigo

GALICIA

Oporto

PORTUGAL

R. Douro

R. Ebro

PYRENEES

R. Garonne

Cevennes

Gulf

Lio

Lisbon

ESTREMADURA

Madrid

CASTILE

ARAGON

CATALONIA

Barcelona

R. Tagus

Badajos

R. Guadiana

SPAIN

VALENCIA

Valencia

BALEARIC IS.

Port

Almanza

Lagos

R. Guadalquivir

Cartagena

Majorca

Cadiz

Malaga

Str. of Gibraltar

Gibraltar

MEDITE

Tangier

Algiers

MOROCCO

ALGER

BIBLIOGRAPHY

MARLBOROUGH, SARAH, DUCHESS OF: *Private Correspondence . . . with Sketches and Opinions of her Contemporaries* (two vols., 1838).

MÉRODE-WESTERLOO, COUNT J. P. E. DE: *Mémoires . . . publiés par le Comte (H.M.G.) de Mérode-Westerloo* (1840).

MILLNER, SERGEANT JOHN: *Journal* (1701–12) (1733).

MURRAY, SIR GEORGE—*see Marlborough, Duke of*.

ORKNEY, GEORGE HAMILTON, EARL OF: (Four) "Letters of the First Lord Orkney during Marlborough's Campaigns" (ed. H. H. E. Cra'ster), *English Historical Review*, April 1904.

PARKER, CAPTAIN ROBERT: *Memoirs* (1683–1718) (1746).

Parliamentary History of England, vol. vi (1702–14) (ed. William Cobbett and J. Wright, 1810) (Hansard).

PELET, J. J. G., and VAULT, F. E. DE: *Mémoires militaires relatifs à la succession d'Espagne sous Louis XIV*, vols. ii–v (1836–42).

RÖDER—*see* Ludwig Wilhelm von Baden.

ROOKE, ADMIRAL SIR GEORGE: *Journal* (1700–2) (ed. O. Browning, Navy Records Society, vol. ix, 1897).

SAINT-SIMON, LOUIS DE ROUVROY, DUC DE: *Mémoires* (ed. Chéruel and Regnier, twenty-three vols., 1881–1907).

SCOT, JOHN: *The Remembrance: a Metrical Account of the War in Flanders* (1701–12) (ed. James Ferguson, 1901) (papers illustrating the history of the Scots Brigade).

SHREWSBURY, CHARLES TALBOT, DUKE OF: *Correspondence* (ed. W. C. Coxe, 1821).

TREVELYAN, G. M.: *Select Documents for Queen Anne's Reign* (1702–7) (1929).

VILLARS, CLAUDE LOUIS HECTOR, DUC DE: *Mémoires*, vol. ii (ed. de Vogüé, 1887).

III. REPORTS OF THE ROYAL HISTORICAL MANUSCRIPTS COMMISSION

Athole Papers, Report XII, Part VIII (1891). (Orkney on Blenheim, etc.)

Bath Papers, vol. i (1904). (Harley correspondence: Godolphin, St John, Marlborough, Shrewsbury.)

Buccleugh Papers, vol. ii, Part II (1903). (G. Stepney (Vienna), Sir L. Blackwell (Florence).)

Cowper Papers, Report XII (appendix), Part III, vol. iii (Coke MSS.) (1888). (Captain Richard Pope, Tallard at Nottingham.)

Downshire Papers, vol. i, Part II (1924). (W. Aglionby, St John).

Frankland-Russell-Astley Papers (Chequers) (1900). (Cutts correspondence: Marlborough, Cardonnel, Hedges, Lamberty.)

Hare Papers, Report XIV (appendix), Part IX (1895). (Francis Hare, Chaplain-General.)

Marlborough Papers, Report VIII, Part I (1881).

Morrison Papers, Report IX, Part II (1884).

Ormonde Papers, Report VII (1879).

Portland Papers, Report XIII, Part II, vol. ii (1983). (Harley-New-castle.)

—— Report XV (appendix), Part IV, vol. iv (1897). (Harley corre-spondence: Cranstoun, Cutts, De Foe, Godolphin, Paterson; news-letters.)

Spencer Papers, Report II (1871).

Stuart Papers (belonging to His Majesty the King), vol. i (1902).

IV. PRINCIPAL BIOGRAPHIES OF JOHN, DUKE OF MARLBOROUGH, AND SARAH, DUCHESS OF MARLBOROUGH

ALISON, SIR ARCHIBALD: *Life of Marlborough* (1848).

ATKINSON, C. T.: *Marlborough and the Rise of the British Army* (1921).

BELLOC, HILAIRE: *The Tactics and Strategy of the Great Duke of Marl-borough* (1933).

CAMPBELL, JOHN: *The Military History of Eugene and Marlborough* (1736).

CAMPBELL, K.: *Sarah, Duchess of Marlborough* (1932).

CHANCELLOR, F.: *Sarah Churchill* (1932).

CHIDSEY, D. B.: *Marlborough* (1930).

COXE, W. C.: *Memoirs of the Duke of Marlborough* (1820) [Coxe].

CREIGHTON, L.: *Life of John Churchill, Duke of Marlborough* (1879).

DOBRÉE, B.: *Sarah Churchill* (1927).

DUMONT, J.: *Histoire militaire du Prince Eugène et du Duc de Marlborough* (1729).

DUTEMS, J. F. H., and MADGETT: *Histoire de Jean Churchill* (1806).

EDWARDS, H. J. and E. A.: *A Short Life of Marlborough* (1926).

FORTESCUE, SIR JOHN: *Marlborough* (1932).

KEARSEY, A. H. C.: *Marlborough and his Campaigns* (1931).

LEDIARD, THOMAS: *Life of John, Duke of Marlborough* (1736) [Lediard]. *Lives of the Two Illustrious Generals, The* (1713).

MAYCOCK, F. W. O.: *An Outline of Marlborough's Campaigns* (1913).

MOLLOY, J. F.: *The Queen's Comrade* (1901).

REID, J. S.: *John and Sarah, Duke and Duchess of Marlborough* (1914).

ROUSSET, J. DE M.: augmentation of *Histoire militaire* (see Dumont, J.) (1747).

TAYLOR, F.: *The Wars of Marlborough, 1702-9* (1921).

THOMAS, P. E.: *The Life of the Duke of Marlborough* (1915).

THOMSON, MRS. A. T.: *Memoirs of the Duchess of Marlborough* (1839).

BIBLIOGRAPHY

V. SECONDARY AUTHORITIES

ACTON, J. E. E. D.: *Lectures on Modern History* (1906).

ANQUETIL, L. P.: *Vie du Maréchal Duc de Villars . . . écrite par lui-même* (1784). (A secondary account based on the original papers.)

BLOK, P. J.: *History of the People of the Netherlands*, vol. v (translated O. A. Bierstadt, 1912).

BRODRICK, T.: *A Compleat History of the Late War in the Netherlands* (1713).

CALLENDER, G. A. R.: *The Naval Side of British History* (1924).

Cambridge Modern History, The, vol. v, "The Age of Louis XIV" (1908).

Campagne de Monsieur le Maréchal de Tallard en Allemagne 1704 (two vols., 1763).

CORBETT, J. S.: *England in the Mediterranean*, vol. ii (1904).

FEILING, K. G.: *A History of the Tory Party, 1640–1714* (1924).

FORTESCUE, SIR JOHN: *A History of the British Army*, vol. i (1889).

FRISCHAUER, P.: *Prince Eugène* (translated A. Smeaton, 1934).

HOPKINSON, M. R.: *Anne of England* (1934).

KLOPP, O.: *Der Fall des Hauses Stuart*, vols. x, xi (1881–85).

LA RONCIÈRE, C.: *Histoire de la marine française*, vol. vi (1899).

LEADAM, I. S.: *The History of England (1702–60)* (1921).

LEGRELLE, A.: *La diplomatie française et la Succession d'Espagne*, vol. iv (1892).

MACKNIGHT, T.: *Life of Henry St John, Viscount Bolingbroke* (1863).

MALLINSON, COL. G. B.: *Prince Eugene of Savoy* (1888).

MORGAN, W. T.: *English Political Parties and Leaders . . . 1702–10* (Yale Historical Publications, 1920).

NICHOLSON, T. C., and A. S. TURBERVILLE: *Charles Talbot, Duke of Shrewsbury* (1930).

NOORDEN, C. VON: *Europäische Geschichte im achtzehnten Jahrhundert*, vols. i, ii (1870).

ROSCOE, E. S.: *Robert Harley* (1902).

STANHOPE, PHILIP HENRY, EARL: *History of the Reign of Anne* (1872).

STRICKLAND, AGNES: *Lives of the Queens of England*, vol. viii (1852).

TINDAL, N. (and DR BIRCH): *The Continuation of Mr Rapin's History of England*, vols. xv, xvi (iii, iv of continuation) (1762–63).

TREVELYAN, G. M.: *England under Queen Anne: Blenheim* (1930).

—— *England under Queen Anne: Ramillies and the Union with Scotland* (1932).

—— *England under the Stuarts* (1904).

WILLIAMS, B.: *Stanhope* (1932).

INDEX

INDEX

measures to recapture, IV: 196; allied troops from, at the Lines of Brabant, IV: 203

ILLER, river, III: 345

Imperial Cuirassiers, at Blenheim, IV: 99, 108; charge by, IV: 100

Imperial forces, under Eugene in Italy, III: 119; IV: 54; deficiency of, in siege material, IV: 142; M.'s disgust with, IV: 183

Imperial Grenadiers, at the Schellenberg, IV: 24

Imperial Infantry, at the Schellenberg, IV: 37

Infantry, English, formation of, M.'s method of, III: 108, 110; M.'s training of, and use of fire-power by, III: 109; IV: 120

Infantry, French, depth of formation of, III: 110

Ingoldsby, Lieutenant-General Richard, IV: 180

Ingoldsby's Regiment, at Blenheim, III: 326; IV: 92 n., 129; at the Schellenberg, IV: 33

Ingolstadt, the one fortress left to the Elector (July 1704), IV: 43; siege of, by the Margrave, IV: 51, 57, 67 et seq., 123; the Margrave's feelings on, IV: 51, 67–68, 69; the Elector unaware of, IV: 80; the Margrave persuaded to raise, IV: 123

Ingria, under Swedish rule, III: 188

Innsbrück, the Elector at, III: 254

Ireland, Rochester as Lord-Lieutenant of, III: 67, 70, 83; William III and Presbyterianism in, III: 92

Irish Brigade, the, in French service, at Blenheim, IV: 99; M.'s scrupulosity concerning, IV: 186

Italy, Eugene's campaigns in, III: 97, 102, 117, 119; IV: 173, 175, 176; Imperial army in, III: 119; command in, sought by the Elector, III: 193–194; Vendôme's successes in, III: 239, 240, 254; reinforcements for the Imperial army in, IV: 54; French forces under Vendôme in, in 1705, IV: 172; M.'s plan of campaign for, in 1705, IV: 175–176

JAAR stream, the, M.'s crossing and re-crossing of, III: 150, 153

Jacobite sentiments of the Tory Party, awakening of, on Anne's accession, III: 85, 119

Jacobites, the, M.'s communications with, III: 181, 296–297

James II, deathbed message from, to Anne, III: 38; Rochester's effort to convert, III: 67; popery of, Nottingham's aloofness from, III: 68; remark of, on Prince George of Denmark, III: 71; and the subterfuge of "national emergency," III: 84; and the Tory Party, III: 180

James Francis Edward Stuart (the Old Pretender), III: 276; attitude to, of Anne, III: 37–38, 39; recognition of, by Louis XIV, III: 38, 84, 85; exclusion of, from the English throne, Article on, added to treaties of Grand Alliance, III: 39, 50, 55, 56, 57, 64, 82; alleged plot to bring in, III: 90; report to, from Hooke, on interview with M., III: 296–297

James, William, book by, cited, III: 114 and n.

Jersey, Edward Villiers, first Earl of, Anne's Lord Chamberlain, III: 72; dismissal of, III: 310

Joseph, Archduke, King of the Romans, on the Margrave's willingness to divide the command, III: 358; at the siege of Landau, IV: 142, 154; accession of, as Emperor Joseph I, IV: 186; letter to, from M., on the fiasco of 1705, IV: 193; and the Margrave, IV: 195, 252; Gallas's report to, on the English temper in 1705, IV: 243–244; mentioned, III: 59, 205, 358

Judoigne, IV: 216

Jülich, III: 120

Jura Mountains and Vosges, gap between, obstructions protecting, III: 104

KAISERSWERTH, siege and capitulation of, III: 121 et seq., 147 n. 1, 156

Kane, General Richard, IV: 23

Kehl, III: 347; IV: 127; captured by Villars, III: 239, 253, 319

Ken, Bishop, and Queen Anne, III: 34

Keppel, Arnold Joost van—see Albemarle, first Earl of

Kessel stream, the, IV: 78

Killiecrankie, battle of, a lesson learned at, III: 108

King's Dragoon Guards at Elixem, IV: 210

King's (Liverpool) Regiment, the, at Blenheim, IV: 326

Kinzig valley, III: 345

Klissow, battle of, III: 190

Klopp, Onno, on the moral worth of M., Godolphin, and Sunderland, III: 36 n.; on M.'s pertinacity, III: 244; on Wratislaw's memorandum for Queen Anne on the desperate state of the Empire, III: 292; on battle of Blenheim, IV: 106 n.; on M.'s pettiness, IV: 139 n.; on M. at his visit to Hanover, IV: 160; on the Margrave's contempt for the French, IV: 252

Kreuznach, IV: 183; reinforcements at, IV: 190

Kron-Weissemburg, stormed by Villars, IV: 252

Kühlseggen, III: 324

INDEX

planned by the Elector, IV : 172; siege of, by Villeroy, IV : 190, 196; M.'s march to save, IV : 195; supplies and siege train from, IV : 228, 229

Lille Saint-Hubert, M.'s halt at, III : 130

Lillo, battle on the causeway of, III : 227, 228

Limburg, III : 144; siege of, proposed, III : 240, 242, 243, 248; conducted by M. in person, III : 246, 251; capture of, III : 250

Limburg dispute, the, III : 251–252

Lincolnshire Regiment, the, at Blenheim, III : 326; IV : 92 n.

Lisbon, fortified harbour, III : 100

Little Bruegel, battle-plan of M. thwarted at, III : 132–133

Livonia, under Swedish rule, III : 188

Lombardy, the Grand Prior in, III : 265

London, M. acclaimed in, on return from exile, III : 160

London, City of, merchants and financiers of, importance of, in Anne's day, III : 43; magnates of, Whiggism of, III : 91; support of the war by, III : 91; money-power of, Tory fury over, III : 271; rejoicing in, over Blenheim, IV : 114; M. entertained by, IV : 167

Lord Keeper, the, thanks of the House of Lords to M., expressed by, IV : 165–166

Lorraine, Charles Alexander, Duke of, nominal neutrality of, IV : 185ⁿ

Lorraine, Duke of, III : 358

Lottum, Count, Guelders taken by, III : 250

Louis XIV, accession of Queen Anne not notified to, III : 34–35; recognition accorded to the Prince of Wales by, III : 38–39, 84, 85; power of, broken by Anglo-Dutch alliance, III : 45; Heinsius's resistance to, III : 53; peace proposals of, rejected (1702), III : 63; war declared against, III : 83; territorial acquisitions of, III : 97; Belgian fortresses occupied by, III : 97; initiative of, efforts to wrest from him, III : 101; military dispositions of (1702), III : 118–119; shock to, of loss of the Meuse, III : 135; great vigour ordered by, III : 136, 143; and M.'s victories, III : 149; and Villeroy, III : 159; and M.'s capture, III : 160; hope entertained by, of gaining Charles XII as ally, III : 190; and schemes of the Elector, III : 192–193; IV : 50; and Rakoczy, III : 197; and the rising in the Cevennes, III : 198–199; relations of, with Savoy, III : 199; Savoy's requests spurned by, III : 201; vengeance designed by, for Savoy, III : 203 (see also Savoy and Vendôme); intentions of, in summer of 1703, three ways of countering, III : 209; re-

capture o⸗ Liége ordered by, III : 214; Guelders offered by, to Frederick I, III : 250; Tallard sacrificed by, III : 257; estimate by, of the results of 1703, III : 259; new armies placed in the field by, III : 265; recognition by, desired by Frederick I, III : 289; plan of, for opening the campaign of 1704 foreseen by M., III : 300; renewal of war by, on all eight fronts, III : 319; letters exchanged by, with his marshals, III : 319; and his marshals, bewilderment of, in June 1704, III : 342 et seq.; plan demanded by, from his marshals, to aid the Elector, III : 342; plan eventually chosen by him, III : 343; orders of, to his marshals, June 23, 1704, III : 345–346; and Tallard, IV : 61, 62; orders issued by, to Villeroy, IV : 64–65; dispatch to, from Tallard before the Schellenberg affair, IV : 80; Tallard's dispatch to, before Blenheim, IV : 87; reception of the news of Blenheim by, IV : 114–115; Tallard's account of Blenheim to, IV : 121; the Elector's doings watched by (May 1704), IV : 125; design of, against the Empire, final end of, IV : 127–128; wish of, to forsake war by, after Blenheim, IV : 128–129; and the loss of Gibraltar, IV : 132, 133; fine behaviour of, in his misfortunes, IV : 140–141; letter of encouragement sent to Villeroy by, IV : 150; M.'s plans penetrated by, IV : 150; and the war in 1705, IV : 172; unity of action of his armies imposed by, in 1705, IV : 172, 173; letter to, from the Elector in August 1705, IV : 232; peace terms offered by, to the Dutch, IV : 251; effect on, of the forcing of the Lines of Brabant, IV : 253; letter from, to Villeroy, on accepting battle, IV : 253–254; Villeroy's reply, IV : 255; mentioned, III : 156, 276

Louvain, Louis XIV's household at, III : 318; suggested allied advance on, IV : 215–216; M.'s intention to march to, IV : 220; garrisoned by the French, IV : 231; French sacrifice of, to save Brussels, IV : 232

Louvois, François, Marquis de, drill uniformity imposed by, III : 109

Low Countries—see Flanders

Lumley, General Henry, at Blenheim, III : 326; IV : 97, 98, 105, 129; at the Schellenberg, IV : 36

Lumley's Regiment (1st King's Dragoon Guards) at Blenheim, III : 326

Lüneberg, subsidy treaty signed with, III : 63

Lutzingen, IV : 89, 90; battle around, IV : 102; set on fire, IV : 107

Luzzara, Eugene's victory at, III : 154, 193

Lyon, Comte de, M.'s wish to help, IV : 249–250

279

INDEX

Hesse and others, on the appointment of Eugene to the Rhine command, III: 350–351; to Schmettau, on Eugene and Tallard, IV: 66; to Eugene, on the Margrave and the siege of Ingolstadt, IV: 67–68; the *projet* enclosed in, IV: 68–69; to Hedges, on Tallard's being shepherded by Eugene, IV: 67; to the Margrave, on his position and plans, IV: 75–76; to Godolphin—*see under* Godolphin, letters to; to Harley—*see under* Harley, letters to

Letters to: from Sunderland, a token of renewed amity, III: 35; from Harley, III: 81; from Opdam, announcing his defeat, III: 228; from his wife, given him at Harwich, stating her imagined grievances, III: 298, 309; from Eugene, on the need for speed in marching to Donauwörth, IV: 76–77 *and n.*; from Leopold I, on creating M. an Imperial Prince, IV: 137–138

Letters to and from: the Duchess of Portsmouth, IV: 179–180; Villars, IV: 188

Military references: appointment of, as Captain-General of Anne's forces, III: 33; military status of, III: 65; interest of his victories eclipsed by Occasional Conformity, III: 94; operations of, conditioned by political considerations, III: 96; proclamation of, on the cause of England's quarrel, and on aliens in England, III: 97–98; strategy of, directed to obtaining command of the Mediterranean, III: 100; IV: 132; wishes of, on employment of the Navy, III: 101; Admiral Rooke's opposition thereto, III: 101; training of infantry by, and formation adopted for, III: 108, 109, 110; fire power developed by, III: 108–109; training of cavalry by, III: 110; battles of, terrain and wide fronts of, III: 111; battle attacks under, III: 112; plans for the campaign of 1702, and for naval action, III: 117; opposition to these, III: 118; appointment of, as Deputy Captain-General of the Dutch Republic, III: 124; appointment of, as Commander-in-Chief, Dutch generals' indignation at, and arguments against, III: 125, 126 (*see also* Dutch generals); proceedings hampered by the field Deputies—*see* Dutch field Deputies; salary of, as Commander-in-Chief, III: 125; views on war ascribed to, III: 126; reserve maintained by, at outset of his commandership-in-chief, III: 126; forces concentrated by, near Nimwegen, and reviewed there, III: 127; move of, to the Meuse, III: 128; the Meuse crossed

by, initiative thereby secured, III: 130; English artillery joining, III: 131; assertion of authority by, III: 132; at the Heaths of Peer, III: 132 *et seq.*; increased forces of, III: 134; private complaints about the Dutch by, III: 135, 139, 142, 144; battle begun by, at the Heath of Helchteren, foiled by the Deputies, III: 137–138; message of, to Boufflers and Berwick, apologizing for not having attacked them, III: 140; and the Dutch ban on battle, III: 141 (*see also* Battles); methods of, advanced, beyond his times, III: 141; attempts of, on the Meuse fortresses, III: 141 *et seq.*; and the siege of Venloo (*q.v.*), III: 142, 143; troops of, in good heart, III: 146; sieges swiftly carried out by, III: 147, 148; outnumbered by Boufflers, III: 148; strain on, in autumn of 1702, III: 148; still prevented from giving battle, III: 149; effect of the Dutch restriction on his warfare, III: 156; and others, boat-journey of, down the Meuse, III: 156; taken prisoner and escape of, III: 157 *et seq.*; on his capture and escape, III: 158; tumult caused thereby, III: 160–161; advice of, on defence in the Cadiz affair, III: 164; return of, to the Army, III: 187; Eugene supported by, against the Elector, III: 193; liking of, for Eugene, views of, on him, shared by Anne and others, III: 193; operations of, in Flanders, effect on opinion in Savoy, III: 200; troops drawn from, for Portugal, III: 207, 208, 253; on not dividing the army, spoken in old age, III: 208; concentration of, round Maestricht in 1703, III: 209; arguments of, with the Dutch, on the plan of campaign, III: 209–210; and his "Great Design," III: 209, 220, 281; bungled by the Dutch, III: 220 *et seq.*; desire of, for battle, banned by the Dutch, III: 221; why quiescent, with larger forces, III: 225; slanders of, put about by Slangenberg, III: 229–230; joined by Slangenberg, and advance of, on the French camp, Villeroy defeats the move by a retreat, III: 234–235; his own comments on the affair, III: 234, 235–236; battle again proposed by, but banned, III: 241; the paper giving his proposals, III: 242; and the siege of Limburg (*q.v.*), III: 242, 244 *et seq.*; report of, on the taking of Huy, III: 243–244; resolve of, to quit his command, III: 245, 249, 250, 262, 266, 267, 269, 283; position of (autumn 1703), III: 246; detractors of, III: 246 (*see also* Slangenberg); and the meeting with Charles, now King of Spain, at Düssel-

INDEX

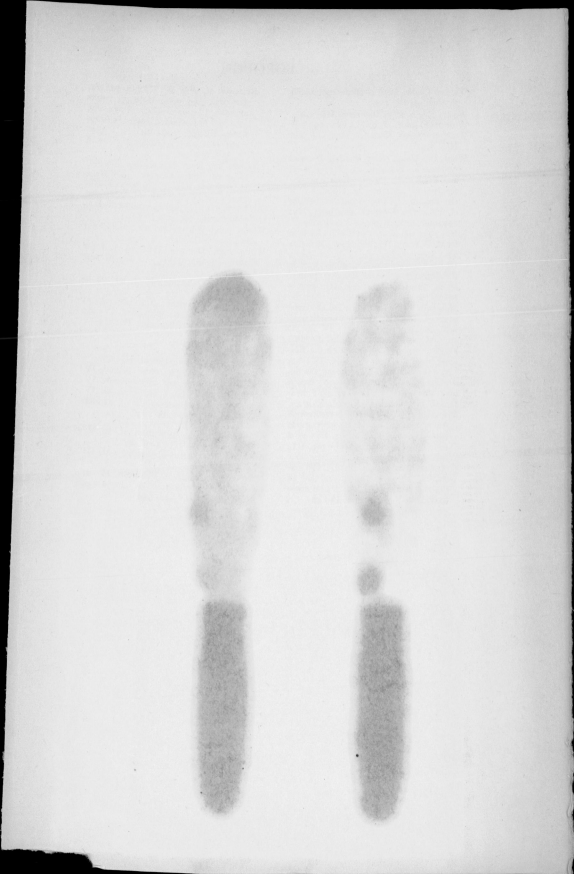

DATE DUE
